MELBOURNE SCHOOL OF THEOLOGY

PARADOSIS

Volume No. 2

Studies in the Psalms

2015

PARADOSIS

No 2. (2015)

ISSN 2203-4951

ISBN 978-0-9924763-4-2

© 2015 Melbourne School of Theology. All rights reserved.

Executive Editor
Justin Tan

Principal Editor
Colin Kruse

Issue Editor
Ted Woods

Assistant Editors
Ben Chenoweth and Andrew Brown

Production and Cover Design
Ho-yuin Chan

A Publication of the Melbourne School of Theology
5 Burwood Highway, Wantirna, Victoria 3152, Australia
PO Box 6257, Vermont South, Victoria 3133, Australia
Ph: +61 3 9881 7800, Fax: +61 3 9800 0121
mstpress@mst.edu.au, www.mst.edu.au

Opinions and conclusions published in PARADOSIS are those of the authors and do not necessarily represent the views of the Editors or the Melbourne School of Theology.

Principal Editor's Introduction to *PARADOSIS*	4
Editorial	6
The Psalms: A Threefold Conversation?	
Edward James Woods..	9
God of all Nations – Reading the Psalms	
John W. Olley...	30
Is it Right to Pray the Imprecatory Psalms?	
Katy Smith..	48
Recently Discovered Greek Papyri and Parchment of the Psalter from the Oxford Oxyrhynchus Manuscripts: Implications for Scribal Practice and Textual Transmission	
Michael P. Theophilos......................................	66
Passionate Pursuit of the God of Redemption: Interpreting Psalm 119 in the Light of its Immediate Context in Book V of the Psalter	
John De Hoog...	86
Psalm 137 and its Canonical Placement	
Gillian Asquith...	107
At the Edge of the Precipice: Psalm 89 as Liturgical Memory	
David Cohen..	127
Psalm 148, Pinnacle of the Psalms	
Andrew Brown...	145
Invitation for Papers	173
Notes for Contributors	
	174

PRINCIPAL EDITOR'S INTRODUCTION TO *PARADOSIS*

The Melbourne School of Theology (MST) is committed to pursuing excellence in learning, research and the highest possible standard of scholarship in theological education, an area in which we are called to make a contribution to the work of the Gospel.

This journal is entitled *PARADOSIS*, a Greek word meaning 'tradition'. *PARADOSIS* is chosen as the title of the journal because it expresses the sense that the theological enterprise is a continuous ministry, the ongoing 'traditioning' responsibility of the Christian church to carry forward the deposit of faith from the past, while rearticulating it in dialogue with the contexts, mindsets and issues of current culture.

Admittedly, 'tradition' can have negative connotations, as in Jesus' criticisms of scribes and Pharisees who broke the commandments of God for the sake of their human traditions. However, it has positive connotations when used in relation to the gospel of Christ and the fundamental Christian teachings received and passed on by the apostles. These form the bedrock of the Christian faith. Early believers were urged to hold fast to, contend for, and pass on this tradition.

The theological implications of the gospel traditions occupied the best minds in Christendom during the early centuries following the apostolic age. The consensual conclusions they reached constitute Christian orthodoxy and the basis of subsequent theological endeavours down through the Middle Ages, the Reformation period, the Enlightenment, and the theological enterprise today.

Christian theology must serve pastoral ministry, evangelism, cross cultural mission and inter-faith dialogue. From the earliest centuries Christian leaders, evangelists and apologists sought to apply theology to the pastoral needs of believers and commend the faith to others. In recent times these disciplines have flourished and are producing their own traditions.

PARADOSIS will showcase articles in biblical studies and theology. A future journal planned by MST, *PRAXIS*, will provide opportunity for the publication of articles in pastoral ministry, evangelism, mission and other living faiths.

Dr Colin G. Kruse
Principal Editor

EDITORIAL

This second issue of *PARADOSIS* contains eight articles, all dealing in various ways with issues relating to Psalm studies and research.

To begin with, Ted Woods (Melbourne School of Theology) has made a response to the journal article by Patrick Miller (1999) that the Psalms have engaged in an important conversation with Deuteronomy. Building upon this observation, but taking it one stage further, it has been argued that the Psalms have also engaged in an important conversation with the book of Isaiah, thus making the whole enterprise a *threefold* conversation. Thus within the Psalms, one *learns* the story and command (Deuteronomy), how to *sing* and *pray* the Lord's songs (Psalms), and how to *see* the broader theological vision (Isaiah). This threefold mix and conversation of Psalms, Deuteronomy, and Isaiah, also reflects the importance of these three dominant books at Qumran, as well as their importance for works like Luke-Acts in the New Testament.

John Olley (Vose Seminary, WA) argues that the Psalms as a whole provide us with prayers that can illuminate our understanding with regard to God's *mission* that covers all nations. Previous studies have argued that kingship (Davidic and Yahweh) and wisdom are key elements in the Psalter's overall structure, but the present study has correctly sought to produce evidence that the place of the nations is inseparably linked to these motifs (e.g. Psalm 96 as a good case in point), as well as to the overall story-line of the Psalter.

One of the continuing 'chestnuts' of Psalm study remains the Imprecatory Psalms. Katy Smith (Bible College of South Australia) asks the question "Is it possible for Christians to pray the Imprecatory Psalms?" This is then pursued with two issues in mind. The first relates to justice (both God's and Israel's), and the second is the overall theological framework of the Bible. It is argued through an examination of Psalms 69, 109, and 137, that the Imprecations are an expression of *covenant faithfulness* in relationship to a sovereign God to whom vengeance belongs. And so, can Christians pray the Imprecatory Psalms? A qualified 'yes' is given, especially for situations of unjust suffering. But, in crying out for justice to be done, we leave any vindication to God's vengeance, whilst at the same time praying that God's love might touch the hearts of those who oppose all that is good.

Next, Michael Theophilus (Australian Catholic University, Melbourne) visits his interest in Papyrology, with particular focus on the Psalter at Oxyrhynchus. He notes that almost half of the Septuagint (LXX) manuscripts discovered at this place are fragments of the Psalter. Amongst other things, this has important interest for the study of the Septuagint (LXX) text as it existed at a certain point in antiquity. Further, from this study it is argued that the scribal process of textual transmission in this place was *dynamic* and *fluid* rather than static and fixed, with several examples given. These examples will no doubt create further interest and implications for textual criticism and the wider interpretation of the Psalms.

In contrast to Bernhard Duhm's negative portrayal of Psalm 119, John De Hoog (Reformed Theological College, Geelong), seeks to address two questions to Psalm 119, relating to its *purpose*, as well as to its *process* (dynamics) by which it achieves its purpose. In answer to the first question, Psalm 119 is designed to commend a life of pursuing the Lord through His Word (Torah obedience). In answer to the second question, Psalm 119 is a multi-faceted portrayal of *what it actually looks like* to pursue the Lord through His Word (which is often not a smooth road). The Psalm achieves its purpose not by admonishing the reader but by painting a portrait of the life of a God-seeker. Finally, drawing upon the work of Erich Zenger in Book 5 of the Psalter, Psalm 107 at the beginning of this book poses the question: "Who is wise?" This is finally worked out through the connections between Psalms 111–112 and Psalm 119 (God's gracious/mighty actions in history, as a reason for his peoples' obedient response through Torah keeping).

Gillian Asquith (Melbourne School of Theology) explores how Psalm 137 can speak within differing historical contexts, both exilic (sixth century BC), as well as within a much later context of the third or second century BC. It is argued that considering the Psalter is finally a book of instruction, exhorting the wise to a Torah-adherence life, Psalm 137 plays a 'cautionary' role, reminding the reader that the divine justice that brings recompense for the victims of the Babylonian period is the very same justice that required their punishment in the first place. Mindful that God watches over those who love him, but destroys the wicked, the final redactors of the Psalter sought to combat Hellenistic apostasy in the Seleucid period by compiling a book of divine instruction, encouragement, and warning, to which Psalm 137 makes a key contribution.

David Cohen (Vose Seminary, WA) makes Psalm 89 his focus of study. It is argued that as an act of liturgical use and memory, Psalm 89 articulates a convergence of four interrelated and critical aspects of human reflection: mythic, parabolic, mimetic, and parenetic qualities. It is these that create a space for significant *dialogue* and *memory* to take place within the 'precipice' of the exilic experience of the sixth century BC.

Finally, Andrew Brown (Melbourne School of Theology) appropriately concludes these articles and our study of the Psalter with a Hallelujah Psalm. It is argued that Psalm 148 (called a 'creation-focused hymn') not only stands at the centre of the final group of Hallelujah Psalms 146–150, but also has a certain pride of place and represents the *pinnacle* of the book. Structurally, Psalm 148 has seven units within, which reflect the seven days of creation. As such, it may be seen as a valuable contribution to a biblical theology of creation reflected at Genesis 1:1–2:3. But finally within its peers (Psalms 146–150), Psalm 148 stands above them all as the greatest expression of *inclusive* and *universal* praise.

Rev Dr Ted Woods
Issue Editor

The Psalms: A Threefold Conversation?

Edward James Woods

Melbourne School of Theology

Introduction

In his article, "Deuteronomy and Psalms: Evoking a Biblical Conversation,"[1] Patrick Miller argues that the books of Psalms and Deuteronomy have much in common with each other at both conceptual and inter-textual levels, especially noting the influence of the Song of Moses (Deut 32) upon Psalms 78 and 106 as *self-indictments* of the community for not obeying the law of the Lord, first presented in Psalm 1 where the law (Torah) is presented as the only path to true happiness. Other themes from Deuteronomy reflected in the Psalms include the *nearness of God* (Deut 4:7), and the *fear of God* (Psa 34:11 [ET]), as well as the pivotal role played by the law (Torah) in Psalms 1, 19, and 119, which Miller argues is the book of Deuteronomy itself (*cf.* Psalm 1:2 with Joshua 1:8). In this way, the hermeneutics of story and instruction (Deuteronomy) are joined with song (Psalms). Thus one learns the story and the command, and how to sing the Lord's song.

But having conceded this much, is it possible to take one further step in this biblical conversation by suggesting that the Psalms have also engaged in conversation with the book of Isaiah, by providing an overall *vision* to that of story/law and song? In one small paragraph of his article, Miller briefly draws attention to Isaiah 2 in his discussion of Psalm 2, but does not develop this any further.[2] Thus, what this article will propose is that in the Psalms, one *learns* the story and command (Deuteronomy), how to *sing* and *pray* the Lord's song (Psalms), and how to *see* the broader vision (Isaiah).

The Evidence of Qumran and the New Testament

As an extension of this claim for the importance of the book of Isaiah within this threefold conversation, it is interesting to note that the three books that appear in the largest numbers of manuscripts at Qumran, Psalms (36), Deuteronomy (29), and Isaiah

---

[1] Patrick D. Miller, "Deuteronomy and Psalms: Evoking a Conversation," *JBL* 118/1 (1999), 3–18.

[2] Miller, "Deuteronomy and Psalms," *JBL* 118/1 (1999), 16.

(21), are also the three quoted most frequently in the New Testament.[3] Especially is this seen in the twofold work of Luke-Acts, in which the book of Isaiah provides an outside frame defining the ministries of Jesus and Paul,[4] and between these framing passages, Deuteronomy and the Psalms play key supporting roles within Luke's overall work.[5] Thus, these three books are never far from each other in terms of final canonical form and influence, and for this reason, have most likely engaged with each other within the Psalter itself at the point of instruction, song, prayer, vision, and worship.

The Overall Structure of the Psalms

Before we begin to say something about the book of Isaiah and its possible relationship to the Psalms, it is worth observing the overall structure of the Psalms in order to map something of the landscape of the 150 individual psalms that now make up the canonical Psalter. As scholars have been correct to point out over recent years, there is evidence that our present Psalter has most likely evolved from smaller collections of psalms to larger collections, and that this process has also been largely determined and shaped by both religious (theological) and historical circumstances as time has gone by. The final shape of the Psalter reveals a fivefold division (1–41; 42–72; 73–89; 90–106; 107–150), most probably reflecting the fivefold books of the Pentateuch. Thus a law (or 'Torah') intention has been finally imposed upon the macro-structure of the Psalter, further illustrated by the positioning of the three Torah psalms (1, 19, 119) within the framing books (1 and 5) of the Psalter. Further, each book within the Psalter concludes with a final doxology, that was most probably the work of a final editor. This may be supported by the fact that the first four doxologies that occur at the end of the first four books reveal a chiastic structure, with 41:13 at Book 1 providing a parallel to 106:48 at Book 4, and 72:18–19 at Book 2 providing a parallel to 89:52 at Book 3. On the basis of this evidence, Zenger plausibly suggests that these four books may well have already existed as a complete compositional entity before

---

[3] J.C. VanderKam, *The Dead Sea Scrolls Today* (London: SPCK, 1994), 32.
[4] With Jesus, Luke 4:18–19 = Isa 61:1–2; with Paul, Acts 13:47 = Isa 49:6; Acts 28:26–27 = Isa 6:9–10.
[5] E.g. Luke 24:44 = law (Deuteronomy), prophets, and writings (Psalms); seen closely together at Acts 2:25–28 = Psa 16:8–11; Acts 2:34–35 = Psa 110:1; Acts 3:22–23 = Deut 18:15–19. See also Rom 15:9–12 where Paul stiches together quotes from Psalms, Deuteronomy, and Isaiah.

Book 5 was added.⁶ Also, within this penultimate structure, there is the note at the end of Book 2 (72:20), "the prayers of David have concluded," which may reveal a further editorial marker within this process. This colophon, coming *after* the doxology of 72:18–19, most probably applies to the entire collection of Psalms 3–72.

Issues Relating to David and Zion

It is further worthy of note that in the following Books 3 and 4, there is only a single Davidic psalm in Book 3 (Psalm 86), and two Davidic psalms in Book 4 (101, 103). But with the addition of Book 5 (Psalms 107–150), we may observe that another large collection of Davidic psalms emerge (108–110, 122, 124, 131, 138–145), paralleling the significant collection of Davidic Psalms in Book 1 (Psalms 3–41). This was probably arranged out of respect for David, first and foremost as the paramount Psalmist, just as other sections of Scripture honoured Solomon as the patron saint of Wisdom in Israel (1 Kgs 4:29–34). But the presence of David in both frames is probably also meant to uphold the *ideals* of kingship (2 Sam 7), including Zion as the place of God's sovereign home and rule over Israel and the nations (2 Sam 6; Psalms 46; 48; 76; 84; 87). It is to be noted that these songs of Zion in Books 2 and 3 belong to Asaph and Korah, the associates of David. Further, one may observe a progression in these psalms like climbing a mountain itself, where to begin with, Psalms 46 and 48 in Book 2 speak of the Lord's defence of Jerusalem and his defeat of the nations through his mighty acts. Finally in Book 3, Psalm 76:11–12 implores Israel to acknowledge God's help with grateful vows, and the nations to acknowledge his sovereign rule with tribute. Then Psalm 84 reminds the pilgrim of the threefold "blessedness" אשרי (*'ašrê*) of dwelling in God's house (verse 4; *cf.* Psa 65:4), going on pilgrimage to Zion (v. 5), and trust in the Lord (v. 12). Then, in Psalm 87:4, all of the nations are represented who have been formerly hostile to the Lord, indicating a widespread conversion to the Lord as those whose names are now registered in Zion. Further, the reference to "fountains" at the conclusion to Psalm 87:7 may be seen as a frame for the opening Zion psalm (46:4) where there is a river whose "streams" make glad the city of God, probably referring to the *source* of life and refreshment as only to be found in Yahweh himself (*cf.* Psa 36:8). Israel and the nations must ultimately experience this for

---

⁶ Erich Zenger, "The Composition and Theology of the Fifth Book of Psalms, Psalm 107–145," *JSOT* 80 (1998), 81.

themselves. This is of some interest for Book 3 itself, for coming as it does at the very centre of the Psalter's five books, it fittingly includes the final *three* Zion Psalms (76, 84, and 87), that also stand as a kind of mountain peak, highlighting the theme of Yahweh's sovereign rule over Israel and the nations.[7] It is in the light of this theme that the issue of human kingship may also be seen. For we have noted that in Book 3, the only Davidic Psalm as such is Psalm 86. What really is this Psalm doing here? A clue may be observed in the link between Psalm 86:9 and Psalm 87:4. The nations will ultimately acknowledge Zion as the city of God in the manner of Isaiah 2:2–5. A similar point is made by Psalm 102, which is framed by the only two Davidic Psalms in Book 4. To these observations we will return later on.

A Further Mountain Peak in Book 3

In the meantime, Psalm 81, which stands at the structural heart of Book 3, proclaims the religious festivals of Israel as a "decree" from the Lord, especially the Feast of Tabernacles (*cf.* Zech 14:16), much in the same way that the seven festivals found in Leviticus 23 stand at the structural centre of the Pentateuch. Every seventh year at this festival the covenant law (Deuteronomy) was to be read to all the people (Deut 31:9–13). In this way Psalm 81:8–10 also takes Israel back to Mount Sinai/Horeb and the Lord's proclamation of the first commandment (Exod 20:2–4; Deut 5:6–8). The main point of this Psalm is framed as a *warning* for Israel to "listen" to the Lord, and if they would do this, Israel's enemies would be subdued before them. But because God's covenant people would not listen to him, he gave them over to their own stubborn hearts to follow their own devices (verses 11–12). Coming as it does at the centre of Book 3, which itself is the centre of the Psalter's five-book structure, we find that Mount Sinai/Horeb and God's covenant law or Torah, especially highlighting the first commandment "You shall have no other gods before me," stands supreme. This Psalm reflects the language and message of Deuteronomy 31:16–18 and the Song of Moses (Deut 32:1–43). As such, it supports the pivotal importance of Deuteronomy and the Torah psalms at the frames of the Psalter as well (Book 1 = Psalms 1, 19; Book 5 = 119). Standing at the very centre of the Psalter, Psalm 81 provides the theological reason why

---

[7] If we include Psalm 122 as a Zion Psalm, which parallels Psalm 132 within the Songs of Ascent in Book 5, then we may notice a further link between Zion as Yahweh's dwelling place, as the place of joyful pilgrimage and peace, as well as the place of Davidic promise and hope.

the *enemy* continues to stand as a constant threat and major theme throughout the five books of the Psalter, and also why Israel (either individual or community) feels that the Lord has "turned his face" from them, or has "forgotten" to be gracious to them, much in the spirit of Isaiah (40:27).[8] The way back within Book 3 is found at Psalm 85, which not only reflects the post-exilic period, but also the prospect of future restoration based upon past mercies (Isaiah 40:1–11). But this time, the Psalmist confesses that he will "listen" to what the Lord might say (v. 8; *cf.* Isa 40:31; 66:2), on the basis that the Lord's salvation and glory is "near" to those who fear him (v. 9). However, this promise of salvation is really a *reiteration* of the salvation prophecy of Isaiah 40–55 (compare v. 9 with Isa 51:5; 55:6). Here we have a situation of the Psalmist recalling the promises of God from the book of Isaiah in order to bring further comfort and reassurance to the dispirited post-exilic community.[9]

The Historical Setting of Book 3

From an historical perspective, Book 3 most probably reflects the rupture represented by the Babylonian exile, evidenced by Psalms 74 and 89 at the frames. This also relates to the eventual disruption of the office of kingship, which figures at the seams with Psalms 1–2, as well as Psalm 72 where the king is understood to be the upholder of "justice" and "righteousness", so that eventually all the nations are to be blessed through him (v. 17; Gen 12:3). But at the end of Book 3, the eternal covenant that God had made with David (2 Sam 7) had been broken through a succession of unfaithful kings, leading to the abandonment of Jerusalem and Babylonian exile in 586 B.C. Psalm 89 ends with a prayer and an appeal to the Lord to remember his former promise made with David (vv. 46–51). At this point, we wait with anticipation to see how Books 4 and 5 of the Psalter will respond to this prayer and theological crisis. But before embarking on this exercise, it will be useful at this point to introduce the book of Isaiah as a possible way forward for the Psalter's way of responding to this crisis.

---

[8] This may prove to be a more convincing centre-point to the Psalter than Walter Brueggemann's argument for Psalm 73 at the beginning of Book 3 in his article "Bounded by Obedience and Praise: The Psalms as Canon," *JSOT* 50 (1991), 63–92. Brueggemann's path "from obedience to praise" must begin with the knowledge that only the Lord is God, and therefore, we must begin by cultivating the art of "listening" to him (Psa 81:8–16), and not to the other gods and competing voices around us. In fact, in Psalm 73:24 it was the Psalmist's ability to be finally led by the Lord's "counsel" within the Temple that enabled him to find an answer to his deep dilemma.

[9] James L. Mays, *Psalms* (Interpretation; Louisville, Kentucky: John Knox Press, 1994), 277.

The Vision of Isaiah

There is much in the broad sweep as well as in the structure of the canonical book of Isaiah to suggest that a two-way conversation has taken place between the Psalms and Isaiah. Especially would this be so for Books 4 and 5 of the Psalter, if it is the case that they reflect the exilic and post-exilic periods of Judaism. It can be assumed, and it will be the working assumption of this article, that the book of Isaiah was completed in its canonical form sometime soon after the recording of Sennacherib's death in 681 B.C. (Isa 37:38), especially as the key hinge chapters of the book (chs. 36–39) reflect both the Assyrian (1–35) and Babylonian periods (40–66). With Webb we can therefore propose the view that the "vision" of Isaiah (1:1) is programmatically presented in 1:1–2:5 in which the transformation of Zion in "justice" and "righteousness" through purifying judgment (1:17–24) is the key to the transformation of the "new heavens and earth", also involving Zion (65:17–25). But at the same time, rebels and sinners will perish, as those who obstruct this grand purpose (1:28–31; 66:22–24). Finally, the nations will come to Zion to share in the salvation that has been realized there (2:1–5; 60:1–3), but the key to all of this will be the transformation of Zion through the work of the royal suffering Servant (52:13–53:12; 61:1–3), who in turn will enable and inspire the righteous remnant of "servants" to go far and wide to proclaim God's glory among the nations (42:6; 49:6; 59:21; 66:19–21). In this way, the entire book moves between the twin poles of history and eschatology, as well as Jerusalem and the New Jerusalem. Finally, Webb also observes that the first part of the book has three units (chs 1–12, 13–27, 28–35), each of which ends with the praises of Yahweh being sung in or en route to the new Zion. After the hinge (36–39)[10], it is then followed by a further three units (40:1–51:11; 51:12–55:13; and 56–66) which end in the same way.[11]

---

[10] Which itself includes Hezekiah's Song of Thanksgiving for his healing toward the end of this section at Isaiah 38:9–20, reflecting much of the spirit and language of the Psalms. See Allan Harman, *Isaiah: A Covenant to be Kept for the Sake of the Church* (Fearn: Christian Focus Publications, 2005), 256–261.

[11] Barry Webb, "Zion in Transformation: A Literary Approach to Isaiah," in *The Bible in Three Dimensions* (eds. D.J.A. Clines, S.E. Fowl, S.E. Porter; JSOTSup 87; Sheffield: JSOT Press, 1990), 65–84. In addition to these structural markers, one may also note Isaiah 48:22; 57:21; 66:24 which all point to "no peace for the wicked", and are also spaced exactly nine chapters apart from each other, beginning with chapter 40, which declares that God's glory was about to be revealed in leading his captive people back to Zion (40:9).

Isaiah within the Psalter

Already we have indicated in previous paragraphs that the canonical book of Isaiah could well have had some influence upon the Psalter, especially the last three books (3, 4 and 5) in particular, because in these books the Babylonian exile in 586 B.C. appears as a *past* event evidenced by Book 3 (Psalms 74 and 89), as well as Book 4 (Psalms 90–106), and finally Book 5 (Psalms 107–150), which looks to life after the exile. As we have already observed in Book 3, one would therefore begin to suspect that if the canonical book of Isaiah was beginning to exert some kind of an influence upon the Psalter, this period in particular would be our first port of call. However, from a final compositional point of view, the book of Isaiah could well have had an influence upon the earlier books of the Psalter (Books 1–2) as well, in the same way that the book of Deuteronomy has influenced most parts of the Psalter in different ways. We will now begin to explore some different lines of argument, both structural, thematic, and lexical, in support of our argument.

Books 1 and 5 of the Psalter, and Isaiah

Firstly, it is of some interest and importance to note how Books 1 and 5 of the Psalter provide a frame for each other, as well as provide a theological direction for the entire corpus. This begins with Psalms 1 and 2 as a wisdom/Torah and royal psalm combination, which sets the theological agenda for the entire Psalter, concluding at Psalm 2:10–12 with a wisdom warning to the kings of the earth not to rebel against the Lord's "anointed" king, and thus against the Lord's sovereign rule over the earth. Rather, the nations are called to "serve" the Lord with fear, as well as submit to the Lord's "anointed" king in Zion. Not to do so will only mean defeat and destruction for these nations (e.g. see Psalm 9). This combination of psalms is then followed by a small group of 'Entrance Liturgy' psalms (15–24), which themselves are also framed by Psalms 15 and 24, which address the question of the pilgrim's *suitability* to ascend the hill of the Lord and "stand" or "dwell" in the Lord's house on Zion. The answer is those who are *morally* righteous in keeping with Psalm 1. Then Psalms 16 and 23 express "trust" in the Lord concluding with joy in the Lord's presence. Psalms 17 and 22 are then pleas for physical deliverance from enemies, which especially express "trust" in the Lord. In the inner frame, Psalms 18 and 20–21 together express prayer and praise for the king's deliverance from his enemies, thus picking up from Psalm 2. The centrepiece in this chiastic arrangement is Psalm 19, which emphasizes creation and the warmth and life-giving nature of the sun in the first half (verses 1–6), as an introduction for the life-giving nature of the law (Torah) in the second half of the psalm (verses 7–14), thus picking up from Psalm 1. Thus, within this group of psalms, not only are the concerns of Psalms 1 and 2 repeated, but they emphasize again the centrality and importance of the law (Torah) as this relates to Zion and the king, even toward the end of Book 1 at Psalm 40:7–8.[12] Already we have noticed the importance of these themes for Book 3, which structurally stands at the centre of the Psalter.

When we come to Book 5, it begins with a Thanksgiving psalm (107) that opens in verses 1–3 in direct response to the prayer for deliverance from exile in Psalm 106:47. Also, as the opening psalm of Book 5, it parallels Psalms 1 and 2 in Book 1 by concluding with a wisdom saying (verse 43) similar to that of Psalm 2:10–12. Then the major part of Book 5 is made up of three sets of Psalms:

(1) *Psalms 110–118* that continue to uphold and look forward to the renewal of the Davidic kingship, beginning with God's *promise* of victory over David's enemies (Psalm 110), as an extension of Psalm 2, and concluding with a hymn of thanksgiving for victory given to the Davidic king (Psalm 118; *cf.* 2 Chronicles 20:27–30). Psalm 118 is also the concluding psalm to the group of psalms known as the Egyptian Hallel, beginning with Psalm 113, in which the Lord helps the needy and helpless, followed by Psalm 114, which tells the story of the exodus deeds of the Lord. Psalm 115 contrasts the Lord as Israel's help with that of the gods of the nations. Psalm 116 thanks the Lord for deliverance from death (*cf.* Psalm 18:5), and Psalm 117 calls on the nations to praise the Lord. Note also that Psalm 118:17–21 reflects an Entrance Liturgy enabling the triumphant king to give thanks to the Lord, anticipating the Songs of Ascent in Psalms 120–134. Then at the centre of Book 5, Psalm 119 stands taller than any other psalm, as a prayer and devotion on the blessings of keeping Torah, which reflects Psalm 1, and Psalm 19 in particular, which stands at the centre of Psalms 15–24.[13]

---

[12] Probably referring to the personal copy of the law that the king is to take at the time of his enthronement to serve as the covenant charter of his rule (Deut 17:18–20).

[13] Note that at Qumran (11QPs^a) Psalm 119 stands at the mid-point of its collection between Psalms 101 and 151, coming immediately after Psalm 132 and before Psalms 135–136. Coming *after* the Songs of Ascent, rather than before them as in the canonical Psalter, has a significant effect. Rather than Torah precipitating pilgrimage to Zion and the Temple,

(2) *The Songs of Ascent (120–134)* can be divided into three sets of five psalms, with each of the centre psalms (Psalms 122, 127, 132) emphasizing a different aspect of Zion, as well as the Lord's promise to David (especially Psalm 132; *cf.* Psa 89:3–4; 2 Sam 7). These songs suggest that the Davidic ideal and hope had not entirely dropped out of favour within the post exilic community, but rather takes on an eschatological and messianic dimension *alongside* of and in the *service* of God's sovereign rule (*cf.* Psalms 2 and 18 in Book 1).[14] Also, these psalms provide a parallel to the Entrance Liturgies (Psalms 15–24) of Book 1, which focus the desirability of making a pilgrimage to Zion, the place of the Lord's presence and rule.

(3) *Psalms 138–145* provide a Davidic collection that reflects the concerns of Books 1 and 2, especially noting the parallels between Psalm 144 and Psalm 18 in Book 1. Finally, the Davidic Psalm 145 not only concludes Book 5 as well as the entire Psalter with the unique term "praise" (Heb. *tehilla*) within its superscription (*cf.* Psa 72:20), but it also serves as an introduction to the final five "Praise the Lord" (Heb. *hallu yah*) Psalms (146–150). This double function is first of all achieved by verse 20 which points back to Psalm 1 and the distinction drawn there between the godly and the wicked. Then, verse 21 points forward to Psalms 146–150, in which the final word is "praise" of the Lord's "holy name" by all his creatures. Thus the final word of the entire Psalter is not that of lament, but rather one of joy and "praise", that also includes "thanksgiving" (*cf.* Psalms 22:3; 50:1–23; 89:14).[15]

---

pilgrimage, in effect, leads to the Torah. This even reflects more the spirit and movement of Isaiah 2:2–4, but the changes may simply be different literary ways of highlighting the importance of Torah. See Gerald H. Wilson, "The Qumran Psalms Scroll (11QPs^a) and the Canonical Psalter: Comparison of Editorial Shaping," *CBQ* 59 (1997), 448–469.

[14] Supported by the importance of the Davidic messiah in the Qumran Scroll (11QPs^a), in which David is also attributed with prophetic status (*cf.* Acts 2:30). But this does not mean with Wilson, "Qumran Psalms Scroll," 464, that this Davidic hope is entirely given up in the Masoretic Psalter by yielding to the kingship of Yahweh within Books 4 (93, 95–99) and 5 (145, 146–150) of the Psalter. Rather, it is the kingship of Yahweh which enables and reinforces this hope and keeps it alive for Israel. For this reason, Wilson's later wisdom frames within the Psalter (Psalms 1, 73, 90, 107, and 145) need not be seen as finally taking precedence over the Royal Psalms (2, 72, 89, 144), by directing our focus to trust in Yahweh. Rather, our trust in Yahweh will in time enable his full plan of salvation to come to completion. In the meantime, God's "righteous remnant" have an important role to fulfil.

[15] Patrick D. Miller, "The End of the Psalter: A Response to Erich Zenger," *JSOT* 80 (1998), 103–110.

Summary of Observations

We may therefore summarize our observations of Books 1 and 5 of the Psalter and their relationship to canonical Isaiah in *three* main ways.

(1) Firstly, Books 1 and 5 of the Psalter reveal a similar structural pattern that especially highlights the concept of *pilgrimage to Zion* (Psalms 120–134; *cf.* Psa 135:2; Isa 66:18–21) and those counted worthy to stand or dwell in the Lord's holy place on Zion (Psalms 15–24). This reflects the programmatic direction of Isaiah 2:1–5 in which the nations will finally engage in such a pilgrimage, for the purpose of being "instructed" in God's law (Torah). This will not only enable the nations to walk in the Lord's "paths" or ways, but the whole process will bring about world "peace" and "justice". The concept of "peace" will only become a full reality when the Prince of Peace reigns from Zion (Isa 9:6–7; 11:6–9,10–12) and brings both "justice" and "righteousness" to the earth. In the meantime, in the absence of such a king, Psalm 122 (attributed to David), prays for the "peace" and well-being of Jerusalem within the Psalms of Ascent (120–134); Psalm 122 has been linked to Psalm 132 within the same set of psalms, highlighting the Lord's choice of Zion as his dwelling place, *alongside* his sworn promise to David of an eternal dynasty (*cf.* Psa 89:3–4; 2 Sam 7:8–16). Further, we have already drawn attention to the importance of the Zion psalms culminating in Book 3 with Psalm 87, and the register of the nations that now belong to Zion as being "born" within her. Again, we noticed that this psalm has a distinct link with the only Davidic psalm in Book 3 (Psa 86:9), in which David remarkably points to the vision of Isaiah 2:1–5 becoming a future reality at Psalm 87.

(2) Secondly, within Books 1 and 5 of the Psalter we may notice a distinct connection between Psalm 18 (Book 1) and Psalm 144 (Book 5) as this relates to the book of Isaiah. Interestingly, in Psalm 18 David experienced the Lord in theophany and divine deliverance from his enemies, in "parting the heavens" and "coming down" as Divine Warrior (*cf.* 2 Sam 22). But now these same words are put into the form of a *prayer* for deliverance in Psalm 144:5–8: "Part the Heavens, O Lord, and come down," reflecting the form of prayer and context of the post-exilic community in Isaiah 63:15–64:12, in which Isaiah pleads for the community that the Lord's anger may

not continue against their collective sin.¹⁶ Also, it is significant that these words come toward the end of both books, especially if it can be correctly argued that Psalm 145 originally closed the Psalter, before the final "Praise the Lord" (*hallû yāh*) psalms were added (146–150). Further, it is highly likely that Psalm 144 has gained its inspiration from the Isaiah text, especially in terms of a form of closure to the Hymns of the Second Temple period. In a Job-like way, both Isaiah and the Psalms finally plead for an experience of *theophany* that will simultaneously involve the Lord coming in salvation and judgment. It is also clear that Psalm 144 reveals evidence of certain modifications from that of Psalm 18 (e.g. the inclusion of Psalm 8:4 possibly indicating the royal nature of the post-exilic community without a king), suggesting that it has been shaped and adapted for a new situation and need. A unique feature of Psalm 144 is the reference to "the evil sword" (verse 10) as a figure of speech for the "words" which the "foreigners" בְּנֵי־נֵכָר (*běnê-nēkār*, *cf.* Psa 18:44–45) were employing as weapons against the welfare of the community, perhaps reflecting a period like that of Nehemiah (6:1–19). Therefore, by re-praying Psalm 18 in a new version and situation, the appeal was made to do for the people what the Lord had done for his servant David. And so Psalm 144 is a prayer in which the community prays as David, and also hopes as David.¹⁷ It is another way of saying, "Do another David, O Lord!"

(3) Thirdly, the final grouping of psalms (138–145) reflects the concerns of Books 1 and 2, especially at Psalm 145:20 with regard to the distinction between the *righteous* and the *wicked*, which virtually provides a frame for the entire Psalter beginning in Psalm 1. In this way, the entire Psalter also mirrors the structure and concerns of the book of Isaiah at its frames (1:2 and 66:24) with regard to those who "rebel" against the Lord. For the book of Isaiah, the rebellious are also those whose chief sins are "pride" and "idolatry", who fail to "trust" the Lord and "listen" to his voice (65:11–12; 66:1–4). Their main sins are listed in Isaiah 1, and at the horizontal level also involve the many sins of social injustice. Like the Psalter, Isaiah can also call those who "rebel" against the Lord

---

[16] Barry Webb, *Isaiah* (BST; Leicester: IVP, 1996), 243, points out that it is likely that later generations of Israelites used this very prayer to lament the destruction of the Temple and seek God's forgiveness. Also see H.G.M. Williamson, "Isaiah 63:7–64:11. Exilic Lament or Post-Exilic Protest?" *Zeitschrift für die alttestamentliche Wissenschaft* 102 (1990), 48–58.

[17] Mays, *Psalms*, 436.

the "wicked" רָשָׁע (rāšā'), beginning at Isaiah 3:10–11 (where the "righteous" are contrasted with the "wicked") and finally the "wicked" are found at the frames of Isaiah 48:22 and 57:21 where "there is no peace for the wicked", which anticipate Isaiah 66:24 and the final death of the "rebellious". The same concept is found toward the end of the Psalter at Psalm 139:19,[18] "If only you would slay the wicked," Psalm 143:12 "destroy all my foes," and then at Psalm 145:20 which speaks of the final "destruction" of the wicked.[19] In this way, the book of Isaiah has provided the Psalter with a similar conceptual and structural framework.

Isaiah 1–12 and Psalm 145

A further structural similarity may be observed between Isaiah 12 and Psalm 145. Miller notes that in Isaiah 12 we encounter a similar kind of ending to a book within a book (Isaiah 1–12) that we seem to have in Psalm 145.[20] As we have already pointed out, Isaiah 1–12 forms the first distinct unit within Isaiah, which ends on a note of "praise". Also, within this unit, most of the important themes of Isaiah are introduced, which are also present within the Psalms, including the importance of Zion implicating the nations (1:2–2:5), followed by alternating oracles of judgment and salvation, separated by the call of Isaiah who announces the peoples' sin as well as the prospect of a righteous remnant (6:1–13). This is then followed by chapters 7–11 that contain parallel passages addressed to Judah and Israel containing a moment of decision (7:1–17; 9:8–10:4), followed by judgment (7:18–8:8; 10:5–15), the remnant (8:9–22; 10:16–34), and glorious hope in terms of a righteous ruler and a New Exodus salvation (9:1–7; 11:1–16). Finally, in the light of this, the people are now called to sing songs of praises, to break forth in a song of proclamation and praise of the name of the Lord (Isa 12:4). Miller concludes, "Like the movement of the Song of Thanksgiving (which can move from individual to community praise), like the movement in Psalm 145 (which concludes with similar themes in Psalms 107–145), and like the movement in Psalms 146–50, the individual who

---

[18] Further, Psalm 139:20 may also reflect Isaiah 66:5 where the wicked "misuse" the name of the Lord by excluding the faithful from worship through sarcastic taunts (*cf.* Isa 5:19).

[19] It should also be noted that Psalm 107:42 contrasts the upright with the "wicked", but uses a different word for "wicked", עולה (*'awlâ*), thus also providing a frame for Psalm 145:20 and Book 5.

[20] Miller, "Response to Zenger," 110.

praises evokes the praise of the many."[21] As a conclusion to Isaiah 1–11, chapter 12 is really a Hymn of Praise, which falls into two sections, clearly marked by the occurrence of the words, "And in that day you will say" (verses 1, 4). In verse 1 the "you" is singular, and in verse 4 it is plural. Thus there is a movement in this Psalm of Praise from the spontaneous outpouring of "praise" (*yādâ*), also found in Psalm 145:10, from each of the Lord's redeemed in verses 1–2 (where the verbs are singular), then in verses 3, and 4–6, (plural) the experience of salvation now prompts the redeemed as a whole to give thanks and "call" (*qārā '*) upon the name of the Lord (verse 4), which probably means to "proclaim" his name and righteous deeds among the nations. Finally, the song comes to a fitting climax in declaring that "great" (*gādôl*) is the Holy One of Israel in your midst (verse 6), as the Immanuel God (*cf.* 7:14), also reflecting the outer frames of Psalm 145 (verse 3 "great"; and verse 21 "holy name").[22]

Isaiah 40–66 and Books 4 and 5 of the Psalter (Psalms 90–106; 107–145, 146–150).

To begin with, we may note some of the conceptual links between Isaiah 40–66 and Book 4 (Psalms 90–106). Three are worth a closer look. First, we have already drawn attention to the only two Davidic psalms in Book 4 (Psalms 101 and 103). What purpose do they serve here in terms of our main inquiry? Psalm 101 is a king's pledge to reign righteously, and Psalm 103 is a hymn extolling God's love and compassion toward his people and their sin. But in between, in Psalm 102, the situation of distress envisaged is most likely that of the Babylonian exile. But at the same time, the Psalmist, most probably representing the wider faith community, voices the plea that the appointed time has now come for the Lord to have compassion on Zion (verse 13). As a result, the nations and kings of the earth will fear and revere the name and glory of the

---

[21] Miller, "Response to Zenger," 110.

[22] Note that as a frame to Psalm 145, Psalm 138 is also a song of praise/thanksgiving using the same verb (*yādâ*), in which the first person style can also be understood as a general song of praise by the post-exilic community in *fulfilment* of the prophecies of salvation first proclaimed at Isaiah 12:1–6 and Isaiah 40–66, especially in carrying out their vocation to be witnesses to the nations of the Lord's sovereignty and salvation, that should also command the recognition of the kings of the nations because they have also now recognized that the words spoken by the prophets have been fulfilled. Indeed, the glory of the Lord has been revealed to all (Psa 138:4–5; Isa 40:5), and the Lord's salvation is the act of the High for the lowly, and the powerful for the weak (Psa 138:6; *cf.* Isa 40:9–11; 57:15; 66:1–2). See Mays, *Psalms*, 424–5.

Lord (verse 15), as the nations assemble to worship the Lord in Zion (verses 21–22). This may well be the hope for which the Psalmist looks in this psalm (verses 17–20). Already we have observed that the only Davidic psalm in Book 3 (Psalm 86) serves the same function alongside Psalm 87 (*cf.* Psa 86:9; 87:4). Both in turn reflect the theological agenda of Isaiah 2:1–5 and may well represent the personification of the exiles in Isaiah 40–55, whose opening complaint, voiced at Isaiah 40:27 (*cf.* 49:14), is that their "way has been disregarded by the Lord." In the meantime, Psalm 102:16 also states that the Lord will rebuild Zion and "appear in his glory", echoing Isaiah 40:5. Further, Psalm 103:5, in close association with Psalm 102, repeats the language of Isaiah 40:30–31 with regard to "youth that is renewed like the eagle's." Even though it is possible that this language may have originally belonged to David, its association with other aspects of Isaiah 40 in Psalm 102 may suggest that the association with Isaiah 40 at both ends of the chapter is not fortuitous.

Another study has made further connections between Book 4 (Psalms 90–106) and Isaiah 40–55 on the basis of particular words and literary structure.[23] In some cases, this common language is present only in these two blocks of material. But of significant interest is the fact that an impressive number of terms shared by Book 4 and Isaiah 40–55 appear in analogous position near the beginning and/or the end of both. For example, Psalm 90:13 and Isaiah 40:1, as well as Psalm 106:45 and Isaiah 54:11, contain the root *nḥm* ("comfort/have compassion"). This is also linked to the word "gather" (*qbṣ*) at Psalm 106:46–47 and Isaiah 54:7. Also, only in these two blocks of material do we find the frailty of humanity compared with the terms "grass" (*ḥāṣîr*) and "flower" (*ṣîṣ*) (Psa 90:5–6; [102:5]; 103:15–16; *cf.* Isa. 40:6–8). Further lexical similarities include "everlasting covenant" (*běrît 'ôlām*) near the end of both sections at Psalm 105:10 and Isaiah 55:3 connected with "servants", and at the end of both blocks of material is the concept of "coming out with joy" (*rinnâ*) at Psalm 105:43 and Isaiah 55:12. Further, whereas the opening Psalm 90:13–14 concludes with Moses' prayer that the Lord might "relent" and have "compassion" on his servants by satisfying them with his "unfailing love" (*ḥesed*), this prayer is finally answered at Psalm 106:44–45 with the same terms (*cf.* Psa 145:8; Exod 34:6–7). In this way, Moses' great

---

[23] Jerome Creach, "The Shape of Book Four of the Psalter and the Shape of Second Isaiah," *JSOT* 80 (1998), 63–76.

intercession for Israel in the past (Exod 32:11–14; Deut 9:18–20, 25–29) has been called into the service of the exiles' present plight, with the hope that the Lord will *continue* to answer their cries for help (Psa 106:47; *cf.* Deut 30:1–10). But, this will also be dependent upon the theophany of the Lord's self-declared character at Exodus 34:6–7 to which Moses makes his appeal, which also concludes the Psalter at Psalm 145:8. Finally, the concept of God's "comfort/compassion" has an equivalent frame within Isaiah 40–55 with God's "word" which stands forever (40:8) and finally accomplishes God's will for his people (55:11; *cf.* Psa 147:15–20). Creach argues that the number of such parallels, and the fact that some terms only appear in these two blocks of material, suggest that some form of interplay has taken place between the psalms in Book 4 and Isaiah, with Isaiah 40–55 most likely providing the model for such interplay. But in the end, Book 4 with its emphasis upon Moses in Psalm 90, and the reference to "secret sins" (verse 8; *cf.* Deut 27:15, 24), framed in the final psalm (106) by the reference to "Horeb" (Deuteronomy's typical term for Sinai) and the "cast idol" (verse 19), followed by the people's sacrifice to "demons" (only elsewhere at Deut 32:17), equally suggest that Book 4 has been deliberately patterned on the basis of "Torah" (instruction and law) as this is found in the book of Deuteronomy. Thus we really find with Book 4 of the Psalter a fine example of the threefold interplay of Psalms, Isaiah, and Deuteronomy, as this will finally lead into Book 5 of the Psalter, with its eschatological perspective of hope and praise.

A third connection between Book 4 of the Psalter and Isaiah 40–66 relates to the theme of the "vengeance" of God. Especially does this relate to Psalm 94 where the Lord is called the "God of Vengeance", which is unique to this psalm within Psalms 93 to 99, which proclaim the kingship of the Lord. Creach has also drawn attention to the connection between the universal rule of Yahweh and idol passages within Isaiah 40–55, reflected in Psalms 96:4–5 and 97:1–7, which also share between them further identical language and themes.[24] But in these same psalms, the Lord comes to judge the earth (Psa 96:13; 98:9) because "righteousness" and "justice" are the foundation of his throne, and all the peoples will

---

[24] Creach, "Shape of Book Four," 68. Phrases and clauses from Psalms 96, 97, and 98 appear in the prophecy of Isaiah 40–55, especially relating to the Lord coming in judgment and salvation, accompanied by the chorus of praise from Heaven and Earth (Isa 44:23; 49:13; 55:12).

see his glory as the fire of his holy presence consumes his enemies on every side (Psa. 97:2–6). One could argue that in the first instance, such a theophany of the Lord's presence reflects Deuteronomy 32:40–43. In fact, Isaiah 58:14 reflects Deuteronomy 32:13–14, and then Isaiah 59:14 follows this up by saying that "justice" is driven back and "righteousness" stands at a distance. And because there was no one to intervene, the Lord armed himself with the garments of vengeance and zeal, to repay his enemies for what they have done (Isa 59:9–20; *cf.* 65:6–16; 66:15–18). Within these passages, it may be the case that the Lord's judgment upon Israel was the *antecedent* to his judgment upon the nations, possibly reflected at Isaiah 66:18. But the burden of the communal lament of Isaiah 59:9–15 was the absence of "justice" (*mišpāṭ*) in verses 9, 11, 14. This meant that deliverance was still far away for God's people, but "justice" was also absent from God's own people themselves, making it difficult for anyone to protest (verses 14–15).[25] Thus, the Lord himself had to intervene and satisfy the need for "justice", by finally repaying the nations for what they had done (Isa 59:18; 63:4–6). On this basis, it is more likely that the prophetic word of Isaiah became the inspiration for the "God of Vengeance" within Psalm 94 and Psalms 96–99 (also framed by the concerns for "justice" and "righteousness"), for it gave these psalms especially a theological rationale for such a God within the context of the Babylonian exile (*cf.* Isa 62:10–12) alongside the God of Psalm 103:6–10 (*cf.* Exodus 34:6–7). Finally, in the book of Isaiah, the day of vengeance is also linked to the day of redemption for God's people (Isa 61:2; 63:1–6), which immediately precedes the final prayer for the Lord to "rend the heavens and come down" (Isa 63:15–64:12), which we have already noted is found in Psalm 144:5–8 (the penultimate psalm before Psalm 145), and then at Psalm 149:6–9 (the penultimate psalm before Psalm 150) in which "vengeance" upon the nations that have attacked God's kingdom will be finally carried out by the Lord's own people, according to the "sentence" (NIV) (*mišpāṭ*; verse 9) already proclaimed by the Lord (reflecting the earlier Deut 32:40–43 and more recent Isa 59:18).

As an extension of the previous paragraph, we may therefore note how Isaiah 40–66 also links up with Book 5 of the Psalter (Psalms 107–150). As we have seen, the main point here is that the penultimate Psalms 144 and 149 reflect the same concerns and

---

[25] Webb, *Isaiah*, 228.

direction as that of Isaiah 59:9–20 and Isaiah 63:15–64:12 for the Lord to finally reign in justice and righteousness upon the earth, with implications for both Israel and the nations. But the movement toward this scenario also involves the second Psalm at the beginning of Book 1, which corresponds to the second Psalm from the end, Psalm 149. Psalm 2 announces that it is through his anointed king that the Lord will claim kings and nations for his rule. But in Psalm 149, the instrument now turns out to be the assembly of the faithful, who now appear to fulfil the vocation of the Davidic king (*cf.* Dan 7:13–22).[26] These concepts also align with the book of Isaiah, where the second chapter from the beginning announces the pilgrimage of the nations to Zion, where the law ("Torah") of the Lord will go forth, instructing the nations in justice, righteousness, and peace (Isa 2:1–5; *cf.* 65:11–12). And like the penultimate Psalm 149:4, the faithful remnant in the penultimate chapter of Isaiah are also the lowly and "humble" servants of the Lord, who await the vengeance and justice of God through the "sword" (65:11–12; *cf.* 59:9–20; 63:15–64:12). In fact, the very last word of Psalm 149 (verse 9) appeals to the "faithful" who recognize God as their "King" (verse 2), who are entrusted with the vocation formerly assigned to the monarchy and articulated as such in Psalm 2 (*cf.* Psa 149:7–9 and Psa 2:8–9), to carry out the judgment "written" against the Lord's enemies, which is a final appeal to remain obedient to God's Word (Torah) (*cf.* Deut 32:40–43; Isa 59:18).[27] On the one hand, this movement in theological thinking aligns with that of Isaiah 55:3–5 where the suspended covenant with David is now democratized and fulfilled in the people as a whole.[28] This also corresponds with the people to whom the Lord finally looks at the beginning of the last chapter of Isaiah (66:2), as those who are "humble" and contrite in spirit, and tremble at his word. As Barry Webb puts it when commenting upon the communal lament of Isaiah 59:9–15, "There is still one element of hope for the people of God, and that is the lament itself."[29] And as we can see with what follows in Isaiah 59:16–20, this was the very thing that the Lord responded to in terms of coming for the faithful remnant as the God of "justice" and "vengeance". In the light of this observation, it is

---

[26] Here, we may also note the reversal of language between Psalm 2:3, and Psalm 149:8.

[27] See J. Clinton McCann, "Psalms," in *Theological Interpretation of the Old Testament* (ed. K.J. Vanhoozer; Grand Rapids: Baker, 2008), 164–65.

[28] The New Testament's application of Psalm 2 to Jesus (Acts 4:25–26) as well as to the believing congregation (Rev 2:26–28) agrees with this.

[29] Webb, *Isaiah*, 228.

not surprising to find the form of communal lament still alive at the beginning of Book 4 of the Psalter (Psalm 90), and within Book 5 with Psalms 123, 126, and 137. Again, this corresponds with the direction of the book of Isaiah within its final chapters, especially relating to 59:9–20 (*cf.* 63:15–64:12; 65:11–12; 66:15–16), as well as to those people to whom the Lord will look as "humble and contrite in spirit, who tremble at my word" (Isa 66:2; *cf.* 2 Chron 7:14). [30]

Erich Zenger has also contributed to this debate by producing a convincing analysis and outline of Book 5 of the Psalter.[31] His thesis relating to Psalms 107–145 is that these Psalms constitute a post-cultic meditation/recital as a "spiritual pilgrimage" to Zion, which is the seat of the universal king Yahweh and of the God of Sinai who teaches his Torah from Zion. This is achieved by the intentional placement of Psalm 119 at the middle of the composition of Book 5. Thus, the Psalms are a means of opening oneself to the living Torah of Yahweh, in accordance with the programme at the beginning of the Psalter (Psa 1:2), and in accordance with the closing Hallel, Psalms 146–50, which interprets the recitation/singing of the Psalms as the actualization of the way of life (Torah) instilled in the cosmos. In drawing attention to the canonical history of Israel,[32] Zenger argues that the poor and needy are being called to praise the God who rescues *in the midst of affliction and suffering* (Psalms 138–144). This way of viewing Book 5 of the Psalter not only supports the vision of Isaiah found at Isaiah 2:1–5 for all the nations involving instruction in the Torah, but it would also appear to offer this "spiritual pilgrimage" to Zion (and the Temple) in the *same* non-cultic (possibly better than Zenger's "post-cultic") terms (*cf.* Isaiah 66:1–24). Further, we have already aligned Zenger's point about the suffering of the poor and needy in Psalms 138–144 with the cry of the poor and needy at Isaiah 63:15–64:12 (*cf.* Psa 144:5–8).

As a final observation, one may surmise that the call of Isaiah featuring the grand vision of God within chapter 6 would also hold something of theological worth for the Psalter.

---

[30] The defining mark of the post-exilic theology of the Chronicler, supported by the placement of the seven Penitential Psalms at Psalms 6, 32, 38, 51, 102, 130, and 143.

[31] See Zenger, "Composition and Theology," 98–102, relating to Psalms 107–145. But see the following article by Miller, "Response to Zenger," 103–10, who correctly relates Psalm 145 to Psalms 146–50.

[32] Exodus = Psalms 113–118; Sinai = Psalm 119; Entry into the Promised Land with Zion as goal = Psalms 120–136, interspersed with the great "Messianic" promises both individual = Psalm 110, and collective = Psalm 144.

(1) First we may observe that Isaiah's entire message is based upon a single foundation: the belief that Yahweh, God of Israel, is the only one who is "high and lifted up" (Isa 6:1).³³ In this respect, no other earthly power can challenge him, nor any other god. This explains why the strong condemnation of everything that is "proud" in Isaiah 2:6–22 comes so early in the book. Further, it is significant that this passage follows immediately after Isaiah's vision for the future in 2:1–5, when the mountain of the Lord's temple (Zion) will be "raised up" above all mountains, and all the nations will come in pilgrimage to it in order to be taught from the Torah about the ways of the Lord. But in the meantime, the Lord has a day in store for the "proud and lofty" who will be brought low (Isa 2:12). This is also the concern of Psalm 94:2 which shares the word "proud" גאה (gē'e) with Isaiah 2:12. This may have provided a further reason why Psalm 94 could confidently pray that God would come in "vengeance" upon the wicked. Along with the only other two psalms where this same word "proud" is used (Psalms 123:4 and 140:5), the context suggests that the wicked use arrogant and deceitful words against the righteous. Psalm 140:3 says: "They make their tongues as sharp as serpents; the poison of vipers is upon their lips." Then in verse 10 the language of judgment is given: "Let burning coals fall upon them," which may well reflect Psalm 18:8 (cf. 2 Sam 22:9). But the context of "burning coals" together with lying and unclean lips makes the conceptual association with Isaiah 6:5–7 an interesting possibility. When confronted with the awesome theophany of God's holiness and presence within the Temple, Isaiah could only make the confession: "Woe is me, for I am a man of unclean lips, and I live among a people of unclean lips, for my eyes have seen the King, the Lord Almighty." Then only after Isaiah's lips were touched by the live coal from the altar was his guilt taken away, and atonement for sin made. The point of this passage is that Israel must also follow Isaiah's lead and experience, as a nation characterized by "unclean lips", before they too can render to the Lord fitting worship and service. This may account for the fact that the Psalms are replete with the enemy using arrogant, deceitful, and harmful "words" against the faithful as their main weapon of attack and destruction. At this point, it is of further interest that the opening psalm of the Psalms of Ascent in Book 5 (Psalm 120) targets the problem of "lying and deceitful lips". Then

---

³³ Gordon McConville, *The Prophets* (Exploring the Old Testament 4; London: SPCK, 2002), 5.

the punishment suggested is the "burning coals" of the broom tree as a means of fighting fire with fire. In this psalm, possibly the Psalmist was discouraged from making his pilgrimage to Zion, thus indicating that the problem of "unclean lips" was not confined to Israel. The Psalms of Ascent conclude at Psalm 134 with the call to the servants of the Lord to render "praise" to the Lord with the lips within his house on Zion's hill, thus suggesting that the only worthy use of the lips in life is praise of the Lord, and not to curse and oppose his people through speech (*cf.* Num 22–24). Finally, it is really a call to become as the Seraphim at Isaiah 6:3, who call, "Holy, holy, holy, is the Lord God Almighty, the whole earth is full of his glory."

(2) As a further extension of this last point, it is worth noting that "the theological heart" of the Psalter for a number of scholars are the so-called enthronement psalms which address God as "King", who desires "justice" and "righteousness" for his world order (Psalms 93 and 95–99).[34] But here again, we cannot dismiss the presence and possible influence of Isaiah's vision in the Temple with Psalm 93 at the beginning of this group, focusing the Lord as a reigning King, "robed in majesty" whose "throne" has been established from all eternity (verses 1–2). Then, like the Seraphim at Isaiah 6:3, here the seas "lift up" their voice (mentioned 3 times), proclaiming that the Lord "on high" is mighty, with his "holiness" adorning his Temple (verses 3–5). Finally, the framing psalm to this collection (Psalm 99) also has a triple refrain (verses 3, 5, 9), which suggests that the entire psalm is meant to be an exposition of the holiness of the Lord[35], again resembling in a literary fashion the threefold call of the Seraphim from Isaiah 6:3. Mays concludes:

> The Hymn is a liturgy for the vision that Isaiah saw in the Temple when he felt the foundations tremble and heard the threefold "holy" sung in praise. He never viewed life and the world in the same way after he said, 'my eyes have seen the king'.

The Psalms seek to preserve that memory for all time.

Conclusion

There is sufficient evidence within the Psalter to suggest that the Psalms have not only engaged in a conversation with Deuteronomy

---

[34] Gerald H. Wilson, "The Use of the Royal Psalms at the 'Seams' of the Hebrew Psalter," *JSOT* 35 (1986), 85–94.

[35] Mays, *Psalms*, 316.

from beginning to end[36], but this conversation has also involved the book of Isaiah at both structural, thematic, and lexical levels. Thus in the Psalms, one *learns* the story and command (Deuteronomy), how to *sing* and *pray* the Lord's songs (Psalms), and how to *see* the broader theological vision (Isaiah). This threefold mix and conversation (Psalms, Deuteronomy, and Isaiah) also reflects the importance of these dominant books at Qumran, as well as their importance for works like Luke-Acts in the New Testament.

---

[36] Miller, "Deuteronomy and Psalms," *JBL* 118/1 (1999), 3–18.

God of all Nations – Reading the Psalms

John W. Olley

Vose Seminary

> Why do the nations conspire and the peoples plot in vain?...
> I have installed my king... "You are my son".[1]
>
> Declare his glory among the nations...
> Say among the nations, "The LORD reigns".[2]
>
> All authority is given to me... make disciples of all nations.[3]
>
> The gospel... regarding his Son, who as to his earthly life was a descendant of David and who through the Spirit of holiness was appointed the Son of God in power by his resurrection from the dead: Jesus Christ our Lord. Through him we received grace and apostleship to call all the nations[4] to the obedience that comes from faith for his name's sake.[5]

The book of Psalms has provided forms and content of prayer for God's people for centuries, shaping and sustaining not only words of worship but life in all its vicissitudes. In response to current practice in many churches, N. T. Wright has called for the reclaiming of the power of the Psalms in contemporary public worship and personal devotion:

> The Psalms represent the Bible's own spiritual root system for the great tree we call Christianity... The regular praying and singing of the Psalms is *transformative*... so that we look at the world, one another, and ourselves in a radically different way.[6]

---

[1] Psa 2:1, 6–7. All biblical quotations are from NIV® unless otherwise stated and references are to psalms unless otherwise specified. Psalm and verse numbers will follow English versions, with MT or LXX numbers in brackets if different.

[2] Psa 96:3, 10.

[3] Matt 28:18–19.

[4] Instead of NIV "Gentiles" for (τὰ) ἔθνη I use "nations" to make explicit shared language with Matt 28:18.

[5] Rom 1:2–5; similarly Rom 16:24–26, an *inclusio* for the letter.

[6] N. T. Wright, *The Case for the Psalms: Why They Are Essential* (New York: HarperCollins, 2013), 5–7.

Recent decades have seen a major shift in academic study of Psalms which is beginning to be expressed in commentaries[7] and has great potential to affect preaching, worship and devotion – and hence life. Previously focus, in both research and preaching, has been on individual psalms, whether exploring possible historical settings of composition (including the life of David) or classifying psalms on the basis of their forms and possible cultic settings. While those approaches have continuing benefit, attention is turning to Psalms as a book. Nancy deClaissé-Walford is representative in asking, "Why these 150 psalms, in this particular order in the Psalter? Why does Psalm 1 begin the Book? Why is Psalm 90 located where it is? And so forth."[8] There is evidence of intentional arrangements that point to theological emphases and desired patterns of response.[9] Here I will argue that Psalms provides us with prayers that can illuminate our understanding of Christ's commission (and Paul's response) and sustain us as we are caught up in God's mission that covers all 'nations'. Individual psalms find their meaning as part of the whole.

Psalms as a Book

As with any area of biblical interpretation, some proposals regarding the structure of Psalms and theological themes gain wider acceptance than others. This is not the place to review and evaluate proposals in detail, but rather I highlight some well-recognised

---

[7] E.g., J. Clinton McCann, Jr., "The Book of Psalms: Introduction, Commentary, and Reflections," in *The New Interpreter's Bible: A Commentary in Twelve Volumes* (Nashville: Abingdon, 1996, Vol. 4), 639–1280; Konrad Schaefer, *Psalms* (Berit Olam; Collegeville, Minnesota: Liturgical Press, 2001); Gerald H. Wilson, *Psalms, Volume 1* (The NIV Application Commentary; Grand Rapids: Zondervan, 2002); and in most detail, Frank-Lothar Hossfeld and Erich Zenger, *Psalms 2: A Commentary on Psalms 51–100* (Hermeneia; Minneapolis: Fortress Press, 2005) and *Psalms 3: A Commentary on Psalms 101–150* (Hermeneia; Minneapolis: Fortress Press, 2011) [*Psalms 1: A Commentary on Psalms 1–50*, forthcoming].

[8] Nancy L. deClaissé-Walford, *Introduction to the Psalms: A Song from Ancient Israel* (St Louis: Chalice, 2004), vii, referring to her earlier *Reading from the Beginning: The Shaping of the Hebrew Psalter* (Macon, Georgia: Mercer University Press, 1997).

[9] Recent overviews are in W.D. Tucker, Jr., "Psalms 1: Book of," and L. Wray Beal, "Psalms 3: History of Interpretation," in *Dictionary of the Old Testament: Wisdom, Poetry & Writings* (ed. Tremper Longman, III and Peter Enns; Downers Grove, Ill: IVP, 2008), 578–93, 605–13; and in more detail, Gordon J. Wenham, "Reading the Psalms Canonically," in his *The Psalter Reclaimed: Praying and Praising with the Psalms* (Wheaton, Ill: Crossway, 2013), 57–79 [reprinted from "Towards a Canonical Reading of the Psalms," in *Canon and Biblical Interpretation* (ed. Craig G. Bartholomew et al.; Scripture and Hermeneutics; Milton Keynes: Paternoster, 2006), 331–51] and J. Kenneth Kuntz, "Continuing the Engagement: Psalms Research Since the Early 1990s," *Currents in Biblical Research* 10, 3 (2012), 321–78.

features that provide a context in which to explore the place of the 'nations'.

That there are collections in Psalms has been long recognised. For instance, superscriptions are clustered: every psalm superscription in Book I (1–41) mentions David, apart from 1–2, 10[10] and 33[11], with a similar collection a major part of Book II (42–72; see 51–65, 68–70, with 72:20 "This concludes the prayers of David son of Jesse"). There are however later psalms with a Davidic superscription, mainly in Book V (107–150).[12] Two other significant collections associate "sons of Korah" (42–49, 84–85, 87–88) and "Asaph" (50, 73–83). Firth comments that the Korahite psalms "have a strong focus on Jerusalem" and "God as the great king over all the earth", with a "dialectic [that] holds together honest complaint and the hope offered by the presence of God", while the Asaph collection "appears to be shaped by concerns generated by the fall of Jerusalem... in which covenant, individual testimony and national reflection can be applied to the sense of loss created by the exile."[13]

Clearly Psalms as we now have the book reached its form after the exile in the Second Temple period and so the question arises as to whether this historical setting has affected the overall collection and not only the Asaph collection. Is there a purpose, a 'story', in the present arrangement? Childs in 1979 was perhaps the first to argue for taking seriously the canonical structure of Psalms, making

---

[10] Psalms 9 and 10 were probably a single psalm (as in LXX). Together they form an alphabetic acrostic; see e.g. *BHS*.

[11] "Ps 33:1 links directly to Ps 32:11 in regard to key words, sentence structure, and liturgical setting. The functional affinity of the two songs was thus clear to the compiler of the collection" (Erhard S. Gerstenberger, *Psalms, Part 1; with an Introduction to Cultic Poetry* (The Forms of Old Testament Literature; Grand Rapids: Eerdmans, 1988), 144).

[12] Psalms 86, 101, 103, 108–110, 122, 124, 131, 133, 138–145. LXX Psalms manuscripts increase the number and content of superscriptions with around 87 titles (mss vary) compared to MT 73. LXX translators apparently did not understand לדוד (*ldwd*) as implying Davidic authorship, seen both in the use of the dative, τῷ Δαυιδ [cf. the genitive τοῦ Μωυσῆ, Psalm 90 (89)] and extended superscriptions such as Psalm 65(64), "A psalm τῷ Δαυιδ [for David], a song: Ιερεμιου καὶ Ιεζεκιηλ [of Jeremiah and Ezekiel] from the record of the sojourning, when they were about to depart."

[13] D. G. Firth, "Asaph and Sons of Korah," in *Dictionary of the Old Testament: Wisdom, Poetry & Writings* (ed. Tremper Longman, III and Peter Enns; Downers Grove, Ill: IVP, 2008), 25–27. Other collections: 111–118 each begin or end הללו־יה "hallelujah" and 120–134 have as superscription שיר המעלות "A song of ascents". 42–83 overwhelmingly use אלהים "God" (201 times, with יהוה "Yahweh", 44 times; contrast 3–41 with the proportion 15:278, and 84–150 with 16:370). There are also doublets, e.g., 14 and 53 (note divine names), and 108:1–13 (2–14) combines 57:7–11 (8–12) and 60:5–12 (7–14).

observations on Psalm 1 as opening and on the scattering of royal psalms providing an eschatological note.[14] This was developed in detail by Wilson[15] who highlighted the significance of both the position of Psalm 2 and the closing psalm of each of the five books, so incidentally supporting the canonical division into five books which has textual evidence as early as the Psalms scrolls from Qumran. Psalms, 2, 72, and 89, are royal psalms, with Book IV (90–106) standing

> as the 'answer' to the problems posed in Ps. 89 as to the apparent failure of the Davidic covenant with which Books One-Three are primarily concerned. Briefly summarized the answer given is: (1) YHWH is king; (2) He has been our 'refuge' in the past, long before the monarchy existed (i.e., in the Mosaic period); (3) He will continue to be our refuge now that the monarchy is gone; (4) Blessed are those who trust in him![16]

Book V is more heterogeneous with an encouragement of trust in Yahweh.[17] "David is seen as modelling this attitude in Psalms 108–110 and 138–145, an attitude which finds expression in obedience to YHWH's Torah, expressed in the massive and centrally located Psalm 119."[18] The final block, Psalms 146–50, each starting with

---

[14] Brevard S. Childs, *Introduction to the Old Testament as Scripture* (London: SCM, 1979), 504–25.

[15] Gerald H. Wilson, *The Editing of the Hebrew Psalter* (SBL Dissertation Series 76; Chico, Calif.: Scholars Press, 1985); "The Use of the Royal Psalms at the 'Seams' of the Hebrew Psalter," *Journal for the Study of the Old Testament* 35 (1986), 85–94; "Shaping the Psalter: A Consideration of Editorial Linkage in the Book of Psalms," in *The Shape and Shaping of the Psalter* (ed. J. Clinton McCann; Journal for the Study of the Old Testament Supplement Series 159; Sheffield: JSOT Press, 1993), 72–82; "King, Messiah, and the Reign of God: Revisiting the Royal Psalms and the Shape of the Psalter," in *The Book of Psalms: Composition and Reception* (ed. P. W. Flint and P. D. Miller, Jr.; Vetus Testamentum Supplements 99; Leiden: Brill, 2005), 391–406.

[16] Wilson, *Editing*, 215.

[17] 11QPsª preserves parts of thirty nine psalms that are in MT and another eleven compositions, seven known elsewhere and four previously unknown. All of the MT psalms are from Books IV and V but with a different order. There is similar lamenting over Jerusalem and expression of hope, but more focus on a Davidic deliverance. The יהוה מלך "Yahweh reigns" psalms are not included. See Gerald H. Wilson, "The Qumran Psalms Scroll (11QPsª) and the canonical Psalter: Comparison of editorial shaping," *Catholic Biblical Quarterly* 59, 3 (1997), 338–64; Ryan M. Armstrong, "Psalms Dwelling Together in Unity: The Placement of Psalms 133 and 134 in Two Different Psalms Collections," *Journal of Biblical Literature* 131, 3 (2012), 487–506.

[18] David M. Howard, Jr., "Editorial Activity in the Psalter: A State-of-the-Field Survey," in *The Shape and Shaping of the Psalter* (ed. J. Clinton McCann; Journal for the Study of the Old Testament Supplement Series 159; Sheffield: JSOT Press, 1993), 63, here summarising Wilson.

הַלְלוּ־יָהּ "hallelujah", praises Yahweh's cosmic sovereignty. The motif of "obedient trust", expressed in following the way of God's "instruction"[19] as in the opening Psalm 1, is reinforced by the structurally framing wisdom psalms, 73, 107 and 145, with 119 dominating the central section of Book V.[20]

A detailed stimulating elaboration of a post-exilic reading of the psalms in order is that of deClaissé-Walford:

> But this "unfettered" praise [Psalm 150] is only possible at the *end* of the story of the Psalter. The postexilic community must understand where it has come from (the "Who are we?") and where it is going (the "What are we to do?") before it can participate in the praise of YHWH the king. Thus the Psalter becomes a story of survival in the changed and changing world with which the postexilic Israelite community is confronted.[21]

In the process of collecting and ordering and placing within the canon of scripture,

> The Psalms underwent a transformation from being the words of humankind to God into scriptural words of God to humankind. They became words of encouragement and hope to a community in turmoil, a community coming to grips with a new life situation.[22]

Psalms 1 and 2 no doubt had separate origins and may appear unrelated but their juxtaposition as 'orphan psalms' before the cluster of Davidic psalms, together with literary links, leads to a composite picture that shapes subsequent reading. The "happy, blessed" (אַשְׁרֵי '*ašrê*) are "the person whose delight is in the תּוֹרָה (*tôrâ*) of the LORD" (1:1–2) and "all who take refuge in him" (2:12), an *inclusio* for the two psalms. They bring together the generic individual (אִישׁ '*îš*, 1:1) and 'the nations' (גּוֹיִם *gōyim*) with their

---

[19] תּוֹרָה *tôrâ*, commonly translated "law", is not so much a set of rules but "instruction in the broadest sense, written tradition that is authoritative for the people of God. Specifically, Psalm 1 introduces the psalms as Scripture to be studied, heeded, and absorbed" (James Luther Mays, *Psalms* (Interpretation; Louisville: John Knox Press, 1994), 15). The New Jewish Publication Society Version (1985) translates "teaching". It includes the whole story of God's involvement with his people and creation, recounted in some psalms. The structuring of Psalms into five 'books' may be a deliberate reminder of the five books of the 'Torah', in which individual 'laws' have as their context a broader historical narrative.

[20] Wilson, *Editing*, 200–28, and 'Shaping,' 78–82.

[21] deClaissé-Walford, *Reading*, 103.

[22] deClaissé-Walford, *Introduction*, 5. See also J. Clinton McCann, Jr., *A Theological Introduction to the Book of Psalms* (Nashville: Abingdon, 1993).

contrasting הָגָה (*hāgâ*): faithful "meditating" (1:2) and rebellious "plotting" (2:1). The contrast in 1:6, between the דֶּרֶךְ (*derek*, "way") of the צַדִּיקִים (*ṣaddiqîm*, "righteous") that Yahweh "watches over" and that of the רְשָׁעִים (*rĕšāʿîm*, "wicked") which will אָבַד (*ʾābad*, "lead to destruction"), leads in 2:12 to the warning to "you kings" to acknowledge God's rule or "your way (דֶּרֶךְ) will lead to your destruction (אָבַד)".[23]

> While Psalm 1 orients the reader to receive the whole collection as instruction, Psalm 2 makes explicit the essential content of that instruction—the Lord reigns. The entire psalter will be about the "happy" / "blessed" life, and it will affirm that this life derives fundamentally from the conviction that God rules the world.[24]

Psalms 1 and 2 thus provide a number of interlocking motifs: the call to delight in Yahweh's 'instruction' as the only way to blessing, Yahweh as ruling the world through his anointed king in Zion, and the fate of the 'wicked' who persist in rebellion against Yahweh. How are the people of Israel to live as vassals within the powerful Persian empire – and later Greek then Roman? They may have some measure of self-rule, but certainly were not a 'nation' with a king reigning in Jerusalem. In Psalms they find expression of hope: it is Yahweh who is 'enthroned in heaven' (2:4) and who has the last word to all nations; their response was to transcend their traditional ideas and to find identity as they "delight in the *tôrâ* of the Lord" (1:2), that was the path to ultimate blessing.

The 'Nations' in Psalms

If they, and we, continue to live among the 'nations', what views of the nations are shaped by worship using Psalms? What kinds of attitudes and expectations are fostered? Looking at Psalms within the wider canon of both Old and New Testaments, in what ways might Psalms contribute to shaping and undergirding response to the commission to "make disciples of all nations" (Matt 28:19), calling all nations εἰς ὑπακοὴν πίστεως "to obedience of faith" (Rom 1:5; 16:26)?

---

[23] The end of 2:11 and start of 2:12 is textually difficult, hence different translations in English versions, "kiss the son" and "kiss his feet" (cf. NIV, NRSV). Irrespective, the context points to submission to Yahweh's appointed ruler.
[24] McCann, "The Book of Psalms," 688–89.

Studies using a canonical approach to Psalms have given little attention to 'nations' other than under the general rubric of Yahweh's kingship and place of the Davidic ruler. On the other hand, Christopher Wright has contended that "the proper way for disciples of the crucified and risen Jesus to read their Scriptures, is *messianically* and *missionally*"[25]. His own work is organised thematically, so he discusses a few specific psalms referring to the 'nations' under the headings: "David: a king for all nations"; "nations as beneficiary of Israel's blessing"; and "the nations will worship Israel's God".[26] In a footnote however he comments, "The growth of interest in the Psalms as a whole may hold further missional significance"[27]. In response to an invitation, Wenham recently explored a canonical reading of "The Nations in Psalms":

> The canonical approach does not ignore discussion of the original author's understanding of each psalm, but it holds that the most accessible and authoritative sense of a psalm is that of the Psalter's editor, a sense that is opened by reading the psalm within its wider context of surrounding psalms.[28]

In a similar vein I explore the topic, with some obvious indebtedness to Wenham and other commentators.

The Nations as Book-ends: Psalms 2 and 144–150

Psalm 2 has boldly placed nations and their kings under the sovereignty of Yahweh, with a call for all to acknowledge him or face destruction. The same motif appears in the concluding Psalms 148–149. Yahweh's cosmic reign ("The One enthroned in heaven", 1:2) leads in conclusion to a call to universal "praise", including that of

> kings of the earth and all nations
> you princes and all rulers on earth (148:11).

Yet there remain those who continue to refuse that call, and so Yahweh's חֲסִידִים (*ḥăsîdîm* "faithful ones"), who as עֲנָוִים (*'ănāwîm* "lowly, humble") have first been the recipients of Yahweh's יְשׁוּעָה

---

[25] Christopher J. Wright, *The Mission of God: Unlocking the Bible's Grand Narrative* (Nottingham: Inter-Varsity Press, 2006), 30 (emphasis his).
[26] Wright, *Mission*, 345, 474–78, 478–84.
[27] Wright, *Mission*, 481, n.28.
[28] Wenham, *The Psalter Reclaimed*, 162. Chapter 8, "The Nations in the Psalms" (161–186) was originally a lecture given in 2010.

(*yĕšû'â* "victory, deliverance"), will be agents carrying out his sentence, in imagery (but not language) reminiscent of 2:9–12:

> To inflict vengeance on the nations
>   and punishment on the peoples,
> to bind their kings with fetters,
>   their nobles with shackles of iron,
> to carry out the sentence written against them (149:4–9).

As in 2:6 Zion is the centre, but there is mention only of Yahweh as "King" (149:2).[29] Here it is the "faithful ones" who enjoy victory and who see the submission of the "nations" and their "kings" as their הָדָר (*hādār*, "adornment, splendour"; 149:9b). Mays notes connections with Isaiah 40–66:

> These are the prophecies that speak overall of the LORD's revelation of his kingship in the world through the victorious salvation of his people (e.g., 40:1–11; 41:21–29; 52:7–10). Specifically, the LORD in these prophecies promises to make Israel a *two-edged* instrument to crush those who war against them (41:11–16) and to *adorn* his people with saving victory (55:5; 60:9)... Something wonderful and strange is afoot here, the lowly becoming the warriors who fight for the kingdom and inherit the earth.[30]

Relevant here is the ending of Isaiah. Isaiah 40–66 has much that is positive concerning "the nations", reflected in Paul's several citations in Romans, but there is also diversity similar to Psalms,[31] and Isaiah, like Psalms, ends with destruction of "those who rebelled against me" (66:24).[32]

David has last been mentioned in the block with Davidic superscription (138–145) that precedes the concluding "hallelujah" psalms (146–150). In particular the concluding pair, 144–145, includes Yahweh giving him victory over others, so leading into the concluding praise psalms. Psalm 144 begins with battle imagery, calling to Yahweh,

---

[29] The parallelism points to the identity of "their King" as being "their Maker".

[30] Mays, *Psalms*, 447–48, citing also Matt 5:3, 5. Linguistic parallels, especially with Isaiah 60–61, are listed also by Leslie C. Allen, *Psalms 101–150* (Word Biblical Commentary; Waco, Texas: Word, 1983), 319–20.

[31] E.g., Rikk E. Watts, "Echoes from the Past: Israel's Ancient Traditions and the Destiny of the Nations in Isaiah 40–55," *Journal for the Study of the Old Testament* 28, 4 (2004), 481–508.

[32] John W. Olley, "'No Peace' in a Book of Consolation—A Framework for the Book of Isaiah?" *Vetus Testamentum* 49 (1999), 351–70.

> my shield, in whom I take refuge (חָסָה ḥāsâ)
> who subdues peoples[33] under me (144:2).

The language recalls 2:12, with its promise of blessing to the one who "takes refuge" (also חָסָה ḥāsâ), following the promise to "my king" of rule over "the nations". There is affirmation of future praise

> to the One who gives victory to kings,
> who delivers his servant David (144:10).

The present stance however is a prayer for deliverance, including a repeated plea to "deliver me, rescue me ... from the hand of foreigners" (144:7, 11). The phrase בְּנֵי נֵכָר (bĕnê nēkār "sons of foreignness") occurs in Psalms only here and in 18:44, 45 (45, 46), a psalm which celebrates the king's victory over foreigners who "cower... obey me... lose heart", and which is replete with language and imagery seen in 144, 145. There may have been victory then (see further below), but as one journeys to the conclusion of Psalms, submission of others is still in the future. So the following acrostic Psalm 145 is an affirmation of Yahweh's kingship, concluding with blessing for "those who fear him" (v. 19; cf. 2:11) but destruction for "the wicked" (v. 20; cf. 1:6; 2:12) and the affirmation: "let every creature [כָּל־בָּשָׂר kol-bāśār "all flesh"] praise his holy name for ever and ever".

At the Seams
Psalms 72 and 89

Psalm 72 not only closes Book II but also "concludes the prayers of David son of Jesse" (72:20). In what may have been a coronation psalm the prayer is that the king will receive the submission and tribute of nations near and far (72:8–11), summarised in

> May all kings bow down to him
> and all nations serve him (72:11).

A result of his reign exercised with justice and righteousness, with care for the "weak and needy", is material prosperity and, in fulfilment of the Abrahamic promise (Gen 12:3),

---

[33] While most MT manuscripts have עַמִּי 'ammî "my people", the masorah notes "one would expect עַמִּים ['ammîm "peoples"]", which is the reading in 11QPsᵃ, also followed in Aquila, Syriac, Targum and Vulgate; cf. 18:47(48).

Then all nations will be blessed (וְיִתְבָּרְכוּ *wĕyitbārĕkû*)³⁴ through him,
and they will call him blessed (יְאַשְּׁרוּהוּ *yĕ'aššĕûhû*)³⁵ (72:17).

Reading this as a prayer of David "for Solomon"³⁶ one can reflect on the possibilities then ahead for the nation with Solomon's reign, with temple, peace, and prosperity, enhanced by tribute brought.

Post-exilic readers knew of the decline that began in Solomon's reign itself, a decline that 1 and 2 Kings repeatedly links with failure to obey God's commands.³⁷ The juxtaposition and order of Psalms 1 and 2 point to the same priority on obedience and relationship. Read now after the exile, "because the rule of God is the ultimate object being praised... [there is an] eschatological dimension."³⁸

Unlike the hope of Psalm 72 at the end of Book I, Book II ends in the lament of Psalm 89 that contrasts Yahweh's kingship and the current distress. Instead of the nations seeing Israel as a nation to be emulated and so be blessed (72:17), now, with repetition adding to the anguish,

> Remember, Lord, how your servants³⁹ have been mocked,
> how I bear in my heart the taunts of all the nations,⁴⁰
> the taunts with which your enemies, LORD, have mocked,

---

³⁴ As in Genesis there is debate as to the best understanding of the hitpa'el form (commonly reflexive/reciprocal), hence NIV alternative "will use his name in blessings (see Gen. 48:20)" (the hitpa'el is also in Gen 22:18; 26:4) and JPSV "invoke his blessedness upon themselves". LXX translates as the passive, εὐλογηθήσονται. Irrespective, nations share in the blessing through identification.

³⁵ The root אשר *'šr* as in 1:1; 2:12 (so NRSV "happy").

³⁶ So interpreting the preposition -לְ *l-* of the superscription in light of the closing sentence; e.g., Childs, *Introduction*, 516.

³⁷ The story of Solomon's reign begins with David's charge that links the promise of blessing with "walk in obedience to him... as written in the Law of Moses", repeated in Yahweh's direct words to Solomon with increasing warning (1 Kgs 2:2–4; 3:14; 6:12–13; 9:3–4-8). Sadly, after his death "the whole assembly of Israel" described Solomon's rule with language echoing the oppressive slavery in Egypt before the exodus (1 Kgs 12:4).

³⁸ Childs, *Introduction*, 517. Childs is perhaps the first to highlight the canonical placing.

³⁹ So NIV alternative, translating the plural עֲבָדֶיךָ *'ăbādeykā* of most MT mss, followed by LXX and Vulgate. Most EVV follow 24 mss and the Syriac which have the singular. The plural may be similar to the plural "faithful people" in v. 19 (20), and the plurals of vv. 15–18 (16–19), so linking people and their king.

⁴⁰ The Hebrew of this line is awkward. If MT כָּל־רַבִּים עַמִּים *kol-rabbîm 'ammîm* is followed it may have the sense "all the many (different) peoples"; see detailed discussion in Marvin E. Tate, *Psalms 51–100* (Word Biblical Commentary; Dallas: Word, 1990), 412–13.

> with which they have mocked every step of your anointed one [89:51(52)].

Again brought together are the life of the people, focussed in an "anointed one" (cf. 2:2), the overarching kingship of Yahweh ("*your* enemies", "*your* anointed one"), and the behaviour of "the nations". A strong expression of dissonance is seen climactically not only in the destruction of Jerusalem *per se* [v. 40(41)] but in the resultant scorn and taunting. There is "shame" [v. 45(46)], but this in turn involves Yahweh and the "nations". One cannot separate the life of God's people from Yahweh's purposes for the nations. The doxology at the end of Book II is now read with Psalm 89. It poignantly brings to the fore the issue, how is Yahweh, to whom "heaven and earth" belong [v. 11(12)], now to be "blessed" by all (בָּרוּךְ *bārûk*) [v. 52(53)]?

Book IV (90–106)

The dramatic change of mood from 90 on has long been recognised. More than fifty years ago Westermann observed that "(t)he first half of the Psalter is comprised predominantly of Psalms of lament, the second predominantly of Psalms of praise"[41]. Psalm 90 pivotally answers the cries of 89 (and 88) and moves forward with its affirmations of God's long-standing compassionate relationship with his people, yet recognising "our iniquities" (90:8; absent from 88, 89), with a willingness to be "taught" and so "gain a heart of wisdom" (90:12). The superscription "Prayer of Moses, the man of God"

> immediately takes the reader back to the time of Moses when there was no land or Temple or monarchy... (Book IV) offers the "answer" that pervades the psalter and forms its theological heart: God reigns... Relatedness to God is still possible as it was in the time of Moses.[42]

In describing the Psalm as a תְּפִלָּה *tĕpillâ* "prayer (supplication, intercession)" is there also a reminder of the occasions when Moses interceded for the people – in Exod 32:11–13 an intercession based on God's reputation among the nations and his promise to Abraham, Isaac and Israel – and God showed his forgiving, restoring compassion? The following psalm affirms the lasting

---

[41] Claus Westermann, *Praise and Lament in the Psalms* (trans. Keith R. Crim and Richard N. Soulen; 2nd ed.; Edinburgh: T. & T. Clark, 1981), 257 (original German article, 1962).
[42] McCann, "The Book of Psalms," 1040.

security of those who say, "The Lord is my refuge" (91:2, 9; מַחְסֶה *maḥseh*; cognate noun of the verb used in 2:12).

The central clustering in Book IV of psalms affirming Yahweh's kingship (93, 95–99) is commonly noted, with Howard adding an argument for the placing of 92 and 94 which "show the wicked and foolish who may flourish for a moment, but who will ultimately be overcome by YHWH and YHWH's righteousness"[43]. The motifs of Psalms 1 and 2 are again brought together.[44]

Significant for our exploration is that Book IV with only 17 psalms, has the plural nouns 'nations, peoples'[45] 25 times (101 in all psalms).[46] To sing of Yahweh as King is to have the whole world in view. It is not only that we[47] are "the flock under his care" (95:7) who must ensure that we "do not harden [our] hearts" (95:8), but at the same time we "declare his glory among the nations, his marvelous deeds among all people" (96:3). To affirm God as creator-king has consequences for how God's people see political structures, imperial power and the many "gods of the nations" (96:5).

Is there more? Psalm 100 opens with a call to joyful worship by "all the earth" (100:1). Zenger argues in detail that, although מלך *mlk*, as either noun "king" or verb "reigns as king", does not appear in 100, yet the language is shaped throughout by "royal theology" and statements from 93, 95, 96 and 98 are cited, and so 100 can be understood as climax and conclusion of the preceding 'YHWH is king' psalms. There are also links between 100:3 and 46–48 (see below on 47). This leads to a striking conclusion:

> If we read Psalms 93–100 as a continuing context, the nations move steadily into the center of the event, drawing closer and closer to Israel and its God... Psalm 100, as the climax of the composition, integrates the nations of the world in worship before the God of Zion:

---

[43] Howard, "A Contextual Reading," 121.

[44] Links with 1 may be seen in 92:12–14; 94:11, 12.

[45] EVV generally translate גּוֹיִם *gōyîm* as "nations"; עַמִּים *'ammîm* as "peoples", but sometimes "nations"; and the less common לְאֻמִּים *lĕ'ummîm* as "nations" or "peoples". Similar variation is seen in LXX ἔθνος and λαός.

[46] גּוֹיִם *gōyîm* 10 (54), עַמִּים *'ammîm* 14 (37), לְאֻמִּים *lĕ'ummîm* 1 (10).

[47] I deliberately switch to 'we' since the songs of the people of Israel have become the songs of the Christian church – and most, if not all, readers of this article will be part of that community.

> they should, and they will, shout aloud to YHWH, serve him (and not the idols; cf. 97:7) with joy, and experience his nearness—like Israel and together with it... This astonishing universalism is found in pointed fashion at the beginning and end of the canonized prophetic corpus but also in the Psalter itself [Isa 2:1–5; 19:21–25; 66:18–23 and Zech 14:9–21; cf. esp. The Psalter's conclusion, Psalms 145–150].[48]

While Wenham notes that "[n]ot all commentators share Zenger's daring reading that makes verse 3 a confession by the nations", he continues, "it is clear that this psalm calls on all of them to join in the true worship of the God of Israel".[49]

Following the flow of the psalms in the movement from the end of Book III into the central cluster of Book IV is to go from the depths of despair, powerlessness and hopelessness into the boldest affirmation of confidence and inclusion possible! Importantly, these psalms follow quite closely from the agonizing cry of 89. To sing these psalms with their focus on Yahweh, his people, and the nations is to live out the dramatic reversal in the middle of Psalm 73 (the first psalm in Book III):

> When I tried to understand all this,
>   it troubled me deeply
> till I entered the sanctuary of God;
>   then I understood their final destiny (73:16–17).

How is an impoverished subject people without political independence, whether living within the Persian province of Yehud or elsewhere in the empire (or subsequently under Greek, then Roman rule), to live as God's people? It may seem counter-intuitive that the answer is firstly to boldly affirm Yahweh's absolute sovereignty and to call all nations and peoples to give glory to him, to recognize that they too are subject to his rule. It also means that one lives as Yahweh's people, faithfully delighting in his *tôrâ* (and so the comprehensive, all embracing Psalm 119). That is the basis upon which and the context within which further cries can be made.

Significantly the same explicit reminder at times of weakness, powerlessness and/or injustice and idolatrous syncretism of God's purposes for the nations is seen throughout the Old Testament. The first statement in Gen 12:3 is given to Abraham when it might seem he had nothing (no child or land and away from familiar

---

[48] Zenger in Hossfeld and Zenger, *Psalms 2*, 494, 497, with n.23.
[49] Wenham, *The Psalter Reclaimed*, 184.

surroundings). God's glory amongst the nations is the basis of Moses' intercession at the time of the golden calf incident (Exod 32:11–12) and similarly Joshua's after the defeat at Ai (Josh 7:8–9). The narrative setting of Deuteronomy is a people at present without land, but again it is through the presence of God and "righteous decrees and laws", which are to be "followed", that "the nations" will be drawn (Deut 4:5–8). Times of blatant injustice and syncretistic worship or economic weakness are addressed with a vision of God's glory amongst all nations (e.g., Isa 2:3–4; Jer 3:17; Zeph 2:11; Hab 2:14; Mal 1:11).

'Nations' Throughout the Psalms

Previous studies have argued that kingship (Davidic and Yahweh's) and wisdom are key elements in the five-book structuring of Psalms and that there is a consequent broad story-line. Here I have sought to present evidence that, inseparably linked with these motifs, is the place of the 'nations'. This does not mean that the "nations" has been an element in the structuring but rather that motifs of kingship and of God's people following his *tôrâ*, walking in his 'way', cannot be spoken of without reference to the 'nations'. The 'nations' are an integral component in the mix. God's sovereignty and his purpose that "all nations" honour him is the context in which Israel is God's people and David is his "anointed one".

This is the context in which psalms of crying to Yahweh for deliverance continue through all the five books. Features of Psalm 86 are representative. After affirming

> All the nations you have made
>   will come and worship before you, Lord;
>   they will bring glory to your name (86:9)

there is a cry

> Arrogant foes are attacking me, O God;
>   ruthless people are trying to kill me—
>   they have no regard for you (86:14).

Wright comments

> The subtext, then, of the implied logic in the psalmist's appeal is that if all the nations are going to have something to praise God for, it should not be too difficult for God to sort out the psalmist's personal problems and give him a more immediate cause for praise (Ps 86:12) … The Abrahamic promise thus becomes not just a majestic vista of

the ultimate mission of God but a very potent engine of personal hopefulness in the immediate saving power of God.[50]

To this can be added the psalmist's plea immediately following the affirmation concerning the nations:

> Teach me your way, Lord.
> That I may rely on your faithfulness;
> give me an undivided heart,
> that I may fear your name (86:10).

Brought together are the nations bringing glory to God, the individual knowing and following God's way, and praying in the midst of present conflict.

The two psalms with greatest number of instances of 'nations/peoples'[51] are 96 (nine times), a psalm in the middle of the Yahweh kingship psalms of Book IV, and 67 (ten times), framed by 66 (twice) and 68 (twice). Read canonically, 66–68 provide a backdrop for the cries for deliverance in 69–71, followed by the royal psalm 72 which has the nations bringing tribute to the Davidic king and "all nations being blessed through him" (72:17).[52] Psalm 72 carries on the motifs of 66–68 that the nations bow down to and praise Yahweh, and share the benefits of his just reign, because of what they see he has done in and through his people—but such hope is not separated from present distress.

The two psalms with the next greatest number are 9 and 44 (each seven times), psalms which speak mainly of the "nations" as those defeated on entry into the land or those that are now enemies and threatening, and so to be defeated. This is a reminder, already noted above regarding 145–150, that those who persist in opposing Yahweh's purposes, remaining "wicked", suffer defeat.

A contrast is 47, which has six instances. Here are brought together the past where Yahweh

---

[50] Wright, *Mission*, 234.

[51] In the following I refer only to psalms that specifically speak of "nations/peoples". The fact that such explicit vocabulary is throughout the book is significant. To these could be added the many references to 'enemies' and the 'wicked', but they may be internal or external to the people of God, just as 'righteous' potentially includes people from the 'nations'. Wenham, *The Psalter Reclaimed*, 168, observes that:

Early Davidic psalms do not mention the possibility of some righteous among the nations who will escape this judgment, but in the light of the programmatic statement inviting them to serve the Lord (2:11), it cannot be ruled out.

[52] See above for previous discussion of this verse.

> subdued nations under us,
>> peoples under our feet [47:3(4)],

the present affirmation of faith that

> God is the King of all the earth...
> God reigns over the nations [47:7–8(8–9)],

and the unexpected

> The nobles of the nations assemble,
> the people of the God of Abraham,[53]
> for the kings (or 'shields') of the earth belong to God [47:9(10)].

For MT עַם אֱלֹהֵי אַבְרָהָם "people of the God of Abraham" LXX has μετὰ τοῦ θεοῦ Ἀβρααμ "with the God of Abraham". Some thus see a case of haplography and so emend to ...עִם עַם "with the people..."[54]. MT as it stands however makes sense, especially given reference to Abraham and use of the early name of God, associated with Jerusalem at the time of Abraham, עֶלְיוֹן *'elyôn* "Most High".[55] A similar unexpected statement of equal inclusion is in 87, also a psalm of Zion, where after a list of nations[56] to be recorded as "those who acknowledge me" (87:4),

> The LORD will write in the register of the peoples (עַמִּים *'ammîm*):
> "This one was born there [i.e., Zion]" (87:7; cf. v. 4).

Such openness to others fits what has been argued above on Psalms 93–100 but may be seen in the very opening of Psalms where the one "blessed" is the generic אִישׁ (*'îš* "person"), set over against rebellious "nations". Similarly Psalm 8 refers to the generic אָדָם *'ādām* "human being, earthling". There is the potential for all

---

[53] Omitting NIV's "as", to reflect MT where the phrases are in apposition.

[54] E.g., *BHS*, P.C. Craigie, *Psalms 1–50* (Word Biblical Commentary; Waco, Texas: Word, 1983). 347; Hans-Joachim Kraus, *Psalms 1–59, A Commentary* (trans. Hilton C. Oswald; Minneapolis: Augsburg, 1989), 466.

[55] E.g., McCann, "The Book of Psalms," 869; Wright, *Mission*, 490. For עֶלְיוֹן see Gen 14:18–22; Deut 32:8.

[56] Predominantly in Psalms 'nations' are nameless. Other than mention of Egypt and neighbouring nations in psalms remembering the exodus and entry into the land of Canaan, the naming of specific nations is seen only here and in 60:8 (10) = 108:9 (10); 68:31 (32); 83:5–8 (6–9) and 137:1, 7–8. Psalm 87 stands out with its geographical spread and positive expectation.

humans to "be blessed" and to share in authority through delighting the Yahweh's "instruction".

Conclusion

In summary, the 'nations' feature in various ways in Psalms. They are an integral part of motifs and the story-line that are commonly seen behind the canonical structure. One cannot speak of "following God's way" and kingship without including the nations. Worship that fosters individual trusting obedience looks out to the 'nations' and Yahweh's glory in all the earth. What is sung now in worship has eschatological fulfilment, seen by the eyes of trust: Yahweh is sovereign over all nations and all nations are to give glory to him. Those who acknowledge him participate in blessings while those who persist in rebellion will perish. Especially after 89 focus is on Yahweh as King, with a somewhat muted but real place for the Davidic king: 110 strongly reinforces the importance of the king, affirming the programmatic perspective of 2, while the Davidic inscriptions of 138–145 leading into the concluding 'Hallelujah' psalms ensure the place of David. In the present God's people face opposition and at times defeat or scorn, and so there are cries to God, but these are based on his rule over all nations. Visions of the future shape the present.

How to live without political, economic or military power? How to live as a minority, subject to foreign powers and surrounded by dominant cultures? Jews in the Second Temple period and beyond faced such questions. Some similarity may be seen in issues faced by churches today, whether in countries that once experienced the political power of Christendom or elsewhere, all living now as minorities, often marginalised. Miroslav Volf contends that "the church has two malfunctions: idleness and coercion... His vision is for a thoughtful faith, practised with integrity in community"[57].

Jewish faith and life amongst the 'nations' was sustained and resourced through corporate worship and private meditation using the book of Psalms. The answer of Psalms is not to retreat into a private world, waiting for some dramatic change. Instead they boldly affirmed allegiance to the God of all nations, relativising the attraction and permanence of empires, and reflected on how to follow God's ways, using Psalms as 'instruction'. They sang of opposition and of the apparent success of foreign ways – and in

---

[57] Sophie Timothy, "Miroslav Volf to visit," *Eternity* 43 (Dec 2013):3.

worship found their answers. The variety of psalms gave language to express diverse experiences, hopes and agonising cries in the midst of the pressures of life in the empire – and the same variety of psalms would not let them forget God and the nations.

The psalms provided a full range of possibilities. The 'nations' may be 'enemies' who were defeated in the past or threaten in the present, but they are people who are called to give glory to God and follow his ways. They could persist in being 'wicked' and so be perish, or else come in worship and allegiance to Yahweh as 'king' and to his 'anointed one' and so share blessing as part of God's people. There was eschatological promise of God's glory being recognised in all the earth.

Through constant singing of and meditation on the whole Psalter, they remembered that, irrespective of how the 'nations' acted, God's people are to follow his ways, for all other ways are doomed to fail. They are to "meditate on his *tôrâ*" – and *tôrâ* was never separate from their relationship with the God of the universe.[58] As God's people they live out now the cosmic rule of God, and so "delight in his ways". Throughout the constant mention of the 'nations' reminded them that God had called them to "the obedience of faith" for the sake of the nations.

---

[58] In Psalm 119 seven synonyms are used as well as *tôrāh*. In every case, except vs. 49, 128 which are commonly emended following the versions, there is a relational possessive: "your" (almost all), "of Yahweh" (v. 1), "his" (vv. 2, 3), "of my God" (v. 115).

Is it Right to Pray the Imprecatory Psalms?

Katy Smith

Bible College of South Australia

Introduction

The usefulness of Imprecatory Psalms as Christian Scripture poses one of the greater hermeneutical challenges to confessing evangelical scholarship. While the Psalter has been a source of blessing for faithful Christians over the millennia in times of thanksgiving, lament, praise, and complaint, this same book contains imprecations that boldly ask for horrific violence to be done to the psalmists' enemies.[1] While evangelical scholars cherish 2 Timothy 3:16–17, a number hold the view that these imprecations should not be appropriated for church use or for believers under the new covenant. Anderson, for instance, calls the imprecations "pre-Christian"[2], while Craigie views the words of imprecation not as oracles of God but as "Israel's response to God's revelation emerging from the painful realities of life" that are "in themselves evil".[3] In contrast, Estes reminds the reader of the Psalter that the psalmists who are crying out for vindication are not "abject pagans"[4] but rather they are the covenant people of God pouring out their painful experiences before their covenant God.

The apparent division of scholarly opinion prompts the question of how we are to both faithfully and helpfully use the psalms that contain these imprecations within Christian worship both individually and corporately. The task of this paper is to first examine whether the psalmist's view of justice within the psalms expressing imprecations is aligned to the view of God's justice that encompasses the whole Psalter. If it is indeed evident that both views of justice are aligned, then the imprecations cannot be seen to be inherently evil. The second task is to suggest a framework to understand the imprecatory psalms theologically. The goal is to

---

[1] Examples of Psalms that contains imprecations are Psalms 5, 10, 28, 31, 35, 40, 58, 69, 109, 139, and 140.

[2] A. A. Anderson, Psalms 1–72 (2 vols; NCB; London: Oliphants, 1972, Vol. 1), 434.

[3] Peter C. Craigie, Psalms 1–50 (WBC; Nashville: Thomas Nelson, 1983), 41.

[4] Daniel J. Estes, *Handbook on the Wisdom Books and Psalms* (Grand Rapids: Baker, 2005), 172.

propose a way forward to resolve the issue at the crux of this hermeneutical challenge, "Is it right to pray the imprecatory psalms?"

Understanding Justice in the Imprecatory Psalms

From the beginning to the end of the Psalter, the psalmists testify to the two-sided justice of Yahweh where God acts salvifically on behalf of those whose allegiance is to his kingship, while he acts mercilessly against those who oppose him. Psalm 1, the hermeneutical gateway into the Psalter, teaches how the one who delights in Yahweh's instruction will be known in the way of the righteous, while the one who walks, stands, and sits in the path of the wicked will perish. Alternatively, Psalm 2, which is considered the first psalm of Book I of the Psalter, suggests the kings of nations who do not submit to God's anointed king will perish in the way, while those who serve Yahweh with reverential fear and who take refuge in him are blessed. Similarly, Psalm 145 before the extended doxology of Psalms 146–150 also declares the same view of God's justice in v. 20, which is that Yahweh acts to preserve the life of those who love him, while he will destroy the wicked. It is after this concluding note that the psalmist then calls all flesh to bless the holy name of Yahweh forever (v. 21). Thus, examining Psalms 69, 109, and 137 as exemplars of imprecatory psalms, we will ask whether the view of God's justice in these psalms is aligned to the view of God's two-sided justice that encompasses the whole Psalter.

Understanding the Imprecations of Psalm 69 in Context

The imprecations of Psalm 69 are isolated to one section in vv. 23–28 [vv. 24–29][5], which structurally is significant. Before the imprecations, David cries out his utter dependence upon his covenant God as he waits in desperate agony for Yahweh to ransom him from relentless opposition (vv. 1–20). David's initial appeal for God to save him in v. 1 sets the tone for the first half of the psalm (vv. 1–18). The metaphorical language of the waters sweeping up as far as David's life Heb. נפש (*nepeš*) in v. 1 [2] conveys that the situation is threatening his very being, which is then accentuated in v. 2 [3] with the imagery of falling into muddy depths with no firm ground. Later in v. 14 [15], David repeats

---

[5] There is a discrepancy in the versification of Psalm 69 between the Hebrew text and English translations. Therefore, for the sake of readership, Hebrew versification is acknowledged in the brackets when it is necessary, otherwise this section will follow English versification.

similar sentiments asking God to rescue him from the mud and not to let him fall. This phrase in v. 14 [15] rendered 'Rescue me from the mud and let me not fall' then has a parallel phrase that repeats the same verb נצל (*nāṣal*) in the cohortative ('let me be rescued') with the indirect objects being the threatening waters and those who hate the psalmist. The use of parallelism in this instance indicates that the situation from which the psalmist is seeking deliverance is from those who hate him. The vivid imagery of the threatening waters suggests that those who oppose him could certainly cause his death.

The use of parallelism in v. 4 [5] to describe the psalmist's adversaries accentuates that those wishing to destroy him (v. 4c) are attacking David with lies (v. 4d) and are doing so without cause (v. 4b). His opponents are described as great (v. 4a) and powerful in their number (v. 4c). The psalmist's perception is that he is being unjustly accused, recognising that God knows his folly and guilt (v. 5). David is implying that his guilt is not the reason why he is bearing reproach. Verse 5 [6] declares that God knows Heb. ידע (*yāda'*) his folly, while v. 19 affirms that God knows Heb. ידע (*yāda'*) David's reproach, his shame, his dishonour, and his enemies. What is clear is that the psalmist is not near to death because of his own guilt, but rather due to the shame and dishonour caused by those who oppose him unjustly. Moreover, the psalmist's concern in his shame is for those who seek Yahweh and he asks that they not be put to shame because of him (v. 6). Verses 7–8 provide the reasons for this concern, which is firstly because the psalmist's shame is for the sake of Yahweh (v. 7) and secondly, due to his zeal for Yahweh's temple. In fact, David almost perceives himself enduring shame on behalf of God, since the reproach was first aimed at God but has now fallen to him to bear (v. 9 [10]). As Wenham highlights, "it is not merely his own discomfort that drives the psalmist's prayer, but the honour of God's name and the perseverance of those who trust in him."[6]

David's understanding of why he is bearing shame unjustly motivates his plea in vv. 13–18 [14–19] for God to answer him. In v. 13, David affirms his trusting confidence that God will intervene in a favourable time. This confidence is in the character of God

---

[6] Gordon J. Wenham, *Psalms as Torah: Reading Biblical Song Ethically* (STI; Grand Rapids: Baker, 2012), 172.

whose abundance of *ḥesed*[7] Heb. חסד will answer the psalmist by means of the faithfulness of his salvation. Similarly v. 16 [17] asks for an answer based in the belief that God's *ḥesed* is good. The psalmist envisions that this answer, founded in God's *ḥesed*, will be manifest in two ways. The first is the psalmist's hope that God will no longer hide his face from him (v. 17). The psalmist knows that if God's face is hidden so is his favour, and thus asking God to reveal his face is akin to asking God to show favour to him. The form of this favour in v. 14 and v. 18 is deliverance and ransom from those who hate him. Thus, in the first half of the psalm, leading to the imprecations, the psalmist views himself as one who faithfully honours God and has been dishonoured because of his faithfulness. This shame however is caused by those who hate the psalmist and who seek to destroy him. Therefore, as one who honours God, the psalmist is seeking favour and salvation from God, established in *ḥesed*, as an answer to his plight.

In contrast to David's expectation that God will redeem him (vv. 1–19), vv. 22–28 give voice to the second way David desires God's intervention, which is for God to remove his favour from those who have caused his plight. This desire for the removal of favour expressed through the imprecations involves making his enemies blind (v. 23a) and for their camp to be desolate so that no one dwells in their tents (v. 25). Then, even more terrifying, is the psalmist's request in v. 27 to give his persecutors guilt upon guilt so that they do not approach in God's righteousness.[8] This then leads to the psalmist asking in v. 28 that they be wiped out from the book

---

[7] The translational meaning and value of חסד (*ḥesed*) is widely debated. Glueck, Snaith, and Sakenfeld argue that when *ḥesed* is active in relationship between Yahweh and his people then the term is inherently covenantal and so should be translated 'covenantal faithfulness' or 'covenantal love' (Norman Snaith, *The Distinctive Ideas of the Old Testament*, London: Epworth, 1947, 98–99; Nelson Glueck, *Hesed in the Bible*, Cincinnati: Hebrew Union College, 1967, 71, 102; Katharine Doob Sakenfeld, *The Meaning of Ḥesed in the Hebrew Bible*, HSM 17, Missoula: Scholars, 1978, 147). In contrast, Andersen states that *ḥesed* is not constrained to a covenantal relationship and has strong connections to the meaning of grace, mercy, and compassion (Francis Andersen, "Yahweh, the Kind and Sensitive God," in *God Who is Rich in Mercy*, Eds. Peter O'Brien and David Peterson, Sydney: Lancer, 1986, 41–51). There is no sufficient English word that conveys the semantic value of *ḥesed*. Moreover, the purpose of this paper is to discuss the debate concerning the hermeneutics of imprecations in the Psalter rather than the meaning and translational value of *ḥesed*. Therefore, this paper will use the transliteration only rather than providing an English equivalent.

[8] Verse 28b in the Hebrew versification can be rendered 'and let them not approach in your righteousness', rather than the rendering of many modern English translations, 'may they have no acquittal from you' (ESV). The second person pronominal suffix modifying צדקה (*ṣᵉddāqāh*) refers to God's righteousness.

of the living and not be recorded with the righteous. Thus, the nature of the imprecations is such that David is asking not only for physical blessing and favour to be taken away from those who hate him, but that any opportunity for the persecutors to be in right relationship with God and thus be counted on the path of the righteous be removed. Essentially, after asking God not to be hidden from him and to act in salvation, the psalmist is now requesting that those who caused his shame be the ones from whom God turns away his favour.

Is the psalmist asking for more than the principle of *lex talionis*[9]? When we understand the imprecations in context, the answer must surely be 'no'. As harsh and vindictive as the imprecations sound, what David is asking for is nothing more or less than what those who are persecuting are desiring for him. Verse 26 provides the reason for the imprecations. It seems that his persecutors are actively hunting those who have already suffered under God's justice. David prays that the recipients of the withdrawal of God's favour are the pursuers of those whom God has already struck down and slain. Thus, just as the psalmist's persecutors are violently adding to God's justice, so the psalmist asks for guilt to be added to them.

Understanding the imprecations within their literary context reminds us that the psalmist is not calling for God's justice to come upon his enemies in cold blood. Rather, he views himself as one of the righteous and therefore is seeking God's justice against those who cause God's people shame. Thus, the psalmist's imprecations are aligned to Psalm 1:6, which states the theological principle of Yahweh knowing the path of the righteous, while the path of the wicked will perish.[10] David's prayer in Psalm 69, including the imprecations, is that this theological truth will be realised in his situation where the righteous are suffering unjustly at the hand of those who are counted among the wicked.

Understanding the Imprecations of Psalm 109 in Context

Part of our westernised reaction to the imprecations is the assumption that words asking for God to destroy the psalmists'

---

[9] The *lex talionis* refers to the 'eye for an eye, tooth for a tooth' principle.

[10] While Yahweh knows the righteous, he is absent in the path of the wicked, where those who are present perish. Yahweh is active in the path of the righteous but absent in the life of those who oppose his rule. Thus, Broyles rightly asserts "the implication of v6b is that without divine intervention life will degenerate into death; it is only with divine aid that it is possible to sustain life" (Craig C. Broyles, *Psalms* (NIBC; Peabody: Hendrickson, 1999), 43).

opponents are motivated by hatred. Yet the motivations giving voice to the imprecations are quite contrary to our assumptions. David begins Psalm 109 with a plea for God not to be silent because he is surrounded by language of hate and opposition, both without cause (vv. 2–3). Verses 4–5 then express David's attitude of love and good towards those who attack him. When his accuser appoints evil against him, his response is to devote himself in prayer (v. 5). Thus, the attitude of the psalmist praying the imprecations is that of dependence upon his God to act in a context where the good he is demonstrating to others is rewarded with evil.

David's recollection of how words are spoken against him unjustly causes him to pray the imprecations in vv. 6–19 and he does so using the language of a legal courtroom setting. For instance, in v. 4 David asks for an evil man to be appointed as a prosecutor against his opposer and for the outcome of the trial to be a guilty verdict (v. 7). This request then leads to the series of imprecations asking for his accuser to be deprived of blessing and favour. This encompasses asking that the days of the psalmist's accuser will be few so that another can take his place (v. 8), for his sons to be orphans and his wife a widow, and that even his family be reduced to poverty (vv. 10–11). In the reversal of circumstances, the psalmist asks that no one will extend *ḥesed* and favour (Heb. חנן) to his accuser or to his orphaned sons. Rather, the psalmist asks in v. 13 and v. 15 that future generations will be cut off so that his name will no longer be in existence. David makes a deliberate contrast in vv. 14–15, using a play on the Hebrew זכר (*zākar*). He asks in v. 14 that the iniquity and sin of the father and mother be remembered (*zākar*), while the remembrance (*zākar*) of their name be cut off from the land. The reason given is that his accuser did not remember (*zākar*) to demonstrate *ḥesed*. Instead of showing *ḥesed*, the accuser pursued the humble and broken-hearted to death. David's opponent does not delight in giving favour or blessing, but rather delights in curse. Thus, the psalmist's logic is that if his accuser did not delight in showing to others favour and blessing, then he should not be a recipient of such *ḥesed*. In v. 20, David pleads that this be the recompense, that is, the just reward, of his accusers who speak against his own life. Thus, the psalmist's prayer is aligned to the *lex talionis*.[11] Just as his accuser seeks to end David's life and by

---

[11] David Firth, *Surrendering Retribution in the Psalms: Responses to Violence in the Individual Complaints* (PBM; Bletchley: Paternoster, 2005), 41. See also, John N. Day, "The Imprecatory

implication his future generations, so too he asks God to put an end to his accuser's life. The difference between David's accuser and David himself is that David has displayed *ḥesed* to his accuser and has surrendered his desire for justice to God, while his accuser pursues David personally in violence without cause. While VanGemeren is right to highlight that we need to understand the psalmist's imprecations in the context of his time[12], it is of even greater importance to understand v. 20 as handing over retribution to Yahweh, whose promise is to curse those who curse his people in Genesis 12:3.[13]

Verse 31 is indeed the "matter of the psalm in a nutshell."[14] The reason for the psalmist's vow of praise is his confidence that God is at the right hand of the one in need in order to deliver him from those who would judge his life. Again, courtroom language is used. In v. 6, the psalmist asks that an accuser be appointed at the right hand of his opponent, while in v. 31 the psalmist affirms that God, who can deliver his life, is at his right hand. God's justice is such that salvation for his people means justice against those who oppose them.[15]

Understanding the Imprecations of Psalm 137 in Context

The violence of the imprecations in Psalm 137 is unpalatable to the point that Zenger calls it "the 'psalm of violence' *par excellence.*"[16] It is critical however that we do not divorce the psalm from its exilic context where the exiles themselves have experienced horrific violence at the hand of the Babylonians, suffering torment and oppression in a foreign land. The psalmist is aware of the widening chasm between the promise of the songs of Zion and the reality of the destruction of Jerusalem and the temple. For instance, the song of Zion in Psalm 46 celebrates Zion's inviolability because God is in the midst of her (vv. 5, 7, 11). Psalm 46:2–3 declares that even

---

Psalms and Christian Ethics," *BSac* 159 (2002), 179: "David asked the divine Judge to extend to his enemy the demands of the lex talionis."

[12] Willem A. VanGemeren, "Psalms", *Expositor's Bible Commentary* (12 vols; Eds. Tremper Longman III & David E. Garland (Grand Rapids: Zondervan, 2008, Vol. 5), 810.

[13] Firth, *Surrendering*, 42, observes "as an expression of covenant faithfulness, that desire for vengeance is handed over to Yahweh since the right of vengeance is exclusively his." Furthermore, Day, "Imprecatory Psalms," 179, perceives echoes of Genesis 12:3 in Psalm 109.

[14] Derek Kidner, *Psalms 73–150* (TOTC; Leicester: IVP, 1973), 391.

[15] Day, "Imprecatory Psalms," 178.

[16] Erich Zenger, *A God of Vengeance? Understanding the Psalms of Divine Wrath* (Louisville: WJK, 1996), 47.

though the mountains of the earth may shake and fall, the city of Zion will not because God is present with her. The song of Zion ends with a universal call to peace (vv. 9–10) because Yahweh, the Lord of Hosts, is present with his people in his chosen city, Zion (v. 11). In contrast, Psalm 137 laments how they cannot sing the songs of Zion in a foreign land (vv. 1–3) and recalls how the Edomites encouraged the Babylonians to tear down the city of Jerusalem to its foundation (v. 7). Underlying the psalm is the uncertainty that if foreign and impure nations have torn down the city, then God must have either abandoned Zion or he is defeated.

Psalm 137 has a simple structure focused on זכר (*zākar* 'to remember') and its antithesis שכח (*šāḵaḥ* 'to forget'). The first use of זכר (*zākar*) is at the beginning of the first stanza in v. 1, recalling how the exiles sat by a river in Babylon and remembered Zion. This act of remembrance then leads the psalmist to recollect in vv. 2–3 how they endured the mocking of their oppressors asking them to sing the songs of Zion. The rhetorical question in v. 4 leads to the psalmist uttering imprecations against his own person. The first imprecation in v. 5 is conditional upon the psalmist forgetting Heb. שכח (*šāḵaḥ*) Jerusalem. In this instance, the psalmist asks that his right hand would forget how to play his instrument. If he forgets Jerusalem, which means that he has forgotten the songs of Zion, then in his view he does not deserve to be able to play. The second imprecation is conditional upon the psalmist not remembering (*zākar*) the city (v. 6). His highest joy would be reflected in his singing. If he no longer remembers, then this would no longer be the case and again, in his view, God should take away the capacity for the psalmist to sing and even to speak.

After the psalmist speaks imprecations against himself in the second stanza, the third stanza (vv. 7–9) is a command for Yahweh to remember (*zākar*) how Edom and Babylon destroyed Jerusalem. In v. 7, although Edom was not involved in the actual destruction of Jerusalem, Edom is portrayed as an accomplice in its encouragement of the Babylonians to wreak destruction in Jerusalem. Then vv. 8–9 focuses upon Babylon and pronounces a two-fold blessing on the one who brings retribution to daughter Babylon. We must note that Yahweh is not explicitly addressed within vv. 8–9, but the call for Yahweh to remember in v. 7 implies he will act upon that which he remembers. It is reasonable to suggest that the psalmist is envisaging Yahweh as the one who is blessed as he acts in vengeance against Babylon by crushing the nation in devastating defeat.[17] Verse 9 is the most problematic, with the psalmist wishing that the retribution would be for the Babylonian children's heads to be smashed against rocks. Yet v. 9 is a "naked appeal for retribution"[18] as the psalmist asks for Yahweh to repay Babylon for the destruction of Jerusalem kind for kind. The focus is upon the merciless justice of Yahweh upon those who destroyed the children of God's people and his city.[19] There is no call for salvation on behalf of the exiles, rather the focus is on surrendering retribution for the evil perpetrated against Jerusalem to God, the one to whom justice ultimately belongs.

Are the Imprecations Inherently Evil?

Although the imprecations may offend our westernised sensibilities, contrary to Craigie this paper cannot affirm that the imprecations are "evil"[20]. To affirm this notion, we would in effect be declaring that God's justice is not inherently good. The Psalter relentlessly portrays God's justice as two sided. Exploring the nature of justice in the imprecatory psalms, it has been observed that the psalmists' imprecations are aligned to this two-sided understanding of justice where each imprecatory psalm asks Yahweh to act in salvation on behalf of those who seek him (69:14, 17, 33–34, 109:22; see also 35:26, 58:11–12)[21] and to act in vengeance against their adversaries (69:25–29, 109:20; see also 35:2–6, 26, 58:9–10, 83:15–18). It is

---

[17] See Kidner, *Psalms 73–150*, 461: "although this is an outburst, not a direct plea to the Judge, and reveals only obliquely what Babylon has done, the words are by implication spoken in the Lord's hearing, continuing from verse 7."

[18] James L. Mays, *Psalms* (Interpretation; Louisville: WJK, 1994), 423. See also Leslie C. Allen, *Psalms 101–150* (WBC; Nashville: Thomas Nelson, 2002), 309; A. A. Anderson, *Psalms 73–150* (2 vols; NCB; London: Oliphants, 1972, Vol. 2), 900; Kidner, *Psalms*, 461; Hans-Joachim Kraus, *Psalms 60–150* (Trans. Hilton C. Oswald. Continental; Minneapolis: Fortress, 1993), 504; Mays, *Psalms*, 423; J. Clinton McCann Jr, "Psalms", *NIB* (Vol. IV, Nashville: Abingdon), 1228; VanGemeren, *Psalms*, 952. *Contra* James Limburg, *Psalms* (Westminster. Louisville: WJK, 2000), 467, who explains the violence of the imprecations of v. 9 as a "violent wish, inexcusable but not atypical for a violent time."

[19] *Contra* Heim who argues that a responsible reading of Psalm 137 understands daughter Babylon as a symbol for the brutal army and the infants being representative of the cruel soldiers who oppressed Jerusalem. There is nowhere in the text that suggests such a degree of symbolic meaning. However, Heim is correct in his observation that the nature of the imprecations is "about expressing the agony and resentment of an exiled and humiliated community about their abusive oppressors." Knut Heim, "How and Why We Should Read the Poetry of the Old Testament for Public Life Today", *Cardus*, http://www.cardus.ca/comment/article/2981/how-and-why-we-should-read-the-poetry-of-the-old-testament-for-public-life-today/ (November 11th 2011).

[20] Craigie, *Psalms 1–50*, 41.

[21] Psalm 137 is the exception, since the psalmist does not ask for God's justice in salvation.

critical to note both aspects of God's justice are present and both are beyond dispute. The imprecations by nature are the psalmists crying out for the kind of justice that is witnessed to from the beginning (Pss. 1–2) to the goal of the Psalter (Pss. 145–150). Firth states in relation to Psalm 64, "there is no need to seek retribution because the world view of the psalm again assumes that Yahweh acts on behalf of the righteous against the wicked."[22] In surrendering the desire for justice to God, the psalmists are imploring God for his favour to be manifest in the life of those who seek him, while asking that those who are complicit in evil be cut off from God's favour. The imprecatory psalms are not just applied theodicy,[23] but they are applied *lex talionis* that moves from the academic to the personal, grounded in the extreme suffering of the psalmists, and caused by the malicious intent of others. Indeed, the imprecations are voiced because of the conviction that "justice must be done – at least, it must be done by a God who has created the world..."[24] Thus, the imprecations are not concerned with bloodthirsty revenge but are motivated by the conviction of God's two-sided justice and ask that the principle of God's justice be applied in their situation.

Understanding the Imprecations of the Psalms Theologically

Before we move towards suggesting ways in which new covenant believers can appropriate the imprecations of the Psalter, it is worth discussing three theological points emerging from the above discussion to form a framework for understanding the imprecations theologically.

1. The Imprecations are an Expression of Faithfulness Within the Covenant Relationship

A dimension of the Abrahamic covenant that is often glossed over is Yahweh's commitment to bless those who bless his people and curse those who curse his people (Gen. 12:1–3). This expression of Yahweh's two-sided justice of blessing and curse is engrained in the covenant relationship between God and Abram from the beginning and is then extended to Israel.[25] In the Mosaic covenant, an

---

[22] Firth, *Surrendering*, 141.

[23] Estes, *Handbook*, 174.

[24] Zenger, *God of Vengeance*, 67.

[25] Carl J. Laney, "A Fresh Look at the Imprecatory Psalms," *BSac* 138 (1981), 42: "On the basis of the unconditional Abrahamic covenant, David had a perfect right, as the representative of the nation, to pray that God would effect what He had promised...The cries for judgment in the imprecatory psalms are appeals for Yahweh to carry out His judgment

expression of the two-sided justice of God inherent within the covenant relationship is the blessings and curses in Leviticus 26 and Deuteronomy 28. The covenant blessings and curses affirm to the nation of Israel how Yahweh will protect and act in justice on behalf of his people when they are in right relationship (Lev 26:1–13; Deut 28:1–14), but in the context of their rebellion, God also affirms that he will cut them off from the land (Lev 26:14–45; Deut 28:15–68). To emphasise this two-sidedness to Yahweh's justice in Deuteronomy in particular, Moses' song in chapter 32 narrates Israel's continuous cycle of faithlessness as they spurn Yahweh's grace in salvation (vv. 5–18). Their faithlessness in turn kindled Yahweh's anger and made themselves the objects of God's wrath to the point that Yahweh desired to destroy them and enact the covenant curses against his own people (vv. 19–27). In this context, Yahweh affirms that he is a God of vengeance, with the implication that he will bring justice against his people but also justice on their behalf (vv. 35–36). The kind of justice that God will enact on his people's behalf is a "vindicating grace,"[26] as Yahweh will contend on behalf of his people. Yahweh's reassurance of vengeance on behalf of his people in a context of faithfulness is a promise of justice that is gracious and merciful, while merciless towards their enemies.

While Moses' song offers the basis for God's people to be confident in Yahweh to act on behalf of his people as the one to whom vengeance belongs, there is a profound consequence for covenantal obedience. Verse 35 is a concluding summary of God's actions in vv. 19–35, where he has threatened to punish his people for their hardheartedness and their refusal to acknowledge his salvific work. Yahweh's work in wiping out his people in vv. 26–27 is his prerogative because Yahweh is their creator. For nations to conspire to blot out God's people is to usurp the rule of God. Furthermore, vengeance is not only Yahweh's prerogative against his people, but against all nations. In v. 36, God promises vindication and compassion for his servants when they are powerless or in bondage. Then v. 43 proclaims how Yahweh will avenge the blood of his children, take vengeance on those who oppose his people, and repay those who hate him. It is Yahweh alone who has the sovereignty to kill and to give life (v. 39).

---

against those who would curse the nation – judgment in accordance with the provisions of the Abrahamic covenant."

[26] Christopher Wright, *Deuteronomy* (NIBC; Peabody: Hendrickson, 1996), 303.

So when David and the other psalmists pray for Yahweh to vindicate them against those who threaten their lives by violent words and actions, they are praying that Yahweh would make good on his promise to act in retribution and vengeance. Their prayers are grounded in the covenant theology of Moses' song and are indeed aligned to Yahweh's sovereign and just rule. Again, the reason why the psalmists' imprecations seem unsavoury and sinful is because, in the rawness of grief and pain, the psalmists boldly ask Yahweh to act in vengeance on their behalf and on behalf of God's people. The psalmists' boldness should not be rejected as 'sinful' but rather is an applied expression of the covenant relationship. The psalmist desires to take refuge in the God who promises vengeance against those who oppose his people and his rule. It is the right response to God's commitment to bless those who bless his people and curse those who curse his people because the imprecations surrender retribution to the only one who has the right to vengeance – Yahweh.[27] In fact, taking vengeance into one's own hands against those causing violence unjustly would be an act of covenant unfaithfulness, since the right response, in accordance with Genesis 12:3 and Deuteronomy 32, is to trust in Yahweh, their covenant God, to act in justice on behalf of his people.[28] The psalmist does not personally act in vengeance, but calls his covenant God to contend for his people.[29] Thus given the nature of the imprecations as an expression of dependence upon the covenant God of Israel, it is reasonable to argue that the imprecations are an outworking of Torah-piety. The psalmists are applying in their contexts what they know to be true of their covenant God, which is first that vengeance belongs to Yahweh and second, that the right response then is to surrender and trust in Yahweh's justice to vindicate those who take refuge in him as their covenant God of *ḥesed*. The imprecations are appealing to Yahweh to make manifest his justice against those who oppose his people and, as such, is a plea with Yahweh to make evident his saving and vindicating grace, which is based in covenant theology, in the life of his people.

---

[27] Michael Wilcock, *The Message of Psalms 1–72* (BST; Leicester: IVP, 2001), 122.

[28] See also Firth, *Surrendering*, 42; Laney, "Fresh Look," 42.

[29] McCann, *Psalms*, 909.

2. God's People Can Confidently Entrust Justice and Pain into the Gracious Hands of God

The motif of Yahweh's two-sided justice in covenant theology gives permission for the psalmist to cry out for justice from the dark context of agony and suffering as a consequence of much violence, physical and verbal. His hope is grounded in Yahweh's gracious promise to act as the God of vengeance on behalf of his people against those who curse them. The psalmists are recipients of curses spoken by their enemies, expressing a desire to see the lives of God's people destroyed. Thus, the psalmists can confidently entrust retribution into the gracious hands of God because they know vengeance belongs only to him and he alone is mighty to save.

Furthermore, the cries of the psalmists for Yahweh to contend on their behalf, to vindicate and save, are cries for Yahweh to manifest his covenant faithfulness based on his *ḥesed* in the life of God's people. In contexts of life or death, the psalmist is utterly dependent upon Yahweh's faithfulness in saving and vindicating his life. As Firth observes, "they seek to model a response to violence which is an adoption of a position of powerlessness, a posture of total trust in God… what matters, though, is the inculcation of an attitude of dependence on God."[30] Throughout the complaints of the psalmists, they plead for Yahweh to listen, to contend, to save, and to vindicate, for without Yahweh's intervention, the psalmist would not survive. The surrendering of retribution is "entrusting pain into the gracious hands of God"[31] because the psalmist knows confidently that Yahweh acts as the God of his *ḥesed* in his favour towards those who seek him. The imprecations are an expression of trust.[32]

3. Imprecations Ask Yahweh to Sever the Wicked from the Path of the Righteous

"What more terrifying prayer could there be than to ask for Yahweh not to show grace?"[33] This is Goldingay's question to the 'chilling' plea of the psalmist in 59:6 where he calls upon Yahweh not to show his favour to iniquitous nations. This is true also of Psalm 69:27–28, where the psalmist asks God to add guilt upon guilt to his

---

[30] Firth, *Surrendering*, 139.

[31] Estes, *Handbook*, 175.

[32] John Shepherd, "The Place of the Imprecatory Psalms in the Canon of Scripture," *Churchman* 111/2 (1997), 43.

[33] John Goldingay, *Psalms 42–89* (3 vols; BCOTWP; Grand Rapids: Baker, 2007, Vol. 2), 216.

oppressor and not to give him righteousness. In essence, David is asking that God does not justify his persecutor so that he cannot stand among the righteous. This raises the question (see below) as to whether it is ethical for a Christian justified by the righteousness of Jesus Christ to pray that those who wish to end the Christian's life not be counted among those justified by Jesus. While some might object to this leap from the Psalms to the New Testament, it must be noted that even though the Israelite worldview represents a more 'realised kingdom' perspective and we live with the tension of the 'already and the not yet', whether we ask for God to give to our oppressors his righteousness in the immediate or for an eschatological future, makes no difference to the outcome. Those whom God does not justify in the 'already', that is between Jesus' ascension and his return, will not be justified in the 'not yet', that is, after Jesus' return.

Is It Right to Pray the Imprecations of the Psalter?

The above discussion gives us a theological framework to understand the imprecations of the Psalms as an expression of covenant faithfulness in relationship to a sovereign God to whom vengeance belongs. The question remaining is how we can appropriate the imprecations of the Psalter as Christian Scripture and at the crux of the issue is whether it is ethical to pray the imprecations of the psalms. It is worth noting first that the first two theological points in the framework are unchanging from the Old Testament to the New.

First, as believers of the new covenant, the God whom we trust is still a God of two-sided justice who will bless those who bless his own or avenge those who curse his own. The first example is Matthew 25:31–46 where the separation of the sheep from the goats reflects the two-sidedness of God's justice. Those on his right are declared blessed by the king and thus receive the blessing of his kingdom. The reason they receive blessing and are counted as righteous is that they blessed those who believe in Jesus (v. 40). Blessing one who bears the name of Jesus is blessing Jesus himself. In contrast, the king condemns those on his left to eternal destruction because they did not bless him who was in need. The objection of those cursed in v. 44 and Jesus' response in v. 45 again reflect that how a person relates to one of Jesus' disciples is relating to Jesus himself. Thus, the people on the left are those who have cursed others who belong to Jesus, and thus this is an application of the principle in Genesis 12:3. With this in mind, it would be right for a disciple of Jesus to pray in a context where blessing offered to another is returned with curse asking God for his justice aligned to Matthew 25:31–46 to be realised. This is exactly what the imprecations are in the Psalter. It is asking God's two-sided justice to be realised in the context of the psalmist. However, it would be wrong with Matthew 25:31–46 in mind for the Christian to enact vengeance instead of surrendering justice to the king to whom justice belongs.

A second example is Mark 9:41–48 where the outworking of God's two-sided justice is different to the above example. In the context of the disciples telling Jesus proudly that they stopped someone performing miracles in his name, Jesus uses the opportunity to teach them the principle of Genesis 12:3. In v. 41, Jesus uses the illustration of someone giving one of his disciples a cup of water as a blessing offered to one of his people and Jesus affirms that in turn the one who blesses will be blessed. Jesus says, 'by no means will he lose his reward'. Then in v. 42, Jesus applies the *lex talionis* directly. The one who causes a believer in Jesus to sin will receive the same in kind. The consequences are so severe that it would be better that the offender be drowned than receive the justice he or she deserves. Then vv. 43–45 applies the same principle to the disciples themselves, which is similar to the self-imprecation of Psalm 137:4–5. In saying that it would be better to cut off the hand that causes you to sin than suffer the just consequence of the sin, Jesus says that it is better to suffer now a lesser punishment than the severity of the consequence in the future. Thus, it is evident from Mark 9:41–48 that Jesus still reflects the two-sided nature of justice that characterised God's justice in the Old Testament. This justice is both for those who cause others to sin and for believers who cause themselves to sin.

These two examples demonstrate that Jesus' justice as taught in the Gospels reflects the two-sided justice evident in the covenant theology of the Old Testament, in which the view of justice in the Psalter is embedded. As argued above, the imprecations are a faithful response within covenant relationship to a sovereign God to whom vengeance belongs. The imprecations are a surrendering of retribution to God. Thus, with the knowledge of Jesus' teaching in the Gospels, it would be permissible for a believer in Jesus to ask that Jesus' justice be done in his or her context that is aligned to his teaching and to the theological framework of the Psalter.

Having established that it would be permissible for a believer in Jesus to ask that God's justice be realised in his or her context, knowing that this justice is not necessarily immediate but when Jesus returns, this gives the believer confidence to entrust justice to the kingly rule of Jesus. This is what we do when we pray in the Lord's Prayer 'Your kingdom come' (Luke 11:2). Moreover, this is exactly the point of the parable of the widow and the unjust judge in Luke 18:1–8. Jesus tells the point of the parable up front in v. 1, which is that his disciples will continue to pray, that is be dependent upon God, and not lose heart. The widow in the parable relentlessly asks the judge for justice in her situation, and the judge only gives the widow justice so that she will not cause him shame by her continuous requests. In v. 7, Jesus highlights that God will give justice to those whom he has chosen and he will not delay. The challenge in v. 8 is whether Jesus will find this kind of faith on earth when he returns. This parable gives new covenant believers permission to ask for God's justice in their situation with boldness and with perseverance, with the full assurance that God will bring about justice. Thus, just as the psalmists surrendered the desire for justice to their covenant God in the Psalter, so too believers in Jesus are to actively ask for God's justice to be manifest on their behalf.

However, with the development of biblical theology from the Old to the New, the third proposition in the above framework concerning the psalmists asking God to cut off those who do evil from the path of the righteous, or from his grace, must be re-assessed. Is it ethical for the believer saved by grace to ask that others (no matter their guilt) be cut off from that same grace? The answer must be both 'yes' and 'no'. Knowing that Jesus' rule reflects that two-sidedness that encompasses the whole Psalter, it is right for the believer who is being persecuted to the point of death to ask for God's justice to be realised in their situation even if the vindication is at the return of Christ. The imprecations of the Psalter along with Luke 18:1–6 give permission for the persecuted to cry out in dependence upon God for justice and for vindication. This however must never be motivated by hatred, but rather concern (as with the psalmists) for the honour of God's name and for his people. This is affirmed by Paul who, when writing his letter to the Romans, instructs believers not to seek retribution themselves and repay evil for evil (12:17–19), but to submit that vengeance to God's anger. In making this point, Paul quotes Deuteronomy 32:35, affirming that vengeance belongs to God who will repay (Rom 12:19).

However, we must also acknowledge a development with the gospel of Jesus Christ being revealed, which is that we are to love our enemies (Matt 5:43; Luke 6:27, 35). Jesus' example as he endured persecution to the point of death on the cross demonstrates compassion towards those who put him to death (Luke 23:34). As his disciples, Christians are to follow his example. Similarly Paul in Romans 12:20–21 commands believers to bless their enemies by supplying for their needs and says 'Do not be overcome by evil, but overcome evil with good.' One of the greatest expressions of that love is to pray that God would indeed change the heart of those who do violence against God's people and bring those who persecute to repentance as he did in the example of the apostle Paul.

Thus, we must hold in tension both dimensions. We have permission to echo the sentiments of the imprecations in crying out to God in contexts of great suffering and shame under persecution because we bear the name of Christ. We can surrender our desire for vindication to Jesus, knowing that he will bring justice to those who oppose his people. However, in asking for God's justice to be done, we are to pray as an expression of sacrificial love that God in his freedom be gracious to the undeserving; that he would change the hearts of those who persecute to be in the path of the righteous. Both dimensions must be held in tension since both reflect the two-sided nature of God's justice in Jesus Christ.

Conclusion

There is an earthiness to God's justice that those of us who do not live under intense persecution to the point of death find hard to comprehend. We have softened the justice of God to love and graciousness rather than seeing the devouring fire of the glory of God who is jealous for his name and for those who bear his name. The imprecations are raw cries for justice in the context of intense persecution. These cries for justice are aligned to the view of justice that encompasses the whole Psalter and are based in covenant theology reflected in the Abrahamic and Mosaic covenants. In surrendering retribution to God, the psalmists acknowledge that both salvation and vengeance belong to the sovereign rule of God and ask that what they know to be true of God's two-sided justice be manifest in their context. However, we must be clear that what is not sanctioned is taking retribution into one's own hands. Moreover, the imprecations are not uttered in a context where the psalmists are suffering because of their own folly and sinfulness. It is when they are suffering without cause. So is it right for Christians to pray the imprecations of the Psalter? In contexts where believers are suffering unjustly because they bear the name of Jesus (and not because of their own folly), it is permissible to use the words of the psalmists to cry out to God for justice to be done. This is an expression of dependence upon our God, whom we believe brings justice to those who seek him. This justice however may not be immediate but may be realised at the return of Jesus. Thus, while striving to respond to evil with good, we have permission in these circumstances to ask for God's justice to be manifest, surrendering our desire for vindication to his vengeance, but at the same time, participating in the greatest act of love, which is to pray that God in his freedom might change the hearts of those who oppose the gospel to acknowledge the Lordship of Jesus Christ.

Recently Discovered Greek Papyri and Parchment of the Psalter from the Oxford Oxyrhynchus Manuscripts: Implications for Scribal Practice and Textual Transmission

Michael P. Theophilos

Australian Catholic University

Introduction

The ancient city of Oxyrhynchus continues to yield a significant and steady number of biblical papyri from the early part of the first millennium. Given the city's early prominence, prosperity, and significant Christian influence, this is perhaps understandable. In light of accounts such as *Historia Monachorum in Aegypto* (*HMA*), the late fourth-century journal of seven Palestinian monks, it is evident that Oxyrhynchus was home to many Christian monks, and hence, significant scribal activity. Illustrative of Christian influence within the city is *HMA* §5, attributed to Rufinus of Aquileia (340–410 CE).

> Eventually we came to a certain city of the Thebaid called Oxyrhynchus, which was so famous for good religious activities that no description could possibly do justice to them all. We found monks everywhere inside the city and also in all the countryside round about. What had been the public buildings and temples of a former superstitious age were now occupied by monks, and throughout the whole city there were more monasteries than houses. There are twelve churches in this very spacious and populous city where public worship is conducted for the people, as well as the monasteries which all have their own chapels. But from the very gates with its battlements to the tiniest corner of the city there is no place without its monks who night and day in every part of the city offer hymns and praises to God, making the whole city one great church of God. No heretics or pagans are to be found there, for all the citizens were faithful and under religious instruction... But how can I possibly describe all the kind acts done to us by the people as they watched us going through the city, greeting us like angels, making us welcome. We were told by the holy bishop of that place that it contained twenty thousand virgins and ten thousand monks. I could not possibly tell you, not even by stretching the truth to its limits, how great was the kindness and hospitality shown to us, to the extent that the clothes

were almost torn off our backs by those who were eager to seize us and take us home as their guests.

Oxyrhynchus was a significant and evidently prosperous regional capital, situated on one of the main trade routes, thus making it a common thoroughfare for merchants and travellers.[1] Being the capital of the Nome, Oxyrhynchus was assumed by Grenfell to be the "abode of many rich persons who could afford to possess a library of literary texts."[2] At its peak it was reckoned to be the third largest city of Egypt and, as already noted above, in the early period of the first millennium CE, became a hub of Christian communities and monasteries.[3] These, and other factors, led two young Oxford graduates, B.P. Grenfell and A.S. Hunt of Queen's College, to this site in the late nineteenth century in search of papyri "for the discovery and publication of the remains of classical antiquity and early Christianity in Egypt."[4] Both the dry climate and the dark underground environment preserved thousands of papyrus texts (some more fragmentary than others) which were covered by the sands of time for nearly two thousand years.

The wealth of papyri was immediately apparent in the first day of official digging (January 11th 1897). The excavation reports indicate that, "papyrus scraps at once began to come to light in considerable quantities,"[5] and that the "flow of papyri soon became a torrent."[6] Even to the extent that, at one point in the report, Grenfell stated that "merely turning up the soil with one's boot would frequently disclose a layer of papyri."[7] Finds included the full spectrum of ancient literature; both literary (epic, lyric, elegiac, tragic and comic poets, orators, historians, writers of romance, geometry, medicine and grammar, and early Christian literature),

---

[1] Naphtali Lewis, *Life in Egypt under Roman Rule* (Atlanta: Scholars Press, 1999); Roger S. Bagnall, *Egypt in Late Antiquity* (Princeton: Princeton University Press, 1993).

[2] B.P. Grenfell, "Oxyrhynchus and Its Papyri," in *Archaeological Report 1896–1897: Comprising the Work of the Egyptian Exploration Fund and the Progress of Egyptology in the Year 1896–7* (ed. F. Ll. Griffith; London: Egyptian Exploration Fund, 1897), 1.

[3] M. Rostovtzeff, *Social and Economic History of the Hellenistic World* (3 Vols; Oxford: Oxford University Press, 1941, Vol. 1). A.H.R.E. Paap, *Nomina sacra in the Greek Papyri of the first Five Centuries* (Leiden: Brill, 1959).

[4] J.S. Cotton, "Egypt Exploration Fund: Graeco-Roman Branch," in *Archaeological Report 1896–1897: Comprising the Work of the Egyptian Exploration Fund and the Progress of Egyptology in the Year 1896–7* (ed. F. Ll. Griffith; London: Egyptian Exploration Fund, 1897), iii.

[5] Grenfell, "Oxyrhynchus," 6.

[6] Grenfell, "Oxyrhynchus," 7.

[7] Grenfell, "Oxyrhynchus," 7.

and documentary (proclamations, contracts, receipts, tax returns, petitions, sales documents, leases, wills, shopping lists, private letters, et al.).[8]

It is estimated that over 500,000 papyrus fragments were brought back to Oxford in the period between 1897 and 1910, all of which (bar a limited exception) reside in the Papyrology Rooms of the Sackler Library, University of Oxford. However, thus far approximately only 1% of material has been published, partly due to the laborious processes involved in reconstructing the fragmentary pieces and partly due to the state of the manuscripts. Several papyri and parchment fragments have ink which is significantly faded, or portions of the manuscript which are oxidized to the point of being charcoal black. It is however, equally baffling as to why so much literature, both biblical and otherwise, was "thrown out" *en masse* by the ancients, only to be found centuries later in the now famous rubbish mounds of Oxyrhynchus. In a recent article, AnneMarie Luijendijk has argued that the deliberate discarding of such material, canonical and otherwise, was unrelated to Christian persecution or issues of canonicity.[9] Consensus on the issue, however, has eluded scholars thus far.

Background and Context

The vast majority of scholars who incorporate discussion of the Septuagint into their research (typically commentary writing and general theological studies) rely almost exclusively on the edited printed critical editions of the text of the early to mid twentieth century.[10] However, the Göttingen enumeration of *Handschriften* lists over 400 papyri of the LXX which are dated at or before the eighth century CE (of which over 120 are dated pre-fourth century CE). The tangible benefit of these discoveries for research on the LXX is the textual and interpretive light shed on the history of the

---

[8] See further Grenfell, "Oxyrhynchus," 11.

[9] AnneMarie Luijendijk, "Sacred Scriptures as Trash: Biblical Papyri from Oxyrhynchus," *Vigiliae Christianae* 64.3 (2010), 217–254. Grenfell had hinted at the possibility in the first excavation reports that "It is not improbable that they [i.e. P.Oxy. 1 and 2] were the remains of a library belonging to some Christian who perished in the persecution during Diocletian's reign, and whose books were then thrown away." (Grenfell, "Oxyrhynchus," 6.)

[10] Typically A. Brooke, N. McLean, and H.St.J. Thackeray, *The Old Testament in Greek According to the Codex Vaticanus* (Cambridge: Cambridge University Press, 1906–1940); A. Rahlfs, *Septuaginta. Id est Vetus Testsmentum graece iuxta LXX interpretes* (2 Vols; Stuttgart: Deutsche Bibelgesellschaft, 1935); *Septuaginta, Vetus Testamentum Graecum: Auctoritate Academiae Scientiarum Gottingensis editum* (20 Vols; Göttingen: Vandenhoeck & Ruprecht, 1931-).

early transmission of the text. In J.M Dines's discussion of this predicament, she laments that it is "extremely difficult to recover the original form of the text; indeed in some places it may have been irretrievably lost."[11] Furthermore, because Origen's work on the LXX changed the text as understood, "any pre-Origenic manuscripts, however fragmentary, are of great importance, especially when they come from a Jewish milieu."[12] In this paper, recently discovered Greek papyri and parchment of the Psalter from the Oxford Oxyrhynchus collection are introduced, discussed and analysed. Particular attention is paid to scribal practice, manuscript transmission, and issues of textual criticism.

Cyperus Papyrus is the name given to a fibrous plant which grew in marshy areas, especially in Egypt, and from which a variety of products were manufactured. In Theophrastus' *Enquiry Into Plants* 4.8.4 (371–287 BCE), he states "ὁ πάπυρος πρὸς πλεῖστα χρήσιμος," (trans. "the papyrus is useful for many purposes" (*ll.* 4–5)), listing no fewer than a dozen applications for the plant, including the manufacture of boats (*ll.* 5–6), woven sails (*ll.* 7–8), ropes (*ll.* 8), food (*ll.* 9–11 "μάλιστα δὲ καὶ πλείστη βοήθεια πρός τὴν τροφὴν ἀπὸ αὐτοῦ γίνεται," (trans. "above all, the plant is also of very great use in the way of food")), but concludes that "καὶ ἐμφανέστατα δὴ τοῖς ἔξω τὰ βιβλία," (trans. "most familiar to foreigners are the papyrus rolls made of it" (*ll.* 8–9)). For an ancient description of the manufacturing process, one may turn to Pliny the Elder's description in *Natural History* 13.68–82, who, writing approximately three hundred years after Theophrastus, states "Praeparatur ex eo charta diviso acu in praetenues, sed quam latissimas philyras. Principatus medio, atque inde scissurae ordine," (trans. "the process of making sheets from papyrus is to split it with a needle into very thin strips made as broad as possible, the best quality being in the centre of the plant, and so on in the order of its splitting" (13.74)). Modern scientific analysis of ancient papyri indicate that each of these strips would be laid in a row in parallel, and then a second row of strips would be laid upon the first in perpendicular fashion. The plant's juices acted as a natural adhesive and "bonded [the strips] into a single flexible cohesive sheet."[13] These sheets of papyri

---

[11] J.M. Dines, *The Septuagint* (London: T&T Clark, 2004), 3.

[12] Dines, *Septuagint,* 3–4.

[13] A. Wallert, "The Reconstruction of Papyrus Manufacture: A Preliminary Investigation," *Studies in Conservation* 34.1 (1989), 2.

were exported from Egypt and used all over the Mediterranean in antiquity, yet despite this wide diffusion and use, papyri have survived into modern times almost exclusively in Egypt (with some rare exceptions), and more specifically in the Nile Valley below the Delta, attributable to the region's dry and virtually rainless climate.

Papyrology (the technical art of deciphering and editing documents written on papyrus, leather and other portable objects such as ostraca and lead amulets) is a relatively young discipline by the standards of Classics. While the first papyrus was discovered in 1788 (the so-called Charta Borgiana, an unexciting list of labourers on an irrigation canal from 192 CE), it was not able to generate significant scholarly or popular interest as most considered the mundane nature of the manuscript to be disappointing. Many had hoped for a text in the grand literary classical tradition, perhaps a new play by Sophocles or the like. The field of papyrology only began to take shape with the voluminous discoveries of papyri in the late nineteenth and early twentieth centuries. Because of the scale of these later finds, the famous historian Theodore Mommsen grandly predicted that the twentieth century would be the century of papyrology, just as the nineteenth century had been the century for epigraphy[14], by which he meant that papyri would have the same revolutionary impact on historical research as inscriptions did in his time. This was certainly the case with the textual tradition of the LXX.[15]

The Psalter at Oxyrhynchus

The rubbish dumps of *Oxyrhynchus* have, thus far, yielded no fewer than 30 LXX fragments, ranging in date from the first to sixth century CE. The oldest LXX published fragment from Oxyrhynchus is that of P. Oxy 3522 (Job 42:11–12) dated to the very early part of the first century CE.[16] It includes several notable features including punctuation by spacing (i. *l.* 4, 5, 7), the Divine Name written as the Tetragrammaton in Paleo-Hebrew script (i. *l.* 2, 5), and a text which "stands closer to the LXX rather than the

---

[14] Peter van Minnen, "The Century of Papyrology (1892–1992)," *BASP* 30 (1993), 5. Cf. N. Gonis, "Mommsen, Grenfell, and 'the Century of Papyrology,'" *ZPE* 156 (2006), 195–196.

[15] For a comprehensive listing of LXX papyri as of 2004 see D. Fraenkel, *Verzeichnis der griechischen Handschriften des Alten Testaments* (Bd. 1: Die Überlieferung bis zum VIII. Jahrhundert; Vandenhoeck & Ruprecht, 2004).

[16] P.J. Parsons, "3522. LXX Job 42:11–12," in *The Oxyrhynchus Papyri, Volume L* (ed. A.K. Bowman et al.; London: Egypt Exploration Society, 1983), 1.

literal accurate version of Symmachus."[17] These and many other scribal features are attested in the papyri of the LXX of the Psalter at Oxyrhynchus. It is noteworthy indeed that almost half of Oxyrhynchite LXX manuscripts are fragments of the Psalter.[18] These include: P.Oxy 845, 1226, 1352, 1779, 1927, 1928, 2065, 2386, 4011, 4931, 4932, 4933, 5021, 5023, 5101. In our analysis below we will evaluate and analyze a representative portion of the Psalter at Oxyrhynchus, and comment upon the variegated scribal and textual contribution of these manuscripts.[19]

Published in 1908, P.Oxy 845 (Ps 68:30–37; 70:3–8) was the first fragment of the Psalter to emerge from Oxyrhynchus within the industrious program of systematic documentation of the finds undertaken by Grenfell and Hunt.[20] The extant fragment measures 12.5 cm (h) x 18.2 cm (w) and is estimated to have originally been part of a codex sheet measuring no less than 22 cm in width. There are legible traces of ink on ten lines on the verso and eight lines on the recto. The manuscript is written in what the first editors refer to

---

[17] Parsons, "Job 42:11–12," 1.

[18] The attestation of the LXX inscriptions displays a similar proportion of references to the Psalter in the papyrological record. Although earlier discussions were aware of the importance of LXX inscriptions (E. Böhl, "Alte christliche Inschriften nach dem Text der Septuaginta," *Theologische Studien und Kritiken* 54 (1881), 692–713; E. Nestle, "Die alten christlichen Inschriften nach dem Text der Septuaginta," *Theologische Studien und Kritiken* 56 (1883), 153–154), Jalabert's 1914 catalogue of biblical inscriptions was the earliest attempt to develop a systematic inventory of the material (L. Jalabert, "Citations Bibliques dans l'épigraphie Grecque" in *Dictionnaire d'archélogie chrétienne et de liturgie* (Vol. III, 2; eds F. Cabrol and H. Leclercq; Paris: Librairie Letouzey et Ané, 1914), cols. 1731–1756). Combined with New Testament quotations, Jalabert provided a total of 247 instances of biblical inscriptions. It is of some consequence that 143 of these are quotations from 48 individual Psalms, with only 16 other quotations covering the remaining portions of the LXX (N. Fernández Marcos, *The Septuagint in Context: Introduction to the Greek Versions of the Bible* (Trans. W. G. E. Watson, Leiden: Brill, 2000), 267). It is truly remarkable that Psalm 120:8 occurs forty-three times; Psalm 117:20 thirty-one times; Psalm 28:3 seventeen times; and Psalm 90:1 fifteen times (P. Head, "Additional Greek Witnesses to the New Testament (Ostraka, Amulets, Inscriptions and Other Sources)" in *The Text of the New Testament in Contemporary Research: Essays on the Status Quaestionis* (eds B.E. Ehrman and M. Holmes; Leiden: Brill, 2013), 445).

[19] P. Oxy 5023 (cento of Psalms) and 5024 (prayer with a quote from the Psalter) are excluded from our analysis due to the parchment manuscripts being stored in a separate location and there being some ambiguity as to whether the fragments were purchased or products of the excavations at Oxyrhynchus, although the two scenarios are not mutually exclusive. As admitted by C.E. Römer in the *editio princeps* there is "no guarantee that they [5023 and 5024] were found at Oxyrhynchus" (C.E. Römer, '5023–5024. Parchment Slips' in *The Oxyrhynchus Papyri, Volume LXXV* (ed. H. Maehler, C.E. Römer and R. Hatzilambrou; London: Egypt Exploration Society, 2010), 8.

[20] B.P. Grenfell and A.S. Hunt, "Psalms lxviii and lxx," in *The Oxyrhynchus Papyri, Volume VI* (ed. B.P. Grenfell, A.S. Hunt; London: Egypt Exploration Society, 1908), 1.

as "a large and clear cursive hand,"²¹ and can be dated paleographically to 350–450 CE. In addition to the standard contractions of θεός and κύριος to their respective *nomina sacra*, the manuscript is arranged stoichiometrically. There is no evidence of versification, sense division, paragraphoi or ekthesis. Textually, the manuscript does not fully cohere with any of the extant major uncials, although it is more closely aligned with Sinaiticus (א [fourth century]) than Vaticanus (B [fourth century]) or the Verona Psalter (R [sixth century]). See, for example, recto *l*. 16 where P.Oxy 845 reads υπομονησις corrected to υπομνησις (as per א), as opposed to B and R's υμνησις. This, however, is not surprising given the assumed Egyptian provenance. P.Oxy 845 verso *l*.3 (Ps 68:33 [LXX]) reads "ἰ[δ]έτ[ω]σαν", the aorist active imperative (see/look), for the MT's qal perfect third common plural רָאוּ (they will see). On no few occasions, contemporary scholars (e.g. M. Dahood,²² Johnson²³, Gunkel²⁴, Kraus²⁵) seem to amend the MT's pointing in light of the LXX reading, in this case רָאוּ (perfect) to רְאוּ (imperative), also reflected in the New English Bible translation. M.E. Tate notes that the MT's perfect can be retained only if read as the precative/optative ("let the poor see").²⁶ This reading, nonetheless, does not resolve the issue of to what the object of the verb refers. The LXX resolves this by encouraging the humble (πτωχοί) to look (ἰδέτωσαν [imperative]), and be glad (εὐφρανθήτωσαν [imperative]).

P.Oxy 1226 (Ps 7:9–12; 8:1–4) is a fragment of the upper right portion of a codex leaf. In its extant form it measures 10.5 cm (h) x 6.8 cm (w), with eleven lines of legible text on the verso and twelve on the recto. Paleographically it is dateable to the late third or early fourth century by the distinct paleographic hand; an upright uncial of medium size, with the cursive tendency to link the ω with the following letter (recto *l*. 4; verso *l*. 2).²⁷ *Nomina sacra* for both θεός

---

[21] Grenfell and Hunt, "Psalms lxviii and lxx," 1.

[22] M. Dahood, *Psalms II:51–100* (Garden City: Doubleday, 1968), 165.

[23] A.R. Johnson, *The Cultic Prophet and Israel's Psalmody* (Cardiff: University of Wales Press, 1979), 394.

[24] H. Gunkel, *Die Psalmen* (Göttingen: Vandenhoeck & Ruprecht, 1968), 295.

[25] H.-J. Kraus, *Psalms 60–150* (Trans. Hilton C. Oswald; Minneapolis: Fortress Press, 1993), 59.

[26] M.E. Tate, *Psalms 51–100* (Dallas: Word Books, 1990), 188.

[27] B.P. Grenfell and A.S. Hunt, "1226. Psalms vii, viii," in *The Oxyrhynchus Papyri, Volume X* (ed. B.P. Grenfell, A.S. Hunt; London: Egypt Exploration Society, 1914), 11.

and κύριος occur throughout (recto *ll*.1, 6, 7, 9; verso *l*.3). The insertion of an iota adscript by a second hand at verso *l*.8 may suggest that the text underwent some kind of textual editing or control. However, the extent, consistency or accuracy of such a process is not known. There is a coronis (κορωνίς) of sorts, in the left margin (on the recto between lines 2 and 3) marking the division of a major section in the poetic text. The title "Ψαλ[μος τω Δαυειδ]," immediately precedes this, above which (recto *l*.1) there are traces consistent with the numeral η (=8) representing the number of the Psalm. Of textual interest is the reading "δικαιοσύνην σου" in verso *l*. 2, for the typical "δικαιοσύνην μου" (א B R et al.).[28] This significantly changes the meaning of the request from "Judge me Lord, according to my righteousness" (א B R et al.) to "Judge me Lord, according to your righteousness" (P.Oxy 1226). With the publication of P.Oxy 1226, a reading which had previously only found minimal support in the later cursives (27, 156, 202, 269, 283, 284) has found significant and early attestation.

The virtually complete parchment codex leaf of P.Oxy 1352 (Ps 82:6–19; 83:1–4) measures 13.1 cm (h) x 10.5 cm (w) and is presented as a single column. There is relative consistency in letter formation, with only an occasional lapse into a sloping style in verso *l*.21.[29] Based on the predominant and distinctive upright pointed majuscule hand, the manuscript is datable paleographically to the early part of the fourth century (300–325 CE). Both P.Oxy 1226 and 1352 denote stoichiometrical divisions, the former using line division and the latter *dicola* (double dots). There is evidence of pagination in the right upper margin on both sides (ροθ [= 179]; ρπ [=180]). Recto *l*.14 has the beginning of Psalm 83 marked with the equivalent Greek numeral (πγ) in left margin. Lines boundaries were drawn to aid the scribe. From these features, one can assume that the codex leaf was a portion of, at least, an entire professional copy of the Greek Psalter. As is typical, θεός and κύριος contract to their respective *nomina sacra*, however verso *l*.8 (82:9 [LXX]) and

---

[28] The Psalmist's apparent appeal to his own righteousness is precisely the issue that Calvin takes up in his commentary (*Commentary on Psalms* §7:8). In attempting to ease the apparent acute theological problem, Calvin states, "The solution is easy, because this does not treat the question how he should respond if God should demand from him an account of his whole life; but, comparing himself with his enemies, he maintains and not without cause, that, in respect of them, he was righteous." Calvin, of course, was unaware of the broader textual tradition which we are treating in our analysis.

[29] B.P. Grenfell and A.S. Hunt, "1352. Psalms lxxxii, lxxxiii," in *The Oxyrhynchus Papyri, Volume XI* (ed. B.P. Grenfell, A.S. Hunt; London: Egypt Exploration Society, 1915), 2.

recto *l.*15 (83:1 [LXX]) do not contract υἱός as the references are to that of the sons of Lot/Kore. The original scribe is actively seen to be checking and editing the text, evident through the cancellation of letters through supralinear dots (verso *l.*14, recto *ll.*7 and 12), erasure of letters (recto *l.*12), and even an attempt to remove a case of dittography 83:17-18 (recto *ll.*5-8), "πλήρωσον τὰ πρόσωπα αὐτῶν ἀτιμίας, καὶ ζητήσουσιν τὸ ὄνομ[α [αὐτῶν ἀτιμίας, καὶ ζητήσουσιν τὸ ὄνομ σου, κύριε]] αἰσχυνθήτωσαν καὶ...." Later scribal activity is also evident in making corrections in a small cursive script at various points including 83:10 [LXX] (verso *l.*11), where the first plural subjunctive ποιήσωμεν (let us make) is amended to the second aorist active imperative, ποίησον (make). Furthermore, this later scribe also introduces a previously unattested reading in the addition of γη after τῇ (verso *l.*11). These and other examples amply illustrate that the scribal process was evidently dynamic and fluid rather than static and fixed.

P.Oxy 1779 (Ps 1:4-6) consists of one fully intact papyrus codex sheet measuring 11.5 cm (h) x 7.7 cm (w). The hand is characterized by several irregularities, but can be safely dated to the mid fourth century CE.[30] The unusually large letter formations result in 7-12 letters per line. Although there is no stoichiometric division, there is evidence of punctuation, in particular the use of high stops on recto *l.*8 (Ps 1:4 after "προσώπου τῆς γῆς") and verso *l.*3 (Ps 1:5 after "ἀσεβεῖς ἐν κρίσει"). A rough breathing mark is found on ὡς of recto *l.*8 (Ps 1:4). Previously unattested before the eleventh century (cursive manuscript 281), recto *l.*4 reads "ὡς χνοῦς" for "ὡς ὁ χνοῦς" (Ps 1:4), a helpful reminder that early readings can indeed be preserved in the singular readings of later cursives. This and other examples like it provide further grounds for caution with regard to the manner in which textual critics often discount the possible contribution of singular readings for reconstructing the "earliest" or "original" text.

P.Oxy 1927 is a liturgical cento of the Psalms measuring 11.1 cm (h) x 30 cm (w), dated paleographically to the late fifth century.[31] The cento phrase segments on the verso are largely drawn from

---

[30] B.P. Grenfell and A.S. Hunt, "1779. Psalm i," in *The Oxyrhynchus Papyri, Volume XV* (ed. B.P. Grenfell, A.S. Hunt; London: Egypt Exploration Society, 1922), 6.

[31] B.P. Grenfell and A.S. Hunt, "1927. Liturgical Fragment," in *The Oxyrhynchus Papyri, Volume XVI* (ed. B.P. Grenfell, A.S. Hunt; London: Egypt Exploration Society, 1924), 206-207.

Psalm 32:21–33:2 [LXX] with only minor additions from elsewhere in the Psalter (*l.*11 [32:15; 16:4; 32:20]; *ll.*12–13 [32:21; 105:48]; *ll.*14–16 [32:22; 33:2; 103:33; 145:2]). Of interest is the substitution of "ἕως ἔτι ὑπάρχω" (as long as I live; cf. 103:3; 145:2) for "ἐν παντὶ καιρῷ" (at all times; 33:2) in the phrase "εὐλογήσω τὸν κύριον ἐν παντὶ καιρῷ" (*ll.*14–16). This reading supports Kraus' suggestion that 33:3 functions as a formal vow,[32] abolished only by the death of the speaker, rather than simply being fulfilled in the recitation of the Psalm. The recto displays greater variety of verse selection, with additions from 34:27 (*l.*4); 65:2 (*l.*4); 32:4 (*ll.*4–5), 13:2 (*l.*6); 101:20 (*l.*6); and 17:7 (*l.*6). Of interest are the multiple hands that have contributed to the eclectic text. Recto *ll.*1–5 are written in a standard cursive of the late fifth century, followed by a more angular second hand in *l.*6. A third hand is apparent on the verso *ll.*1–6 and displays some formal features of a sloping script. There is only minimal evidence of punctuation; a high stop after "ἠλπίσαμεν" on verso *l.*12 and "ὑμᾶς" on *l.*14. Given these reading aids, and some liturgical type phrases on the verso, "ἡ ψυχὴ ἡμῶν ὑπομένει σε κύριε" (*l.*11; cf. PS 32:20), "γένοιτο ἔλεός ἐφ' ἡμᾶς" (*l.*14; cf. Psa 32:22), one might assume an ecclesiastical use for the composition. There is one typographical correction on recto *l.*6, where the initial τ has a cancelling diagonal stroke through the vertical. The reconstructed reading, however, is uncertain due to the fragmentary nature of the preserved manuscript.

P.Oxy 1928, measuring 21.5 cm (h) x 30 cm (w) contains an almost complete late fifth century copy of Psalm 90 [LXX] on the verso. In the history of the Psalm's interpretation, several scholars have assumed an apotropaic use of the text, although, one must distinguish between the original *Sitz im Leben* and later use. W. Oesterley describes the genre as a "polemic in devotional form... to counteract the assaults of demons."[33] This view is supported by Rabbinic interpretation, which identifies it as a "song for evil encounters"[34], with specific reference to averting the attacks of demons. It is, therefore, not surprising that there are distinct horizontal and vertical fold marks in P.Oxy 1928, typical of texts folded and worn or carried as amulets. Textually, the manuscript displays affinity toward agreement with the second corrector of

---

[32] H.-J. Kraus, *Psalmen* (Neukirchen-Vluyn, Germany: Neukirchener Verlag, 1978), 419.

[33] W. Oesterley, *The Psalms* (London: SPCK, 1959), 407.

[34] Babylonian Talmud, *Shebuoth* 15^b

Sinaiticus and Alexandrinus and against Vaticanus: the omission of "καὶ" (*l*.5 v.5) in P.Oxy 1928, and the second corrector's supralinear dots of Sinaiticus (folio 113, *l*.22) indicating erasure; the word order of "ἐν σκότει διαπορευομένου" (*l*.6 v.6) and the corresponding second corrected reading in Sinaiticus from "διαπορευομένου ἐν σκότει" to "ἐν σκότει διαπορευομένου" (folio 113, *ll*.23–24). Also of interest is the *nomen sacrum* "ΚΩ" (κυρίῳ) in "ἐρεῖ τῷ κυρίῳ" (*l*.1 v.2), and the corresponding correction in Sinaiticus from "ΘΩ" to "ΚΩ" (folio 113, *l*.12).

P. Oxy 2065 is a further example of the popularity of Psalm 90, and preserves two consecutive sides of a late fifth century parchment codex leaf measuring 4 cm (h) x 5.7 cm (w), containing verses 5b-10a. The smaller dimensions of the codex could be attributed to its use as an amulet. The sixteen verses of the Psalm, with similar letter size and format could be accommodated on a single quire of four sheets. The vocative "κύριε" of verse 9 (recto col. 2, *l*.26) identifies the empathic you "אתה" of the MT (Ps 91:9) as Yahweh, rather than those who are encouraged to trust in Yahweh.[35] This however introduces a textual problem as to the subject of 9b, which seems to refer to humanity rather than God. M.E. Tate resolves the issue by suggesting that verses 1–2 and 9a form an inclusio around verses 3–8, and that 9b "begins a new section of the Psalm."[36] Despite the attractive suggestion that the pagination of P.Oxy 2065 supports this hypothesis (verse 9b begins in line 1 of the second column of the verso), the uneven carryover of "μου" from 9a on the same line makes this, at best, an ambiguous proposal.

P.Oxy 2386 is a papyrus roll measuring 12.5 cm (h) x 13.5 cm (w). The recto consists of the concluding verses of Psalm 83 (vv. 9–13) and the beginning of Psalm 84 (v.1). The text is written in squarish letters with a slight slope to the right, paleographically consistent with the late fourth or early fifth century (cf. P.Oxy 1078 for a comparable hand).[37] The verso, written in a different and unrelated hand, preserves a private letter in three lines. The text of the Psalter is not formatted in any particular fashion, however, stoichiometric divisions are indicated with two diagonal strokes. "Διάψαλμα", the

---

[35] Tate, *Psalms 51–100*, 448.

[36] Tate, *Psalms 51–100*, 449.

[37] E.G. Turner, "2386. Psalms 83(84)-84(85)" in *The Oxyrhynchus Papyri, Volume XXIV* (ed. E. Lobel, C.H. Roberts, E.G. Turner, and J.W.B. Barns; London: Egypt Exploration Society, 1957), 6–7.

Greek equivalent of the Hebrew "סֶלָה" (*selâ*), is preceded by a single diagonal stroke alerting the reader to the pause. A horizontal line is drawn between *l*.12 and *l*.13 to divide one Psalm from the other. The standard *nomina sacra* occur, "ΘΥ" (*l*. 7); "ΘC" (*l*. 9); "ΚΕ" (*ll*. 11, 13); and "Χ[ΟΥ]" (*l*. 4). There is one curious case of an otherwise unattested *nomen sacrum* from Oxyrhynchus, namely the uncontracted "ΘΕΟC" (*l*.3) with superliner bar. Textually, the manuscript has no particular affinity with major codices, twice siding with Vaticanus (*ll*.6–7 "παραριπτεῖσθαι" [v.11]; *l*.11 omits "ὁ θεός" after "κύριε" [v.13]), twice with Sinaiticus (*l*.7 addition of "μου" after "θεοῦ" [v.11]; *l*.7 addition of "με" after "οἰκεῖν" [v.11]), and, on occasion, neither (*l*.5 "κρίσσων" [v.11]).

P.Oxy 4011 recto consists of a Christian version of Psalm 75, albeit in an intercalated, abbreviated and periphrastic presentation. The order and arrangement is as follows: *ll*.1–2, Psalm 75:2; *ll*.2–3 paraphrase of Psalm 75:3, linking Isaiah 40:9; 52:7 and Acts 10:36 through the key terms of "Σιων", "εἰρήνη", and "εὐαγγελίζω"; *ll*.3–4 continue with a free rendition of Psalm 75:6; *ll*.4–5 intercalate a reference to "ἐσταύρωσαν αὐτὸν" (crucified him), reminiscent perhaps of any number of New Testament passages (Mk 15:25; Lk 23:33; 24:19–20; Jn 19:16–18, 23; 1 Cor 2:6–8; Gal 5:24); *ll*.5–6 conflate three passages (Zech 1:11, 1 Pet 3:16, and Ps 49:14). After a clear paragraphos division in *l*.8, the scribe returns to Psalm 75:4, before a final plea for God to arise and scatter the enemy in no uncertain terms, "ὁ θεός, καὶ διασκορπισας πάντες τούς ἐχθρούς ἀπὸ προσώπου αὐτοῦ" (cf. Ps 67:2). To the modern reader or exegete, this conglomeration of apparently unconnected Scriptural intercalations with Psalm 75 may seem somewhat peculiar. However, P.Oxy 4011's fascinating amalgamation of texts preserves an authentic example of someone actually creatively engaged in the theological process. In it we see the interconnected thought of an individual who sought to bring together apparent disparate biblical textual traditions into a narrative of its own. One which begins by declaring the greatness of God's name, recalls the work accomplished through Christ, and concludes with an eschatological note of hope for future divine intervention. As to how successful the author was in cohesively achieving this end, we will allow the reader to adjudicate.

P.Oxy 4931 consists of a papyrus codex sheet measuring 8.5 cm (h) x 5.8 cm (w), containing Psalm 90:3–8 in a formal mixed medium-sized hand, dateable to the mid fifth century CE.[38] There is evidence on both the recto (*l.*8) and verso (*ll.* 2, 5) of dicola marking stoichiometric division. Other punctuation is evident in recto *l.*8 with a lower dot and a space between verses 4 and 5. Textually, there are two minor omissions. First, recto *l.*5 omits "αὐτοῦ" in the phrase "ἐν τοῖς μεταφρένοις αὐτοῦ ἐπισκιάσει" (Ps 90:4). Second, verso *ll.*1–2 omits a portion of verses 5–6. Depending on how one restores verso *l.*2, either a. "[ἐν σκότ]ει" or b. "[ἡμέρα]ς", the scribe has either erred in homoioteleuton (skipping from "πετομένου" [v.5] to "διαπορευομένου" [v.6]), or homoioarchton (skipping from "ἀπὸ βέλους" [v.5] to "ἀπὸ πράγματος" [v.6]) respectively.[39]

P.Oxy 4932 is dated to the fourth or first half of the fifth century and consists of a papyrus leaf measuring 6 cm (h) x 14.1 cm (w) inscribed on one side with Psalm 72:21–23 written in a sloping majuscule, and on the other, an account of the gods.[40] The text on both sides runs with the fibers as the fragment for the Psalm text was cut, and turned ninety degrees to the left and written by a different hand.[41] Left (1.3 cm), upper (1.1 cm), and lower (1.7cm) margins are preserved, so that one can assume that we have here the beginnings of the three written lines. Assuming a standard text, the original dimensions of the manuscript would have been unusually wide (6 cm x 30 cm), however, given the characteristic fold marks, one can assume use as an amulet. A small diagonal line (mid *l.*2) divides the two stoichiometric lines in verse 22. Of textual interest is the reading in *l.*1 "ηὐφράνθη" [rejoice, 72:21], which was also the original reading in Sinaiticus before it was corrected to "ἐξεκαύθη" [burn]. P.Oxy 4932 preserves a heterogeneous Greek tradition in comparison to the MT's "חמרץ" (to be embittered).

P.Oxy 4933 is a papyrus codex leaf (10.1 cm [h] x 5.1 cm [w]) of the late third or early fourth century, consisting of a collection of excerpts from the Old Testament (verso *ll.*1–6, Jer 27:24–26; *ll.*6–18, Amos 11:11–12; recto *ll.*1–21, Ps 17:1–11).[42] Such *Testimonia* were

---

[38] D. Colomo, "4931. Psalm XC 3–8," in *The Oxyrhynchus Papyri, Volume LXXIII* (ed. D. Obbink and N. Gonis; London: Egypt Exploration Society, 2009), 1.

[39] Colomo, "4931," 7.

[40] D. Colomo, "4932. Psalm Amulet: Psalm LXXII 21–3," in *The Oxyrhynchus Papyri, Volume LXXIII* (ed. D. Obbink and N. Gonis; London: Egypt Exploration Society, 2009), 8.

[41] Colomo, "4932," 8.

[42] D. Colomo, "4933. Collection of Biblical Excerpts," in *The Oxyrhynchus Papyri, Volume LXXIII* (ed. D. Obbink and N. Gonis; London: Egypt Exploration Society, 2009), 12–13.

common in both Early Christianity (P.Ryl 3.460; P.Oslo 2.11)[43] and Second Temple Judaism (4Q175, 4Q176 cf. 4Q379). Commonly attested themes include eschatology and Messianism, with a particular Christian interest in the persecuted yet vindicated sufferer as prefigurement of Christ. Such is the case with P.Oxy 4933, for in drawing together Amos 11:11–12 (restoration of the house of David), Jeremiah 27:24–26 (God as redeemer of his people), and Psalm 17:1–11 (God's "κατέβη" [coming down, *l.*29 = v.10] to rescue David from his enemies), the author has prefigured Christ's mission in terms of redemption, restoration and future coming.[44] The lack of any stoichiometric divisions, or indeed any textual marker dividing the passages may indicate that the manuscript originated or was used in a private context. D. Colomo suggests that the smaller format of the codex would have been "very practical for travelling teachers and missionaries."[45] The standard *nomina sacra* occur on recto *ll.*1–3, 6, 10–11, 16, although *l.*10 omits the article before "KN" (v.7).

P.Oxy 5021 consists of a papyrus codex leaf measuring 14 cm (h) x 10.1 cm (w) dated to the fifth century and inscribed with Psalm 90:12–16 (verso *ll.* 1–14, recto *ll.*1–4) and Odes 7–8 (recto *ll.*5–12).[46] There are traces of ink consistent with an "η" in the top left margin, indicating at least eight pages in the codex. Apart from several irregular spaces aiding word division there are no *nomina sacra* or stoichiometric marks on the manuscript. Although a common apotropaic text, the editor of the *editio princeps*, Cornelia Römer, suggests that both the dimensions of the codex and the multi-page format weighs against the possibility of this manuscript having been used as an amulet *per se*.[47] Rather, it was a personal copy to be consulted in a time of physical or mental infirmity.[48] At the conclusion of Psalm 90, the scribe adds "ἀλληλουεϊα" a common introductory refrain found in LXX Psalms 104–106, 110–118, 134–

---

[43] See further Alessandro Falcetta, "A Testimony Collection in Manchester: Papyrus Rylands Greek 460," *BJRL* 83 (2002), 3–19; Martin Christian Albl, *And Scripture Cannot Be Broken: The Form and Function of the Early Christian Testimonia Collections* (Leiden: Brill, 1999).

[44] Colomo, "4933," 11.

[45] Colomo, "4933," 12.

[46] C.E. Römer, "5021. Psalm XC 12–16 and Excerpts from Odeas 7 and 8," in *The Oxyrhynchus Papyri, Volume LXXV* (ed. H. Maehler, C.E. Römer and R. Hatzilambrou; London: Egypt Exploration Society, 2010), 3–4.

[47] Römer, "5021," 3.

[48] Römer, "5021," 3.

135, 145–150, derived from the transliteration of the Hebrew "הַלְלוּ־יָהּ" (lit. praise Yahweh). Two rows of arrows, one left facing and the other right, divide the Psalm text concluding on recto *l*.4 from the selection of Odes on recto *l*. 5 and following.

P.Oxy 5101 consists of Psalm 26:9–14; 44:4–8; 47:13–15; 48:6–21; 49:2–16; 63:6–64:5 and is dated to the late first or early second century CE. The editors note that "it is probably the earliest extant copy of the Septuagint Psalms."[49] Its present fragmentary state is exceedingly complex and consists of four main fragments (A-D) covering six columns of a papyrus roll.[50] One of the significant features of the manuscript is that the Tetragrammaton is recorded in Paleo-Hebrew script, "𐤉𐤄𐤅𐤄" (frag. A *ll*.12, 14; frag. D *l*.14). Although this is not an unattested feature at Oxyrhynchus, as noted above in our discussion of Job 42:11–12 (P.Oxy 3522), there are several notable elements in P.Oxy 5101 which deserve attention. First, the Tetragrammaton is preceded by the Greek definite article, which may indicate that "κύριος" was used in the Greek *vorlage* and was replaced with the Paleo-Hebrew form in P.Oxy 5101. Second, D.B. Capes raises the possibility that even the spaces around the divine name were treated differently[51], perhaps evident in the excess physical space into which the Tetragrammaton is inserted. Third, there is a growing body of evidence from first century Jewish writers that "κύριος" functioned as the oral substitute for יהוה.[52] There are no attested *nomina sacra* in P.Oxy 5101, but there is a curious abbreviation of τε^λ for τέλος in frag. D *l*.13. It has been noted that textually "several readings…correspond more closely to the Masoretic Text (MT) than…Rahlfs's edition."[53] However, at other points, certain readings are not in accord with the MT, for example frag. C iii. *ll*.20, 27.

---

[49] D. Colomo and W.B. Henry, "5101. Psalms (Fragments)", in *The Oxyrhynchus Papyri, Volume LXXVII* (ed. A. Benaissa; London: Egypt Exploration Society, 2011), 1.

[50] Colomo and Henry, "5021," 1.

[51] D.B. Capes, "YHWH Texts and Monotheism in Paul's Christology," in *Early Christian and Jewish Monotheism* (ed. Loren T. Stuckenbruck and Wendy North; London: T&T Clark International, 2004), 124.

[52] Martin Rösel, "The Reading and Translation of the Divine Name in the Masoretic Tradition and the Greek Pentateuch," *JSOT* 31 (2007), 411–428; James R. Royse, "Philo, Kyrios, and the Tetragrammaton," *The Studia Philonica Annual* 3 (1991), 167–183; Albert Pietersma, "Kyrios or Tetragram: A Renewed Quest for the Original Septuagint," in *Studies in Honour of John W. Wevers on His Sixty-Fifth Birthday* (ed. Albert Pietersma and Claude Cox; Mississauga: Benben Publishers, 1984), 85–101.

[53] Colomo and Henry, "5021," 2.

P.Oxy 5127 (Psalm 90:4–13) is the most recently published text of the Psalter from Oxyrhynchus and consists of a late fifth century parchment codex leaf measuring 3.8 cm (h) x 8.6 cm (w). The roughly bilinear slightly sloping hand displays no punctuation or other textual divisions. Both the popularity of Psalm 90 as an amulet text and the fold marks indicate that the manuscript was folded into a small packet of approximately 1.1 cm x 3.8 cm, and possibly carried on the person inserted in a tubular capsule.[54] Miniature amulets of this kind were common in the period, and have been thoroughly explored by recent commentators.[55] Textually, the manuscript displays high levels of heterogeneous readings throughout, with several verses omitted (vv. 9, 10a) or displaced from their typical sequence (v. 8). There is an interesting conflation pertaining to verse 6 where both word orders of "ἐν σκότει διαπορευομένου" (P.Oxy 1928; P.Oxy 2065; P.Ryl 1.3; P.Laur 141; P.Bodm XXIV), and "διαπορευομένου ἐν σκότει" (P.Gen 6; BKT VIII.12; BKT VIII.13; P.Vondob G.348; P.Duke 778) appear as "ἐν σκότει διαπορευομένου ἐν σκότει" (ll.12–15). F. Maltomini suggests the fascinating possibility that the conflation has arisen because of the use of two exemplars.[56]

Table 1. Summary of Manuscript Evidence

Manuscript	Reference	Date (circa)	Form	Material	Features
P.Oxy 845	68:30–37; 70:3–8	350–450 CE	Codex	Papyrus	Stoichiometric divisions; nomina sacra
P.Oxy 1226	7:9–12; 8:2–3	275–325 CE	Codex	Parchment	Stoichiometric divisions; nomina sacra; editing; larger first letter, title number

---

[54] F. Maltomini, "5127. LXX, Psalm XC 4–13 (Amulet)" in *The Oxyrhynchus Papyri, Volume LXXVIII* (ed. R.-L. Change, W.B. Henry, P.J. Parsons and A. Benaissa; London: Egypt Exploration Society, 2012), 1.

[55] M.J. Kruger, "P.Oxy 840: Amulet or Minature Codex?" *JTS* 53 (2002), 81–94; T.S. de Bruyn and J.H.F. Dijkstra, "Greek Amulets and Formularies from Egypt Containing Christian Elements," *BASP* 48 (2011), 163–216.

[56] Maltomini, "5127," 3.

Manuscript	Reference	Date (circa)	Form	Material	Features
P.Oxy 1352	82:6–19; 83:1–4	300–325 CE	Codex	Parchment	Stoichiometric divisions; nomina sacra; editing; page numbers; dicola
P.Oxy 1779	1:4–6	350 CE	Codex	Papyrus	Breathing marks; high stops
P.Oxy 1927	13:2; 16:4; 17:7; 32:4, 15; 32:20–33:2; 34:27; 65:2; 101:20; 103:33; 105:48; 145:2	475 CE	Codex	Papyrus	Cento; multiple hands; high stops; editorial marks
P.Oxy 1928	90:1–16	475 CE	Codex	Papyrus	Amulet; nomina sacra
P.Oxy 2065	90:5b–10a	475 CE	Codex	Parchment	Amulet
P.Oxy 2386	83:9–84:1	375–425 CE	Roll	Papyrus	Stoichiometric divisions; spaces; nomina sacra
P.Oxy 4011	75:2–3, 4, 6	550 CE	Roll	Papyrus	Paragraphoi; nomina sacra; intercalation
P.Oxy 4931	90:3–8	450 CE	Codex	Papyrus	Amulet?; stoichiometric divisions; punctuation
P.Oxy 4932	72:21–23	350–450 CE	Roll	Papyrus	Amulet; paragraphoi
P.Oxy 4933	17:1–11	275–325 CE	Codex	Papyrus	Nomina sacra; *testimonium*

Manuscript	Reference	Date (circa)	Form	Material	Features
P.Oxy 5021	90:12–16	450 CE	Codes	Papyrus	Amulet; page number; paragraphoi
P.Oxy 5101	26:9–14; 44:4–8; 47:13–15; 48:6–21; 49:2–16; 63:6–64:5	75–125 CE	Roll	Papyrus	Tetragrammaton
P.Oxy 5127	90:4–13	475 CE	Codex	Parchment	Amulet

Summary, Implications, and Conclusion

The Psalms from Oxyrhynchus are an exceptional and fertile area of Septuagintal research. We have seen in our analysis that the scribal process of textual transmission was dynamic and fluid rather than static or fixed. The papyrological record demonstrably illustrates scribes actively participating in the theological enterprise. Attention to the Greek text of the Psalter offered clarifications or resolutions to certain grammatically ambiguous Hebrew traditions (P.Oxy 845; P.Oxy 1927; P.Oxy 2065), or even alternatives to it (P.Oxy 1226; P.Oxy 4932). Scribes were seen to be actively involved in the mechanics of editorial revision, either during or after the copying process (P.Oxy 1226; P.Oxy 1352; P.Oxy 1927). Text critically, variant readings previously unattested before the eleventh century minuscule, found attestation in much earlier manuscript traditions (P.Oxy 1226; P.Oxy 1779). Several curious cases of correspondence between the Oxyrhynchus papyri and the second corrector of Sinaiticus were evident (P.Oxy 845; P.Oxy 1928), although not unanimously so (P.Oxy 2065; P.Oxy 4932). Without a fuller analysis, and larger textual papyrological base, it would be difficult to go beyond this observation and posit a connection, albeit tentative, between the two streams of tradition. Scribes were seen to be creatively involved in the theological endeavor, both in the construction of theological narratives (P.Oxy 4011; P.Oxy 4933), and readily drawing on Psalm 90 for apotropaic purposes (P.Oxy 1928; P.Oxy 2065; P.Oxy 4931; P.Oxy 5021; P.Oxy 5127).

As noted above, there remains a vast amount of excavated, yet unpublished, material that requires scholarly attention. The current curator of the Oxyrhynchus papyri estimates that of the papyri excavated by Grenfell and Hunt in the late nineteenth and early twentieth centuries, approximately ten percent is theological in nature, including such items as biblical fragments, Christian private letters, and liturgical texts. Of continued need are able scholars trained in biblical studies, ancient languages, paleography and ancient history to devote themselves to the careful and painstaking process of analysis and publication of the *editions principes*. The raw data of these newly published fragments is crucial in the study of ancient societies as it continually refines, expands and sometimes redefines our understanding of textual traditions and the way new ideas were developed and old ideas were preserved.

Related to this endeavour, the discipline is also in need of a thorough discussion on what constitutes a quotation from the LXX. That is, to what extent is a 'quotation' governed by a strict definition of verbatim reproduction? Quantifiable and transparent criteria must be established so as to more carefully nuance and distinguish a quote, allusion, echo, or indeed the complexity of the oral dimension. In particular, further research is required of the definition of a quotation from a meaningful ancient perspective.

Attention is also required as to the definition of LXX papyri as being 'Jewish' or 'Christian'. Several discussions have provided helpful clues,[57] however the criteria are often muddied by the less than clear boundaries between the two groups in the early Christian period. A recent article by E.L. Gallagher has explored the possibility that Christian scribes preserved the representation of the Tetragrammaton in Paleo-Hebrew within the Septuagintal tradition (cf. P.Oxy 5101).[58] Further work on the paleography of Greek during the relevant periods would help to bring sharper definition to this debate.

Our present study also seeks to stimulate commentators to consider more closely the nature of relationship between the current form of the MT and the ancient Greek translations. H.-J. Kraus notes, "It is striking especially in the commentaries of the Psalter how drastically the basic positions and methods of treating the text differ

---

[57] C.H. Roberts and T.C. Skeat, *The Birth of the Codex* (London: Oxford University Press, 1983); Larry W. Hurtado, *The Earliest Christian Artifacts: Manuscripts and Christian Origins* (Sheffield: Eerdmans, 2006).

[58] E.L. Gallagher, "The Religious Provenance of the Aquila Manuscripts from the Cairo Geniza," *JJS* 64 (2013), 283–305, see especially pages 303–304.

from one another."[59] A. Salvesen provides the most recent methodological treatment of this issue and brings her wealth of knowledge to bear in analysis of particular passages in eight major commentaries on various biblical books.[60] Salvesen encourages commentators to go beyond harvesting the Greek versions for pre-Masoretic vocalizations, and semantic information regarding the MT, to a more thoroughgoing engagement and analysis of the Jewish and Christian Greek traditions in their own right.

As can be readily appreciated from our overview, papyri of the Psalter are variegated and fascinating. Complications abound in almost every dimension of investigation. Despite this however, it is difficult to overestimate the importance of the papyrological testimony in providing an admittedly fragmentary, but genuine snapshot of the LXX text as it existed at a certain point in antiquity.

---

[59] H.-J. Kraus, *Psalms 1–59: A Commentary* (Trans. H. C. Oswald; Minneapolis: Augsburg Publishing House, 1988), 13. See further, R.J.V. Hiebert, C.E. Cox and P. Gentry, *The Old Greek Psalter: Essays in Honour of Albert Pietersma* (Sheffield: Sheffield Academic Press, 2001); E. Tov, *Textual Criticism of the Hebrew Bible* (Minneapolis: Minneapolis: Fortress Press, 2012); A. Schultz, *Kritisches zum Psalter* (Munster : Aschendorffschen, 1932).

[60] A. Salvesen, "The Role of Aquila, Symmachus, Theodotion in Modern Commentaries of the Hebrew Bible," in *Let Us Go Up to Zion* (ed. Iain Provan and Mark Boda; Brill: Leiden, 2012), 95–109.

Passionate Pursuit of the God of Redemption: Interpreting Psalm 119 in the Light of its Immediate Context in Book V of the Psalter

John De Hoog

Reformed Theological Seminary

Introduction

Psalm 119 has often received a bad press. Perhaps the most damning comment I have come across comes from Bernard Duhm (1899) who found "no redeeming features in its art, thought or piety. It is useful only in illustrating the perils of book-religion. It stands as the most empty product that ever blackened paper."[1] R.A.F. Mackenzie wrote, "One could start with the last verse and recite it backwards, and the general effect would be the same."[2] Can a sympathetic reading of Psalm 119 with an eye to its canonical context provide a more positive reading?

The Character of Psalm 119 – Purpose and Process

The person portrayed in Psalm 119 is involved in an 'I-You' conversation with God. Apart from the opening three verses, every verse of Psalm 119 is personally addressed from the first person to God. And in virtually every stanza the psalmist expresses intense neediness. Far from being a dispassionate treatise on the law of God, it rather has the character of a cry from the heart; a cry from the mind, conscience, will and passion of a person who has nowhere to go but God to find the resources needed to live in a godly way in a fallen world. Ministry from Psalm 119 must reflect this character of the psalm. How does Psalm 119 teach or rebuke our minds, test or convict our conscience, train and correct our wills, stir our love and inspire our passions?

---

[1] Duhm, *Die Psalmen* (1899), quoted in John H. Eaton, *Psalms of the Way and the Kingdom : Conference with the Commentators* (Sheffield: Sheffield Academic Press, 1995), 24–25.

[2] MacKenzie, cited in C Stuhlmueller, Psalms, 2 vols. Wilmington: Glazier, 1983, as quoted in Will Soll, *Psalm 119: Matrix, Form and Setting* (The Catholic Biblical Quarterly. Monograph series 023; Washington: Catholic Biblical Association of America, 1991), 87.

Two significant aspects of answering these questions are *purpose* and *process*. What is the purpose of Psalm 119 – what does it set out to do? And what is the process by which it achieves its purpose? If we can prise open the purpose of Psalm 119 we will know what the application of Psalm 119 in ministry should look like. And understanding how Psalm 119 achieves its purpose will help us to know how to work with Psalm 119 towards that outcome.

Psalm 119 Is Not a 'Cry of the Moment'

Even though Psalm 119 expresses a cry of the heart, it is almost the opposite of being a spontaneous composition 'dashed off' in a moment of desperate need. Rather it displays significant and highly disciplined poetic artistry; it is a carefully and patiently composed meditation. This aspect of the character of Psalm 119 must be appreciated in coming to terms with its purpose and process. As Erich Zenger wrote in 2008, "… it must be quite clearly asserted that this psalm is a work of literary artistry whose uniqueness one must appreciate in order to grasp its theological dynamics."[3]

Psalm 119 is an alphabetic acrostic of 22 stanzas, all of which consist of eight verses. The verses are almost invariably bicola.[4] There are eight 'law words' that are used as virtual synonyms throughout Psalm 119. If you exclude words which are not thematically significant from the analysis,[5] then eight of the 11 most frequent words in Psalm 119 are the 'law words'. They are תּוֹרָה *tôrâ* ("law, instruction"), דָּבָר *dābār* ("word"), מִשְׁפָּטִים *mišpāṭîm* ("judgments, ordinances"), עֵדוּת *ēdût* ("testimonies"), מִצְוֹת *miṣwôt* ("commandments"), חֻקִּים *ḥuqîm* ("statutes"), פִּקּוּדִים *piqqûdîm* ("precepts") and אִמְרָה *imrâ* ("word, promise").[6]

---

[3] Frank-Lothar Hossfeld and Erich Zenger, *Psalms 3: A Commentary on Psalm 101–150* (Hermeneia; trans. Linda M. Maloney; Minneapolis: Fortress Press, 2011), 257.

[4] Fokkelman identifies three tricola, vss 48, 145 and 176. J. P. Fokkelman, *The Psalms in Form: The Hebrew Psalter in its Poetic Shape* (Tools for Biblical Study 4; Leiden, The Netherlands: Deo Publishing, 2002), 170. Various modern translations take different approaches, sometimes in keeping with Fokkelman's suggestion about these three verses and sometimes not. The other verses in Psalm 119 are invariably treated as bicola. Zenger states that there is only one tricolon: vs 176. See Hossfeld and Zenger, *Psalms 3*, 261.

[5] See a method for developing frequency analysis word lists in John de Hoog, "A Canonical Reading of Psalm 119" (Melbourne School of Theology, 2011), 68–70.

[6] Most of these words are either exclusively singular or exclusively plural in their uses in Psalm 119. A simple gloss is provided, but note the comments about meaning that follow.

The eight 'law words' are always in Psalm 119 related to Yahweh with a suffix or in a construct expression with the Tetragrammaton. All eight terms appear in six of the 22 stanzas, and not less than six appear in every stanza. There is no regular pattern for their use; they are not used with unique meanings in relation to each other. The terms do not appear only in vv. 3, 37, 90 and 122. In v. 84 *mišpāṭ* appears but it is used in a different sense ("judgment"). In vv. 3, 37 a synonym "ways" takes the place of the law word. In v. 90 "faithfulness" performs this role. Hence, only in vv. 84 and 122 are there no 'law' words or synonyms at all. This construction speaks of a highly disciplined attention to form, and it also speaks eloquently to the purpose of the psalm.

There is further evidence that the psalmist took great care in creating Psalm 119. The use of the number eight stands out: There are eight verses in each stanza. The eight 'law words' are used in statistically remarkable ways. There are 176 instances of the use of these words (8x22), 88 in stanzas 1–11 and 88 in stanzas 12–22. The four masculine law words are used 88 times, the four feminine law words are used 88 times.[7] In addition, the number of I/me/my morphemes is precisely the same as the number of you/your morphemes in which the psalmist addresses God: 315 in both cases.[8] Psalm 119 is clearly not a spontaneous 'cry of the moment'.

Personal and Procedural; Purpose and Process

Psalm 119 has a dual character as both intensely personal and methodologically 'procedural'. Some commentators have felt that the procedural character of the psalm poses the danger of the process of composition becoming an end in itself, such that the communication of meaning in the psalm is relegated by the author a position of secondary importance. For example, Sigmund Mowinckel argued that the procedure of filling in the acrostic and the aim of using the eight law words in a consistent way resulted in a psalm that is almost random in its composition. He wrote:

> In a late psalm like Ps. 119 prayer and lament and hymnal motives so intermingle as to make interpreters feel at a loss with regard to the character and purpose of the psalm. When a psalm was tied down to

---

[7] Hossfeld and Zenger, *Psalms 3*, 259.
[8] Fokkelman, *The Psalms in Form*, 170.

an artificial 'alphabetic' pattern… it very often resulted in a rambling and obscure train of thought and a loose composition.[9]

However, this opinion overstates the effect of the 'procedure' on communication of thought in the psalm. In a critical study of Psalm 119, Will Soll tackles the common opinion that Psalm 119 has little internal coherence. He makes a good case for seeing Psalm 119 as an individual lament on a large scale, with the typical movement of lament psalms being repeated several times in the course of the psalm.[10] Soll argues persuasively that the individual stanzas have more coherence than often supposed, and so does the psalm as a whole. For example, seeing Psalm 119 as an individual lament, he finds the psalm reaching its nadir in the *Kaph* stanza, followed by its zenith in the following *Lamedh* stanza.[11]

While it is true that patterns in the overall flow of Psalm 119 can be difficult to discern, such patterns are not entirely absent. For example, David Powlison notices the same dynamics in the *Kaph* and *Lamedh* stanzas that Soll points to, but he extends the analysis in a useful way. He notes that every stanza in Psalm 119 mentions "situational suffering" except the first two and the last, but that vv. 81–88 (*Kaph*) are unique in Psalm 119 in focusing solely on distress, and that the following verses 89–92 (the first half of *Lamedh*) are unique in Psalm 119 in affirming the stability and certainty of the Lord.[12]

Older critical studies of Psalm 119 that tended to focus on the form of the psalm were prone to seeing the psalm as focused on 'filling in' the acrostic at the expense of thematic content. Newer approaches aimed more at literary analysis are better placed to take up the matter of thematic content. As already mentioned, one of the most prominent features of the content of Psalm 119 is the consistent use of the 'law words'. The eight words are used 'stereometrically'[13], that is, while the individual terms can be differentiated from each other, they are not precisely defined in the psalm and so overlap

---

[9] Sigmund Mowinckel, *The Psalms in Israel's Worship. 2 Vols.* Nashville: Abingdon, 1963, 2.77–78, quoted in Soll, *Psalm 119*, 63–64.

[10] Soll, *Psalm 119*, 71.

[11] Soll, *Psalm 119*, 90.

[12] David Powlison, "Suffering and Psalm 119," *Journal of Biblical Counseling*, no. Fall (2004), 10.

[13] To slightly modify a term Gerhard von Rad used to refer to the way various 'wisdom' terms are used in the Book of Proverbs. See Gerhard von Rad, *Wisdom in Israel* (trans. James D. Martin; London: SCM, 1972), 13, 27.

with each other in meaning. The intention seems to be to express in a larger and more comprehensive way the 'meaning field' that could be expressed by the eight words individually.

The first and most frequently used of the words is תּוֹרָה (tôrâ). The 220 uses of this word in the OT fall into three main categories: (1) teaching or instruction to be learned, (2) commands to be obeyed, and (3) guidance about how to live in specific situations.[14] When one takes the eight 'law words' used in Psalm 119, all three of these categories of meaning are attached to the words. In what follows I will use the word 'Torah' to refer to the collection of law words in Psalm 119. The meaning of the word 'Torah' in this general sense is well captured by Kent Reynolds as "any verbal expression of God's desires."[15] The author of Psalm 119 creates a 'persona' who loves Torah, longs for Torah, delights in Torah, loves to contemplate Torah and desires to obey Torah, not simply to avoid punishment but because of an intense joy in obedience.[16] Reynolds has shown how Psalm 119 creates a portrait of an exemplary Torah student in order to persuade the reader of the value of being such a student. "In the process of reading Psalm 119, the reader begins to think like the speaker."[17]

Psalm 119 constantly makes a particular 'move' in relating the reader to Torah. The 'Psalm 119 move' is to take words and themes that concern a person's attitude to God and to apply those words and themes to an attitude to God's Torah.

For example, the Book of Deuteronomy (the other place in the Hebrew Bible where 'law words' are used 'stereometrically' e.g. Deut 4:1; 5:1; 6:1–2; 11:1, etc.) repeatedly calls upon Israel to "love" (אהב 'hb) the Lord. The Psalm 119 move is to 'divert' that love to Torah.

> V. 97 Oh how I love your law! I meditate on it all day long.
>
> V. 113 I hate double-minded men, but I love your law.
>
> V. 163 I hate and abhor falsehood, but I love your law.

---

[14] Martin J. Selman, "Law," in *Dictionary of the Old Testament: Pentateuch* (eds. T. Desmond Alexander and David W. Baker; Downers Grove, Ill.: IVP, 2003), 498.

[15] Kent A. Reynolds, "Psalm 119: Promoting Torah, Portraying an Ideal Student of Torah" (University of Wisconsin, 2007), 20.

[16] Reynolds, "Psalm 119," 20.

[17] The quote is from Reynolds, "Psalm 119," 113. See pages 66–113 for the full argument.

> V. 165 Great peace have those who love your law, and nothing can make them stumble.
>
> V. 47 For I delight in your commands because I love them.
>
> V. 48 Because I love your commands more than gold, more than pure gold...

Psalm 119 contains ten uses of the verb "love", and all of them are directed to Torah. Moreover, Psalm 119 contains the only verses in the Hebrew Bible where Torah, the 'law words', are the objects of the verb "love" (אהב *'hb*).

Throughout the Hebrew Bible God's people are commanded to "trust" (בטח *bṭḥ*) only in the Lord. Trusting in anyone or anything else is idolatry. Trusting in God is also a common theme in the Psalms. But in Psalm 119:

> V. 42 Then I will answer the one who taunts me, for I trust in your word.

There are many other examples of this typical Psalm 119 'move':[18]

> Clinging to God → clinging to Torah (e.g. v. 31)
>
> Hoping in God → hoping in Torah (e.g. v. 42)
>
> Believing in God → believing in Torah (e.g. v. 66)
>
> Fearing God → fearing Torah (e.g. v. 120)
>
> Seeking God → seeking Torah (e.g. v. 45)
>
> Setting God before me → setting Torah before me (e.g. v. 30)
>
> Raising up hands to God → raising my hands to Torah (e.g. v. 48)

While the 'move' documented here is typical of Psalm 119, its significance must not be exaggerated. The psalm is also *filled up* with expressions of exuberant pleasure, open admiration and blunt need *for God himself*. Nearly always these expressions of passion are connected with Torah in some way, but as Powlison reminds us, the 'I-You' language (expressed mainly in pronominal suffixes) is four times as prevalent in Psalm 119 as the law words combined.[19]

> V. 7 I will praise you with an upright heart...
>
> V. 10 With my whole heart I seek you...

---

[18] See Reynolds, "Psalm 119," 42–49.
[19] Powlison, "Suffering and Psalm 119," 4.

V. 12 Blessed are you, O Lord…

V. 174 I long for your salvation, O Lord…[20]

In Psalm 119 there is no conflict in expression between loving and seeking and hoping in and fearing the Torah of the Lord and doing the same towards the Lord himself. The strong suggestion from the language of the psalm is that these are one and the same thing. According to Psalm 119, seeking the Lord is not a mystical process for which people need special techniques that are difficult to learn. Pursuing the Lord involves chasing after him in the manner he has ordained – through the Torah, the word in which he reveals himself. As the New Testament confirms with great clarity, it is the living word that teaches, rebukes, trains, corrects, tests, convicts, encourages and exhorts God's people (2 Tim 3:16; 4:2; 1 Cor 14:3; Rom 15:4; 7:7; Heb 4:12–13; 1 John 5:13).

We are now approaching an understanding of the *purpose* of Psalm 119. Psalm 119 constantly emphasises to the reader the importance of Torah, God's word, the verbal expression of God's desires, and its purpose is to commend that Torah as the premier resource for pursuing God.

The first three verses set the agenda for Psalm 119.

> Blessed are they whose ways are blameless, who walk according to the law of the LORD.
>
> Blessed are they who keep his statutes and seek him with all their heart.
>
> They do nothing wrong; they walk in his ways.

Verse 4 contains a shift to second person address that continues through the rest of the psalm. The shift is marked by an emphatic use of the pronoun "You": "You, you have commanded your precepts to be obeyed wholly and exactly." These first four verses celebrate an ideal image of perfection. But in v. 5, and for the rest of the psalm, the author is plunged into the reality of his own life, with all its agonies and joys.

His life is *not* the ideal that he paints in vv. 1–4. In fact, his life is full of inconsistencies. For example, in v. 110 he declares that he has not

---

[20] A quick survey of Psalm 119 suggests that expressions directly addressed to the Lord appear at vv. 7, 10, 11, 12, 26, 32, 38, 40, 41, 49, 55, 57, 58, 62, 64, 65, 68, 73, 76, 77, 81, 94, 102, 108, 114, 116, 117, 120, 122, 123, 124, 125, 132, 137, 145, 146, 147, 149, 151, 153, 154, 156, 159, 166, 169, 170, 171, 173, 174, 175.

"strayed" from the Lord's precepts, but in v. 176 he declares that he has "strayed" (same word) like a lost sheep and asks the Lord to seek him. In verse after verse he declares that he has obeyed Torah. But in v. 88 he asks that his life be preserved *so that he can* obey the Lord's statutes. In v. 52 he declares that he has found comfort in Torah, but in v. 82 he cries out "When will you comfort me?"

There are many of these kinds of tensions in Psalm 119, but none of these things are contradictions. They are the stuff of everyday life for someone who is trying to be obedient. All who have some experience of the committed life know that life is like that. A life of obedience is full of joy and disappointment, certainty and uncertainty, confidence and despair, communion with God's people and opposition from God's enemies, and so on. Psalm 119 is a vivid demonstration of what the life of a godly person actually looks like, with all the ups and downs of that life portrayed in Psalm 119's subject's first person experience and longing after the Lord through the medium of his Torah.

The life of obedience is not a smooth road, but the subject repeatedly commits himself to delighting in and observing Torah so as to pursue the Lord. So we come to a summary of the purpose of Psalm 119. *Psalm 119 is designed to commend a life of pursuing the Lord through his Word.*

It is also possible now to summarise the process by which Psalm 119 achieves its purpose. *Psalm 119 is a multi-faceted portrayal of what it actually looks like to pursue the Lord through his Word. It achieves its purpose not by admonishing the reader but by painting a portrait of the life of a God-seeker.*

Summary: Purpose and Process

A step by step pattern of communication of thematic content is not the chief concern of the author of Psalm 119. It has the content of a personal cry of the heart to God. As Powlison puts it, "Psalm 119 is torrential, not topical. It's relentless, not repetitive. It's personal, not propositional."[21] Psalm 119 is written in the highly disciplined form of an all-encompassing acrostic and the extensive use of eight law words. Within that strictly-enforced structure its great intention is to portray the life of a committed God-seeker, so as to encourage the reader to emulate the model Torah student so portrayed.

---

[21] Powlison, "Suffering and Psalm 119," 4.

Psalm 119 within Book V of the Psalter

Book V and the Canonical Approach to the Psalter

One of the burgeoning areas of Psalms study since the mid-1980s, stimulated in part by the publication of Gerald Wilson's work *The Editing of the Hebrew Psalter*,[22] has been the rise of what has been called "final form studies of the Psalms"[23] or the "canonical approach to the Psalter."[24] Jamie Grant provides a useful summary of this approach.[25] We will not air it further in a general sense beyond saying that the canonical approach is based on a fundamental conviction that the order of the psalms in the Psalter and especially the placement of certain psalms at significant locations in the Psalter are not random. Rather, Psalms is regarded by this approach as having been shaped by its final redactors to communicate themes that were crucial to Israel's faith and very existence as a community in the post-exilic situation.

Psalm 119 dominates Book V of the Psalter by its sheer size. Psalm 119 alone has more verses than all the neighbouring Songs of Ascents (Psalms 120–134) put together. We now turn to some observations of Book V, which provides the wider canonical context for Psalm 119.

Psalms 146–150 are widely recognised as constituting a doxological ending to the Psalter as a whole. Psalms 146–150 all open and close with הַלְלוּ־יָהּ (*hallelu-yah*). The distribution of this phrase in the Psalter bears consideration. הַלְלוּ־יָהּ is found 23 times in the Psalter, 19 times in Book V and also in Psalms 104–106, which are the final three psalms of Book IV (the closing words of Psalms 104 and 105 and the opening and closing words of Psalm 106). So the words *hallelu-yah* appear only in Book V and in the three psalms leading up to Book V.

The question raised by the exceptional presence of the phrase in the three psalms outside of but leading up to Book V is: What is the

---

[22] Gerald H. Wilson, *The Editing of the Hebrew Psalter* (Dissertation Series (Society of Biblical Literature) 076; Chico, Ca.: Scholars Press, 1985).

[23] David C. Mitchell, "Lord Remember David: G.H. Wilson and the Message of the Psalter," *Vetus Testamentum* 56, no. 4 (2006), 526.

[24] Jamie A. Grant, *The King as Exemplar: The Function of Deuteronomy's Kingship Laws in the Shaping of the Book of Psalms* (Society of Biblical Literature Academia Biblica 17; Atlanta: Society of Biblical Literature, 2004).

[25] Grant, *King as Exemplar*, 11–19.

function of this phrase in Psalms 104–106? In applying some of the insights of linguistics to biblical interpretation, Cotterell and Turner identify a number of stages in the development of discourse, including the role of "stage-setting"[26]. The appearance of the phrase *hallelu-yah* in Psalms 104–106 appears to be setting the stage for the frequency of this theme of considering and responding to God's work in Book V.

There are further stage-setting features to be observed in Psalms 105 and 106. Psalm 106:1 – (after *hallelu-yah*) "Give thanks to the LORD, for He is good; for His lovingkindness is everlasting" – is identical with Psalm 107:1. These words are repeated again in the opening and closing lines of Psalm 118 and again in the opening line and the (nearly identical) closing line of Psalm 136. These features suggest that the post-exilic editors wanted the reader/hearers to discern a strong link between the end of Book IV and Book V, and that the feature of Book V that they wanted to emphasise at the end of Book IV is its theme of rejoicing in the goodness and everlasting lovingkindness of Yahweh.

There is a third stage-setting function discernible in Psalms 105 and 106. They review God's work in Israel's history from the points of view of the perfection of God's work (105) and the failure of Israel to respond perfectly to that work (106), pointing to the importance this theme will have in Book V.

A fourth stage-setting function lies in the way Psalm 107, the first psalm in Book V, responds to the end of Psalm 106, the final psalm in Book IV. Apart from the doxology, Psalm 106 ends with the plea

> Save us, O Yahweh our God,
>
> And gather (קבץ *qbs*) us from the nations
>
> To give thanks (ידה *ydh*) to your holy name
>
> And glory in your praise (106:47)

Psalm 107 responds by beginning

> Oh give thanks (ידה *ydh*) to Yahweh, for He is good,
>
> For His lovingkindness is everlasting.
>
> Let the redeemed of Yahweh say so,
> Whom He has redeemed from the hand of the adversary

---

[26] Peter Cotterell and Max Turner, *Linguistics & Biblical Interpretation* (London: SPCK, 1989), 247.

And gathered (קבץ *qbṣ*) from the lands,
From the east and from the west, from the north and from the south. (107:1–3)

This response to the question of Psalm 106 is cast in terms of an invitation for the "redeemed" to give thanks for Yahweh's lovingkindness (חֶסֶד *ḥesed*). The invitation is then supported in the rest of the psalm by four illustrations of Yahweh's חֶסֶד in four examples of redemption (vv. 4–9, 10–16, 17–22, 23–32), concluding with a hymnlike summary based on the four examples (vv. 33–42) and an admonition to be wise by continuing to pay attention to the message about Yahweh's חֶסֶד. The psalm contains two refrains repeated four times each (vv. 6, 13, 19, 28 and vv. 8, 15, 21, 31). In each of the four circumstances of distress, the people cry out to Yahweh and he rescues them. In each of the four circumstances, they are called to thank (ידה) the Lord for his חֶסֶד and his wondrous deeds (נִפְלָאוֹת *niplā'ôt*) which have been done "for the sons of men" (לִבְנֵי אָדָם *libnê 'ādām*).

Significant links between Psalms 107 and 145 exist. The last mentioned repeated phrase from Psalm 107, לִבְנֵי אָדָם ("for/to the sons of men"), appears in the centre of Psalm 145 (v. 12). Other key words from the fourfold refrains, ידה, חֶסֶד and נִפְלָאוֹת also appear in Psalm 145 (vv. 5, 8, 10). Just as Psalm 107 ends with a call to be wise, so Psalm 145, which is an acrostic, ends with a wisdom note (vv. 19–20).[27] Wilson argued that this connection between Psalms 107 and 145 put a "wisdom frame" around Book V.[28] (Wilson sees Book V as concluding with Psalm 145, with Psalms 146–150 forming the final doxology of the Psalter as a whole.[29])

Zenger, who follows Wilson in regarding Psalms 107–145 as Book V of the Psalter followed by a doxological conclusion, argues that

---

[27] Gerald H. Wilson, "Shaping the Psalter: A Consideration of Editorial Linkages in the Book of Psalms," in *The Shape and Shaping of the Psalter* (ed. J.C. McCann; vol. 159 of JSOTSup; Sheffield: JSOT Press, 1993), 79.

[28] Wilson, "Shaping the Psalter," 79.

[29] Gerald H. Wilson, "The Structure of the Psalter," in *Interpreting the Psalms: Issues and Approaches* (eds. P.S. Johnston and D.G. Firth; Leicester: IVP, 2005), 232.

these links between Psalms 107 and 145 put a frame around Book V which emphasises its overall "hymnlike structure"[30].

The call to be wise at the end of Psalm 107 is actually framed as a question. Translated a little more literally than most English versions, Psalm 107:43 reads:

> Who is wise? Let him give heed to these things,
>   and consider the "lovingkindnesses" (*ḥesed* plural) of Yahweh.

To summarise, Psalm 107 opens Book V of the Psalter by responding to Psalm 106. It is strongly interconnected with several other psalms in Book V in its repetition of words, sentences and themes, and it opens Book V by asking the question, "Who is wise?" Psalm 107 can be seen as setting an 'agenda' for Book V that is crucial for the identity and survival of Israel in a post-exilic setting. Book V of the Psalter is concerned with answering the question at the end of Psalm 107: "Who is wise?"

Erich Zenger has suggested that Book V of the Psalter has an overall "theological program" and has summarised that program in the following diagram:[31]

R A		A		R A
107, 108–10, 111 and 112	113–18	119	120–136.137	138–144.145
David (eschatological/messianic)	Exodus (Pesach)	Torah (Shabuoth)	Zion (Sukkoth)	David (eschatological/messianic)

(R = royal psalm; A = acrostic psalm)

In v. 43 Psalm 107 gives an initial answer to its own question "Who is wise?" The wise person is the one who considers the "lovingkindnesses" of Yahweh. Book V of the Psalter then 'actualizes' the wondrous deeds (נִפְלָאוֹת) of Yahweh in the exodus (Psalms 113–118 are often called the 'Egyptian Hallel'), in the giving of the law at Mt Sinai (Psalm 119) and in his establishment of his kingdom centralized in Zion (120–136 are the "songs of Zion" that the exiles in Psalm 137 think they cannot sing in a

---

[30] Erich Zenger, "The Composition and Theology of the Fifth Book of Psalms, Psalm 107–145," *JSOT* 80 (1998), 101.
[31] Zenger, "Fifth Book," 98.

foreign land). So Yahweh is praised as "the God of the Exodus who rescues, and the God of Zion, who blesses."[32]

The allusions to the canonical history of Israel in Psalms 113–137 are framed at beginning and end by psalms connected in their titles with David (108–110 and 138–145), thus reinforcing the messianic hope of a Davidic king who will reign under Yahweh. Including a short Davidic collection (Psalms 108–110) as the first group of psalms following immediately after Psalm 107 and concluding Book V with another Davidic collection suggests that the redactors wished the reader to understand that Book V of the Psalter includes the idea that a Davidic king would participate in some way in answering the question of Psalm 107.

The three acrostics, Psalms 111–112 and Psalm 119, are themselves strongly connected verbally and thematically (more on this below); together they suggest that paying careful attention to the law of Yahweh is also part of the answer to the question of Psalm 107.

The overall three-fold answer to the question of Psalm 107 provided by Book V of the Psalter is as follows:

Who is wise?

- The person who meditates on the mighty redeeming works of Yahweh in Israel's canonical history (Psalms 113–137)

- The person who remembers that a Davidic messiah will be involved in the working out of God's purposes for Israel (Psalms 108–110, 138–145)

- The person who makes a commitment to obedience to Yahweh (Psalms 111–112 and 119).

The third of these responses to the question of Psalm 107 receives more support as a likely connection from the particular links between the end of Psalm 107 and Psalm 119. When the 'frequency analysis' words noted above are used to analyse the particular verbal connections between Psalms 107 and 119[33], it turns out that the final two verses of Psalm 107 have a dense concentration of Psalm 119 language.

---

[32] Zenger, "Fifth Book," 99.

[33] As done in de Hoog, "Psalm 119," 73–80, 158–160, see also Appendix, 13–14.

Psalm 107: 42–43 "The upright (יָשָׁר) see it (רָאָה) and are glad (שָׂמַח); but all (כֹּל) unrighteousness (עַוְלָה) shuts its mouth (פֶּה). Who is wise? (a verb from same root, חכם, is used in Psalm 119) Let him give heed (שָׁמַר) to these things, and consider (בִּין) the lovingkindnesses (חֶסֶד) of the LORD (יהוה)."

Of the 13 'frequency analysis' words in these two verses, 11 are also found in Psalm 119, and several of them are significant words in Psalm 119. This usage would draw the thought of the attentive reader to Psalm 119. It seems distinctly possible that the end of Psalm 107 is designed, in part, to point the reader to Psalm 119 as giving part of the answer to the question with which Book V of the Psalter opens.

The Connections of Psalm 119 to Psalms 111–112

A detailed comparison of the use of words in Psalm 111–112 and Psalm 119 reveals that Psalm 119 has a stronger lexical, formal and thematic overlap with Psalms 111–112 than with any other psalm or group of psalms in Book V.[34] For example, four of the eight Torah words in Psalm 119 also appear in Psalms 111–112. The links between these three psalms are more than the coincidence of shared lexemes. All three are acrostics. The three psalms also have strong thematic links. The thematic links can be demonstrated by a careful analysis of the way in which the shared lexemes are used. The significantly shared language between the psalms falls into the following categories.

Words that are used in Psalm 119 in the same way as they are used in Psalms 111–112 without variation:

    a. ירא ("fear") and cognates. Although these words are relatively common in the Psalter, they play a significant role in Psalms 111–112 in that the end of Psalm 111 (v. 10) and the beginning of Psalm 112 (v. 1) are linked by this word group, with 111:10 affirming that the fear of Yahweh is the beginning of wisdom, and 112:1 declaring how blessed is the one who fears Yahweh. The uses of these words in the

---

[34] De Hoog has shown that of all the 'frequency analysis' words in Psalms 111–112, fully 63.4% of them also appear in Psalm 119; which is the highest 'overlap' with Psalm 119 of all the psalms in Book V and compares with an average 'overlap' for all of the other psalms in Book V with Psalm 119 of 50.7%.

Psalter as a whole are widely varied, but their use in Psalms 111–112 and Psalm 119 are highly consistent.

    b. צְדָקָה ("justice, righteousness"). For example, what is affirmed of Yahweh in Psalm 113:3 is almost synonymously affirmed of Yahweh in Psalm 119:142. (See also category 4 below.)

    c. מִשְׁפָּט ("ordinance"). One of the four Psalm 119 Torah words that appear in Psalms 111–112, מִשְׁפָּט is used once each in 111:7 and 112:5, uses which are in keeping with two of the uses of this word in Psalm 119. In fact, both these verses are so full of Psalm 119 words that they sound as if they could come from Psalm 119.

    d. אַשְׁרֵי ("how blessed"). Psalms 112 and 119 use this word in identical fashion.

    e. דָּבָר ("word") is used in Psalm 112:5 – see note on מִשְׁפָּט.

    f. הוֹן ("enough, riches"). Yahweh's Torah is as great (119:14) as the riches of the righteous man in Psalm 112:3.

    g. חפץ ("take delight in"). Identical kind of use.

    h. מִצְוָה ("commandment"). Identical kind of use.

    i. פִּקּוּדִים ("precepts"). Identical kind of use.

Words that are used in Psalm 119 in the same way as they are used in Psalms 111–112 with the variation of adding uses of words that relate to Yahweh's Torah:

    a. עוֹלָם ("forever") and עַד ("forever, perpetuity"). Yahweh's righteousness is eternal in both Psalms 111–112 and Psalm 119, but Psalm 119 goes on to express the eternity of Yahweh's Torah and of its benefits and of a desire to keep Torah forever. (See also category 5 below.)

    b. כֹּל ("all, every"). Identical kind of use.

    c. דרש ("seek with care"). The word is used in the same way in both Psalm 119 and 111, but the object of seeking in

Psalm 111 is Yahweh's works, while in Psalm 119 it is Yahweh himself (twice) or Yahweh's Torah (three times).

Words used to affirm things about Yahweh in Psalms 111–112 that are used to affirm the same things about Yahweh's Torah in Psalm 119:

a. יָשָׁר ("right, upright"). Where Psalm 111:8 attributes uprightness to Yahweh's work, Psalm 119:137 says Yahweh's Torah is upright.

b. אֱמֶת ("firmness, truth"). Again Psalm 119 applies what Psalm 111 affirms about Yahweh's works to Yahweh's Torah.

Words used to affirm things about Yahweh in Psalms 111–112 that are used as the basis of petition in Psalm 119:

a. צְדָקָה ("justice, righteousness"). Psalms 111:3 and 119:142 declare that Yahweh's righteousness endures forever (see also category 1 above). Psalm 119:40 turns that affirmation into a prayer that the psalmist be preserved in Yahweh's righteousness.

b. סמך ("lean upon"). In Psalm 112:8 this word is used to denote the security of the godly person. This use is turned into a prayer in Psalm 119:116.

c. זכר ("remember"). What is affirmed in Psalm 111:5 is the basis of a petition in Psalm 119:49.

Word used to affirm something about the godly man in Psalms 111–112 that is used to express the commitment or orientation of the psalmist in Psalm 119:

a. עוֹלָם ("forever"). Psalm 112's godly man's righteousness endures forever. The author of Psalm 119 promises four times to keep Torah forever (vv. 44, 93, 98, 112), so becoming like the godly man of Psalm 112.

Word used to describe the godly man in Psalm 112 used as a basis for petition in Psalm 119:

a. חנן ("be gracious"). Used to describe the godly man in Psalm 112:5, Psalm 119 uses the word three times to ask for grace from Yahweh (vv. 29, 58, 132), each time on the basis of a commitment to keeping Yahweh's Torah (and so be like the righteous man in Psalm 112).

It is very likely that Psalms 111–112 and Psalm 119 were intentionally linked. We do not know when Psalms 111–112 and Psalm 119 were composed or located within Book V of the Psalter. But whatever their history, the consistent amount of shared language and theme between every section of Psalms 111–112 and Psalm 119 is almost certainly not coincidental.

It is difficult to judge how well we can reconstruct the intentions of the redactors of the Psalter in placing psalms where they are now located. But it is possible to make suggestions about what impact the nature and the placement of these psalms has on the message of Book V as a whole.

Psalms 111 and 112 are twin psalms. They both begin with *hallelu-yah*. Psalm 111 is a song of praise about the Lord's righteousness, his redemption, his covenant and his mercy. Psalm 111 ends with the words, "The fear of the Lord is the beginning of wisdom; all who follow his precepts have good understanding. To him belongs eternal praise."

This theme of fearing the Lord is then immediately picked up in v. 1 of Psalm 112 "How blessed is the one who fears the Lord, who finds great delight in his commands." Psalm 112 is a psalm about the godly person's righteous response to God's work. There are many parallels between the two psalms – see for example the exact coincidence of language between 111:3b and 112:3b. But fundamentally, Psalm 111 is about Yahweh and his redemptive work and Psalm 112 is about his people and their response to his redemptive work.

The connection between Psalms 111 and 112 reflects a similar connection between Psalms 105 and 106, which are the final two psalms of Book IV, which also contain the phrase *hallelu-yah* and which perform a stage-setting function for Book V. Psalm 105 is about Yahweh and his redemptive work, and Psalm 106 is about his people and their response to his redemptive work. In Psalms 105 and 106 the depiction is of Yahweh's *good* work and his people's *disobedient and rebellious* response; in Psalms 111 and 112 the picture is of Yahweh's *good* work and his people's *obedient and faithful* response. This is how things should be. Godly people, as they grow in godliness, begin to reflect God's character, and that growth is part of the answer to the question of Psalm 107.

This analysis allows us to suggest a function for Psalm 119 within Book V. The way the shared language is used suggests that *Psalm 119 is trying to demonstrate what Psalm 112 obedience might look like in real life*. In real life, an obedient response to Yahweh, as called for and *idealised* in Psalm 112, is brought down to earth in Psalm 119.

As we have already noticed, Psalm 119 is utterly realistic about the struggles of living a life in pursuit of God. Book V calls for Psalm 112 type obedience and only Psalm 112 type obedience can be pleasing to God. Through the connections between Psalms 111–112 and Psalm 119, Book V directs the reader to Psalm 119 to demonstrate what Psalm 112 obedience begins to look like in real life.

Psalm 119 is a vivid demonstration of what the life of a godly man actually looks like, with all the ups and downs of that life portrayed in Psalm 119's subject's first person experience and longings after Yahweh through the medium of his Torah. In Psalm 119 the wicked have not yet disappeared; indeed, they pose a genuine threat to the psalmist. Psalm 119 clearly shows that the pious life is not a smooth road. The subject of Psalm 119, speaking mostly in the first person, repeatedly emphasises his dependence upon Yahweh as he commits himself to delighting in and observing Torah in all of life.

The Group of Psalms 111–119

Psalms 113–118, often called the 'Egyptian Hallel', is a group of psalms bounded by the acrostics Psalms 111–112 and Psalm 119. We have noted the strong lexical and thematic connections between Psalms 111–112 and Psalm 119. They appear to function as 'brackets' around Psalms 113–118. However, at first sight there appears to be a jolting discontinuity between Psalms 113-118 and Psalm 119.

Psalms 113–118 certainly 'fit' well within Book V of the Psalter. Psalms 113–117 (not 114) share the phrase הַלְלוּ־יָהּ (*hallelu yah*) with Psalms 111–112 and with Book V more widely, and Psalm 118 opens and closes with the opening words of Book V in Psalm 107:1. Psalms 113–118 provide one perspective on the call of Psalm 107:43 to be wise and give heed to Yahweh's redemptive work, in particular by considering the lovingkindness (חֶסֶד) of Yahweh. Psalms 113-118 answer that call by such devices as encouraging the reader to remember the Exodus account and Yahweh's redemption of corporate Israel, affirming that there is no comparison between

Yahweh and other so-called "gods" and rejoicing in kings acting in the name and authority of Yahweh. All these connections serve to tie Psalms 113–118 tightly into the structure and main themes of Book V.

However, the particular phrases, sentences and many of these themes appear to be entirely absent from Psalm 119, which leads to an initial perception of radical discontinuity between Psalms 113–118 and Psalm 119. But can a connection between Psalms 113–118 and Psalm 119 be drawn on the basis of a more careful analysis of shared language?

The Use of the Divine Name Yahweh

The very frequent use of divine names in Psalms 113–118 is a feature of this corpus. The portrayal of Yahweh in Psalms 113–118 has several dimensions, including the following: (a) Statements that have Yahweh as the direct object of praise using verbs like הלל ("praise"), ידה ("give thanks") and ברך ("bless"): e.g. 113:1, 2, 9; 115:1, 18; 116:19; 117:1–2; 118:1, 28–29; (b) statements attributing glory, greatness, honour, etc to Yahweh: e.g. 113:4, 5; 115:16–18; 117:2; (c) statements that request or place confidence in Yahweh's grace and blessing: e.g. 113:6–9; 115:12–15; 116:5–9; 118:2–4, 6–9, 17–18; (d) statements affirming the power of his redemptive work and calls to rejoice in it: e.g. 114:1–8; 116:3–4, 6; 118:5, 19–27; (e) statements mentioning Yahweh's incomparability: e.g. 113:5; 115:2–8; (f) calls to trust in Yahweh: e.g. 115:9–11; (g) statements of personal commitment to Yahweh: e.g. 116:1–2, 12–19; (h) Yahweh as a warrior and help against enemies: e.g. 118:10–16.

All these themes (a–h) can be found in Psalm 119, but not one of them occurs without the characteristic adjustment of including Yahweh's Torah in the reference. For example, the author of Psalm 119 includes 32 ascriptions of praise, adoration and commitment to Yahweh that are scattered throughout the psalm, but he does so in the following way: ten times he says he "loves" (אהב – vv. 47, 48, 97, 113, 119, 127, 140, 159, 163, 167) Yahweh's Torah,[35] nine times he says he "delights" (חפץ, שעע and שַׁעֲשֻׁעִים – vv. 16, 24, 35, 47, 70, 77, 92, 143, 174) in it; five times he "praises" (הלל, תְּהִלָּה, and

---

[35] As already noted, these are the only places in the whole Hebrew Bible where Torah words are the object of the verb אהב.

ידה – vv. 7, 62, 164, 171, 175) Yahweh for his Torah and twice he "rejoices" (שוש – 14, 162) in his Torah. Further, virtually the whole of Psalm 119 is taken up with theme (g) above, 'Statements of personal commitment to Yahweh', but again almost entirely in terms of appreciation for, meditation upon or execution in life of Torah.

None of the explicit means of stating direct praise or confidence or praise or trust in Yahweh in Psalms 113–118 are found in Psalm 119 without either a superimposed or an intervening reference to Torah. Moreover, the major emphases in Psalm 119 of relating to Yahweh through meditation upon Torah, through delighting in and rejoicing in Torah, by obedience to Torah, through hope in Torah, by being delivered and vindicated through Torah and in the face of the enemies of Torah obedience are entirely absent in Psalms 113–118.

Nevertheless, the overall portrayal of Yahweh in Psalms 113-118 is crucial for Psalm 119. A comparison of the use of divine names between Psalms 113–118 and Psalm 119 reveals a consistent pattern. The eternal glory, greatness, goodness and power ascribed to Yahweh in Psalms 113–118 are ascribed to Yahweh's Torah in Psalm 119. The reliance on Yahweh and his help in trouble affirmed in Psalms 113–118 are stated in terms of reliance on and help given by Yahweh's Torah in Psalm 119. On every occasion the character of the God who stands behind the Torah is assumed. If Yahweh were not who he is described to be in Psalms 113–118, then affection for, trust in and obedience rendered to his Torah would be pointless.

Relationships within Psalms 111–119

The analysis above relates only to the use of the divine name Yahweh in Psalms 113–118 and Psalm 119. We do not have space in this article to consider the use of other words, but a pattern consistent with the connections established here emerges. The picture of Yahweh and his redemptive work painted in Psalms 113–118 is assumed in Psalm 119. Perhaps this could be said of many portraits of Yahweh from many parts of Scripture, but the fact that Psalms 113–118 are contiguous with Psalm 119 and are sandwiched between Psalms 111–112 and Psalm 119 suggests that the final redactors of the Psalter wished the particular portrait of Yahweh in Psalms 113–118 to be taken note of when reading Psalm 119.

The connections can be summarised in the following diagram:

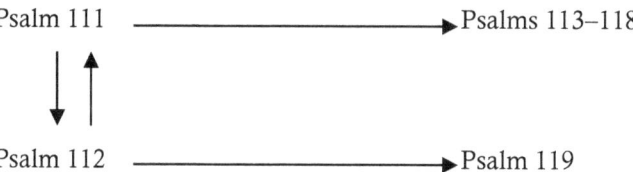

Psalm 111 provides a précis of the redemptive work of Yahweh that is expanded upon in Psalms 113–118. Psalm 112 provides an outline of the response of the godly person to Yahweh's redemptive work that is expanded upon in Psalm 119. This closely connected structure provides a *two-fold exemplary response* to the call of Psalm 107:43. One aspect of the response focuses on praising Yahweh for his redemptive work; the other aspect encourages paying loving attention to Yahweh's Torah. Moreover, the interconnections between these psalms suggest that these two aspects must not be separated but tightly held together.

Final conclusions

In contrast to Duhm's position, it is possible to affirm that Psalm 119 blackens paper in a rich and literarily complex manner. Its passion points to the pursuit of God as the preoccupation of the godly person. Its precision and focus on Torah suggest that such pursuit can be executed through disciplined engagement with God's self-revelation. And its canonical context points to the God being pursued as the God of redemption. His acts of redemption ("lovingkindnesses") are the material most prominent in that passionate, disciplined pursuit.

Psalm 137 and its Canonical Placement

Gillian Asquith

Melbourne School of Theology

Introduction

Psalm 137 is one of the better known psalms for two reasons: first, vv. 1–4 have the dubious honour of ranking sixth in the list of million-selling singles in the UK, with Boney M's cover of *By the Rivers of Babylon* beating The Beatles' *She Loves You* by two places, and sitting only narrowly behind *You're the One that I Want* from the movie Grease. Second, and more significantly, the psalm's concern with loss, grief and anger mixes some of the most evocative and poignant imagery in Scripture with what has been described as the most offensive line in the Psalter: 'happy are those who repay you for what you have done to us – those who seize your infants and dash them against rocks' (137:8b–9).[1]

Western Christians struggle to reconcile such a graphic and violent image of vengeance with the New Testament's commandment to love one's enemies. Where is the theological coherence between an apparently bloodthirsty desire for revenge and the teachings of Christ? How may a Christian appropriate such sentiments as Scripture? These are the concerns that tend to spring to mind upon a reading of this psalm, but there are further challenges to interpreting Psalm 137 beyond the fact that contemporary, Western Christian sensibilities struggle with imprecatory psalms. These challenges appear when we seek to explain the canonical placement of Psalm 137. How does a psalm that speaks so graphically of the Exile function in a literary context that in its final form dates to around the third or second century B.C.?

This essay will offer some suggestions that shed light on the canonical position of Psalm 137 and how it contributes to the theology of the Psalter. We will start with an overview of Psalm 137. An introduction to canon criticism of the Psalter will lead into a discussion of the function of Book V. The canonical placement of

---

[1] John Goldingay, *Psalms Volume 1: Psalms 1-41* (BCOTWP; Grand Rapids: Baker Academic, 2006), 66-67.

Psalm 137 will then be considered on two levels: first in terms of its relationship to its immediate neighbours, and second in terms of its function within Book V and, by extension, the whole Psalter.

Overview of Psalm 137

The opening verses speak of the pain experienced in exile in Babylon, but the psalm was most likely composed back in Jerusalem. The repeated שָׁם (šām) "there" in vv. 1 and 3 suggest that the psalmist is removed from the rivers of Babylon and writes retrospectively, the series of perfect verbs confirming the locative and temporal distance from the Exile itself.[2] Thus the psalm is most likely dated to the period when Cyrus of Persia allowed the Jews to return to Jerusalem to rebuild the Temple (573–516 B.C.).

The references to harps and songs suggest that the collective "we" in vv. 1–4 refers to Temple musicians or Levitical singers. The deportation by the Babylonians focused on the upper echelons of Judahite society to which the Temple musicians and singers belonged. The psalm opens with expressions of the loss and shame experienced by those deportees who would have previously been responsible for leading the worship celebrations at Temple festivals. The psalmist himself may or may not have been a deportee himself. If he were, he would have returned to Jerusalem an elderly man, struggling to reconcile the present state of the Temple ruins with the vibrant worship festivals of his younger days. If he were a second-generation exile, then the emotion conveyed through the psalm demonstrates the extent to which the exilic experience was seared into the post-exilic inherited memory.

The psalm falls into three sections, although there is disagreement regarding the exact division of these. The relationship of v. 4 to what precedes and follows is problematic: does it answer the question of v. 3? Or does it introduce the pledge of commitment in vv. 5–6? Numerous English versions (e.g. NIV, NRSV, NASB, ESV, NKJV) divide the psalm after verse 3, but there is good reason to extend the first strophe to include verse 4.[3] The geographical

---

[2] Occasionally, שָׁם functions as a locative adverb denoting near rather than distant events e.g. Psalm 48:6, 76:3. There is, of course, some fluidity in the way the perfect should be understood in Hebrew poetry, reflected by the NET Bible's translation of all these perfects into English presents.

[3] So Frank Lothar Hossfeld and Erich Zenger, *Psalms 3: A Commentary on Psalms 101–150* (Hermeneia; Minneapolis: Fortress, 2011), 513; Leslie C. Allen, *Psalms 101–150* (WBC; Waco: Word, 1983), 235, John Goldingay, *Psalms Volume 3: 90–150* (BCOTWP; Grand

markers "By the rivers of Babylon" and "on foreign soil" both use the preposition עַל (*'al*) and form an *inclusio* around that part of the psalm characterized by nine instances of the first person plural suffix נוּ (*-nû*). The psalmist switches usage of the first person plural to the singular in vv. 5–6 (the second strophe), calling down curses upon himself should his commitment to Jerusalem ever waver. The final strophe shifts gear further into an impassioned plea for vengeance. The two sub-units 7a–b and 8–9 in this strophe are thematically connected through the imprecations against the parallel Sons of Edom (not reflected in many English translations) and Daughter (of) Babylon.

Strophe 1

Clay tablets found at Nippur and Niru show an extensive system of irrigation canals in Babylon. Psalm 137 depicts the deportees beside these canals as they remember Zion, weeping over the loss of their home and the crisis of faith and identity. The juxtaposition of Babylon and Zion in the opening sentence is programmatic for the whole psalm; the psalm is predicated upon the polarities symbolized by these two cities. If יָשַׁבְנוּ (*yāšabnû*, 137:1) is intended as "sit" then it is possible that the psalmist is describing a posture and location associated with mourning (see Neh 1:4 and Ezra 8:21). The verb may also be understood more broadly as "dwell" in which case these opening verses could refer to the general life situation of the deportees as they worked beside the canals, maintaining them or watering crops.[4]

Musical instruments are designed to be played; therefore the dismal image of harps hanging unused in the trees appears to complete the picture of abject mourning (137:2). However there is worse in store for the deportees. Not allowed to weep in peace, they are tormented by their captors mockingly demanding that they sing songs of Zion for their entertainment. The causal conjunction כִּי (*kî*) "for" indicates that this is the real reason for the silent harps. They are now much more than a physical testimony to the deportees' pain and sorrow; rather they are symbols of protest against the

---

Rapids: Baker Academic, 2008), 604, pace Geoffrey W. Grogan, *Psalms* (Grand Rapids: Eerdmans, 2008), 215; Allan Harman, *Psalms* (Ferne, Scotland: Mentor, 1998), 427.

[4] Hossfeld and Zenger, *Psalms 3*, 515.

conquerors' demands for the subordination of the Judahites and their cult to pagans and their gods.

The anguish stirred by the memory of Jerusalem is exacerbated by the taunts of the captors and emphasised by syntagmatic and phonological parallelism of the poetry in v. 3. The stiches show a progression of thought that intensifies the demands of the Babylonians and the humiliation of the exiles. The Qal participle שׁוֹבֵינוּ (šôbênû) "our captors" simply expresses the hierarchy created when one person holds others against their will. שׁוֹבֵינוּ (pronounced 'shovenu') though, gives way to תוֹלָלֵינוּ, (pronounced 'tolalenu', note the assonance), a problematic *hapax legomenon* most likely meaning "tormentors" or "mockers", that fills out the way in which the captives were treated and heightens the portrayal of their misery.

This "parallelism of greater precision"[5] is developed further in the series of demands imposed by the captors. The neutral term "song" is defined more specifically as שִׂמְחָה (śimḥâ), a word that normally means joy or joyfulness, but by extension can refer to a song of joy, or even a song of military victory.[6] The prescribed content of the song is next defined as a song of Zion, the kind of song exemplified by Psalms 48, 76, and 87 and characterized by the exaltation of Zion as God's enduring city. The demand for such a song was a particularly cruel taunt, intended to humiliate via the bitter irony of a conqueror's songs on vanquished lips. The development of thought in the stiches of v. 3 can thus be expressed as:

> Our captors asked us for a song; our mockers a joyous victory song, "Sing for us about your impregnable city and your God who lived there!"
>
> (my paraphrase)

Verse 4 answers the demand imposed by the Babylonians. It most likely provides an explanation to the psalm's Jerusalem audience for the captives' resistance and has a modal sense "How *could* we sing Yahweh's song on foreign soil?"[7] There is an interesting reversal of

---

[5] David J.A. Clines, "The Parallelism of Greater Precision," *in Directions in Biblical Hebrew Poetry* (ed. Elaine R. Follis; JSOTSS 40; Sheffield: JSOT, 1987), 77-100.

[6] Lenowitz Harris, "The Mock-Simha of Psalm 137," in *Directions in Biblical Hebrew Poetry* (ed. Elaine R. Follis; JSOTSS 40; Sheffield: JSOT, 1987), 149-160.

[7] Hossfeld and Zenger, *Psalms 3*, 516.

the parallelism of precision from the previous verse: the psalmist broadens "Songs of Zion" to the more general designation "Yahweh's song". For the exiles, the Babylonians' mockery exposed the theological crisis of the Exile. The ironic demand for a Song of Zion was the equivalent of a playground taunt that cuts deeply. "Our god's bigger than yours, nah-nah-na-na-nah" was the effective cry, and it struck at the very heart of the Judahites' self-understanding.

The presence of Yahweh in the Temple, and the presence of his chosen people in the land he had given to them, were central to the Judahites' covenant identity. The removal of those covenant markers created an existential crisis additional to the trauma of having been conquered and exiled. Therefore it was not simply victory songs that could not be sung by this conquered people, it was *any* kind of God-song. No song that had previously been sung in Jerusalem, and more specifically in the Temple, to the praise of God whose presence dwelt therein, could be sung to entertain pagans whose gods now appeared more powerful than their own. The integrity of the Judahites could not be compromised by fusing their religious identity with that of foreigners.

Strophe 2

The theme of remembering from v. 1 is continued in the second strophe. Whereas the first strophe comprised a retrospective portrayal of exilic abandonment and desolation, the second strophe brings the psalmist's experience into the present and expresses his current and future commitment to Jerusalem.

The double self-curse involving hand and tongue are suggestive of a musician invoking a punishment that will render him unable to play an instrument or sing. However, the hand and tongue may also be metonyms for action and speech more generally: if the psalmist fails to make Jerusalem the centre point of his affections then may he be struck dumb and paralysed. The self-curse thus extends beyond the psalmist's likely profession to fundamental elements of life itself.[8]

Remembering is a major device used in this psalm to link past, present and future: the psalmist looks back to the past and expresses the sense of desolation and alienation felt in Babylon as the exiles

---

[8] Hossfeld and Zenger, *Psalms 3*, 518. George Savran, "How Can We Sing the Song of the Lord? The Strategy of Lament in Psalm 137," *Zeitschrift für die Alttestamentliche Wissenschaft* 112/1 (2000), 50.

remembered the glories of their former homeland; he invokes curses upon himself if he fails to remember his commitment to Jerusalem in the present time; yet he also looks forward to the future when God will remember the suffering of his people and fulfil his promises to them.

Strophe 3

The psalm now changes from remembering as an action performed by the psalmist and his community to remembering as an imperative directed at God. Although the involvement of the Edomites in the destruction of Jerusalem is not mentioned in the biblical historical narratives, Obadiah 10–14 confirms their presence and solidarity with the Babylonians. It is not clear who the addressees of the direct quote are. Are they the Edomites spurring one another on? Or are the Edomites urging on the Babylonian troops in their destruction of the city? Either way, the psalmist invokes the principle of *lex talionis*: the punishment meted upon the Edomites should match what they had done to Jerusalem. Since the Edomites called for the total destruction of Jerusalem, the psalmist likewise wishes the same upon them, although he leaves the agency of their punishment for God to determine.

Whereas 137:7 constitutes a plea to God against the Edomites, 137:8a expresses the utmost confidence that Babylon will receive its just desserts. The city is doomed to destruction. Babylon is addressed in identical terms ("Daughter Babylon") in several prophetic texts (Is 47:1; Jer 50:42; 51:33) that speak of the downfall of the city which is a metonym for the Babylonian empire as whole. This form of address thus evokes these prophecies and the audience is thereby reminded that the psalmist's confidence is based upon God's prior promises and he may have complete assurance that God will fulfil them. The beatitude of 137:8b explicitly states the principle of *lex talionis* and establishes the expectation that whatever follows in 137:9 is, therefore, an illustration of what the Babylonians did to the Judahites. Once again, the agent of the enemy's destruction is left unnamed. However, the linking of this beatitude with the prior plea to God in v. 8 makes it clear to the reader that it is God who is ultimately responsible for justice.

The shocking language of 137:9 has its roots in Ancient Near Eastern war practices and a number of OT texts refer to similar acts of violence (2 Kings 8:12; Hos 10:14; 13:16; Nah 3:10). The killing of children points to the removal of the enemy's means of continuation as a nation. In this respect, the psalm fills out with graphic detail the prophecies that had already been spoken of Babylon's destruction. As a representative of the powerless, the psalmist cries out to God, not only seeking recompense for the atrocities experienced by his people, but also handing over responsibility for that recompense to God as the only source of legitimate justice.[9]

Having examined the psalm itself, we may now move on to considering its position within the Psalter. We will start with an introduction to the application of canon criticism to the Book of Psalms.

Canon Criticism of the Psalms

For many years the Psalter was regarded as the Hymnbook of Second Temple Judaism, a 'Liquorice Allsorts' collection of songs and prayers for Israel's cult, with a purely cult-functional purpose. However, Brevard Childs' development of the canon-critical method demonstrated the value of working within the interpretative structure that Scripture received from those who formed and used it in its final state.[10] When Child's doctoral student, Gerald Wilson, applied this newly developed method to the Psalter, he made some astonishing discoveries about the way in which the final form of the book affects its interpretation.

Wilson examined forty-two Sumerian third millennium BC stereotyped hymns dedicated to temples, arranged according to apparent political and geographical motivations, and a Catalogue of Hymn Incipits comprising twenty-two cuneiform tablets cataloguing numerous hymns by their opening lines. Wilson persuasively argued a precedent from such hymn collections and catalogues for similar editorial activity in the Psalter that infuses the book with theological reflection and didactic purpose.[11]

Prior to the Exile, Israel had been a nation whose identity was bound up with her king and cult. When she could no longer look to the monarchy or Temple for leadership and identity, she turned to

---

[9] For a detailed discussion of the imprecatory psalms see Erich Zenger, *A God of Vengeance? Understanding the Psalms of Divine Wrath* (Louisville: Westminster John Knox, 1996) or John L. Day, *Crying Out for Justice: What the Psalms Teach Us about Mercy and Vengeance in an Age of Terrorism* (Grand Rapids: Kregel, 2005).

[10] Brevard S. Childs, *Introduction to the Old Testament as Scripture* (London: SCM, 1979), 73.

[11] Gerald H. Wilson, *The Editing of the Hebrew Psalter* (SBL Dissertation Series 76; Chico: Scholars Press, 1985).

adherence to the Torah (e.g. Neh 10:29). Torah-obedience, therefore, became the 'hermeneutical underpinning' for the post-exilic community.[12] Torah should not be restricted to the Mosaic law, however, but more widely defined as 'instruction'. Consequently, the exhortation of Psalm 1:2 to read what follows as Torah, divine instruction, provides the hermeneutical lens through which to read the Psalter and indicates how Israel's songs and prayers *to* God became words to the wise *from* God. As James Sanders notes, "In crisis situations, only the old, tried and true has any real authority"[13], and so it appears that the nation's sacred songs, already authoritative for worship, were loosened from their cultic context and subordinated to a new theological function, namely to provide a meaningful rationale for the post-exilic community in their quest for survival as the people of God.[14]

Thus Wilson pioneered an interpretation of the Psalter as a literary and canonical whole with a coherent message and structure. In the thirty years since the publication of Wilson's ground-breaking work, many have sought to define the content and shape of that coherent message and structure, albeit with differing results.[15] Jerome Creach sees a concern for the destiny of the righteous as the unifying factor, whereas James Mays suggests that the world and humanity be understood in terms of the reign of God.[16] Wilson preferred a development in thought from the failure of the Davidic kingship to the celebration of Yahweh's kingship. All of these elements are present in the Psalter and the challenge remains to identify a structure and message that gives adequate recognition to the nuances at play in the book. The overview that follows is based on Wilson's work, with additional input from more recent scholarship.

---

[12] Nancy deClaissé-Walford, *Reading From the Beginning:The Shaping of the Hebrew Psalter* (Macon, GA: Mercer University Press, 1997), 78.

[13] James A. Sanders, *From Sacred Story to Sacred Text* (Philadelphia: Fortress Press, 1987), 21.

[14] Childs, *Introduction*, 514-5; deClaissé-Walford, *Reading*, 120.

[15] It is important to note that acceptance of editorial shaping to the Psalter with hermeneutical significance is not universal. Notable deniers include John Goldingay and Craig Broyles. Broyles argues that the psalms' original function was to help God's people in their worship, and removing them from this encounter denies the purpose for which they originally came to be (Craig C. Broyles, *Psalms* (NIBC; Peabody, MA: Hendrickson, 1999), 8). Likewise, Goldingay asserts that "[i]nstead of looking for a structure in the Psalter, a more fruitful way of seeking a grasp on the Psalms as a whole is the more traditional approach of seeking to understand the types of psalms that recur, categorizing them into various ways of speaking to God and being addressed by God (Goldingay, Psalms 1, 37).

[16] Jerome F.D. Creach, *The Destiny of the Righteous in the Psalms* (St Louis, Missouri: Chalice, 2008); James L. Mays, *The Lord Reigns: a Theological Handbook to the Psalms* (Westminster: John Knox Press, 1994).

Wilson's evidence for intentional editorial activity includes explicit indicators such as psalm superscriptions and the postscript at Ps 72:20, tacit indicators such as the grouping of psalms with doxologies, the grouping of the Hallelujah psalms and the placing of certain psalms at the 'seams' of the five-book divisions. The absence of psalm superscriptions is also significant. For example, the position of Psalms 1 and 2 as untitled psalms at the head of a section dominated by psalms with author designations and superscriptions suggests that they are to be viewed separately from the other psalms. The identification of wisdom psalms at key points led Wilson to postulate a wisdom-orientation to the Psalter with Psalms 1 and 145 forming a wisdom framework around a book of divine instruction.[17]

Within that wisdom framework, Wilson noted that Books I to III of the Psalter appear to trace the development and ultimate failure of the Davidic covenant. By the end of Book III Psalm 89 remembers the Davidic covenant in dim and distant terms (89:19–20; 49), and despite God's promise to extend that covenant to future generations (89:4, 29, 36), the covenant is viewed as failed (89:44). The powerful description of the failure of that covenant in 89:38–44 sets the scene for Books IV and V to offer a new perspective and theological resolution, namely a return to the Mosaic covenant and a focus on the kingship of God. Now that the Davidic covenant is gone, a reliance on God alone is Israel's mandate.[18] Book IV in particular celebrates the kingship of God with the cluster of יְהוָה מָלָךְ ('Yahweh reigns') psalms (93, 96, 97, 99), and the Psalter concludes with a resounding expression of praise (Psalms 146–150).

---

[17] Book I contains a cluster of Davidic wisdom psalms (Psalms 32, 34 and 37) and although not normally considered wisdom, Psalm 41 closes Book I with the אַשְׁרֵי "blessed" formula used in Psalm 1. Wisdom psalms cluster again in Book V (Psalms 112, 127, 128, 133), along with the wisdom-influenced Psalm 111 and the great Torah Psalm 119. Along the way, Psalm 49 appears in Book II; Psalm 62 also bears wisdom influences. The sapiential vocabulary of Psalm 73 justifies its position in opening Book IV, whilst wisdom influences also appear in Psalms 78, 92 and 94. Interestingly, in post-exilic Israel, Torah piety and wisdom became so closely linked that by the early second-century BC, wisdom and Torah had become indistinguishable; in fact, Ben Sira links Wisdom, who proceeds from mouth of God with the written Torah (Sir 24:3, 23). See Anthony R. Ceresko, "The Sage in the Psalms," in *The Sage in Israel and the Ancient Near East* (eds. John Gammie and Leo G. Perdue; Winona Lake: Eisenbrauns, 1990), 217-230.

[18] Gerald H. Wilson, "Shaping the Psalter: A Consideration of Editorial Linkage in the Book of Psalms," in *The Shape and Shaping of the Psalter* (ed. J. Clinton McCann Jr.; JSOTSS 159; Sheffield: JSOT, 1993), 75.

Wilson's overall approach has garnered much support with subsequent scholarship refining and amplifying his work. For example, J. Clinton McCann Jnr. notes that the answer to the problem posed by the Exile is not restricted to Books IV and V, but is anticipated earlier in the Psalter. Psalms in Book III alternate between expressions of lament and hope whereby God is either celebrated as universal judge or his deeds on behalf of Israel despite her past faithlessness are recounted.[19] Thus trust in the Davidic covenant, the traditional basis for hope, is rejected in Book III, but hope itself is not entirely abandoned.

Other scholars have sought to reconcile the enduring presence of royal psalms within a corpus that places so much emphasis upon the failure of Davidic kingship.[20]

Biblical evidence outside the Psalter demonstrates that expectations did continue for the future restoration of David's line (Zech 12:7–9) and Psalm 2's lack of superscription, plus the thematic and linguistic links between Psalms 1 and 2, suggest a dual introduction to the whole Psalter including a messianic orientation. If then, at the time of the Psalter's final redaction, the royal psalms were understood along eschatological and messianic lines, then right from Psalm 2, the Psalter addresses the question of the continuing validity of the divine promises with the expectation that Yahweh's kingship will eventually result in the fulfilment of those promises.[21] This helps explain the puzzling number of Davidic psalms in Books IV and V. Perhaps these point to the modelling of David as the ideal person who trusts in God, but they may equally point to a strongly messianic theology.

---

[19] J. Clinton McCann Jr. "Books I-III and the Editorial Purpose of the Psalter," in *The Shape and Shaping of the Psalter* (ed. J. Clinton McCann Jr.; JSOTSS 159; Sheffield: JSOT, 1993), 93-107.

[20] In his early work, Wilson noted that the strategic placing of royal psalms (especially Psalms 2 and 144) gives the Psalter not only a wisdom frame but also a royal-covenantal focus. However, he postulated that the former takes precedence due to the primary positioning of wisdom Psalms 1 and 145, and the wisdom shaping of covenantal Psalms 2 and 144 (which form an inclusio around the covenantal framework). In later discussion, Wilson allowed for a greater messianic thrust to the Psalter although he maintained it was still to be understood within the wider framework of the kingship of God, the role of the 'anointed servant' being to usher in God's reign. (Gerald H. Wilson, *Psalms Volume 1* (NIV Application Commentary; Grand Rapids: Zondervan 2002), 711).

[21] Harry P. Nasuti, *Defining the Sacred Songs: Genre, Tradition and the Post-critical Interpretation of the Psalms* (Sheffield: Sheffield Academic Press, 1999), 203; David C. Mitchell, *The Message of the Psalter: an Eschatological Programme in the Book of Psalms* (JSOT Supplement Series 252; Sheffield: JSOT Press, 1997), 255.

Thus the Psalter is far more than a rough collection of songs for various circumstances, grouped by type or superscript. The songs drive a narrative that is intended to inform and transform, and the narrative charts a trajectory from lament to praise. Individual psalms play their part in the overarching narrative through various linking devices: they might be connected by the absence or presence of superscripts; lexical similarities between preceding or subsequent psalms might emphasise a particular theme; or psalms of a similar form *Gattung* might flavour a certain book or book section. For example, the predominance of lament psalms in Book I sets the tone of grief and despair experienced by the exiles, whilst the 'Yahweh reigns' Psalms in Book IV inspire confidence and hope through the sovereignty of God.

Within the five divisions of the Psalter, Book V presents the most challenges for the reader wanting to discern the theological focus of its editors. Book IV presents the kingship of God as the only enduring hope for Israel and there is a sustained, thematic unity to the book. It concludes with the possibility that within the divine kingship is provision for a future Davidic hope, so long as Yahweh's sovereignty is upheld.[22] Book V, however, as Wilson notes, is more diverse, with few roadsigns and landmarks.[23] There are several obvious groupings of psalms identified by superscripts (the Songs of Ascents Psalms 120–134, and two Davidic groups, Psalms 108–110 and 138–145), plus the concluding grouping of Hallelujah Psalms (146–150). Psalms 113–118 form an additional grouping known as the Passover Hallel. The challenge is to identify a theological structure to the book that also takes account of the psalms in Book V that fall outside these groupings, especially the two 'awkwardly placed' psalms, 119 and 137.

Book V

In essence, Book V acts as a response to the kingship of God as set out in Book IV.[24] The call to thanksgiving for the enduring love of the Lord in Psalm 107:1 is programmatic for the rest of Book V.

---

[22] See Lindsay Wilson, "On Psalms 103–106 as a Closure to Book IV of the Psalter," in *The Composition of the Book of Psalms* (ed. Erich Zenger; Leuven: Uitgeverij, 2010), 755–766 for a discussion of how Psalms 103–106, in closing Book IV, leave open the possibility of a future Davidic hope.

[23] Wilson, "Shaping the Psalter," 79.

[24] I am indebted to Erich Zenger, "The Composition and Theology of the Fifth Book of Psalms, Psalms 107–145," *JSOT* 80 (1998), 77–102 and Hossfeld and Zenger, *Psalms 3* for their insights into the overall structure of Book V.

Lexical and thematic similarities plus the wisdom orientation of their respective conclusions indicate that Psalms 107 and 145 form an *inclusio* around the content of Book V, with Psalms 146–150 serving as a final doxology, an extended crescendo of praise.

The three Davidic psalms (108–110) take up the theme of Books I–IV. Psalm 108:6–11 contrasts the promises of God with the present reality of foreign domination. Psalm 109 furthers the cry of distress and plea for deliverance. Psalm 110 answers those cries with the promise of judgement over the nations and a renewed messianic role for the king. It is striking that already in these early psalms of Book V we see echoes not only of the dominant themes of Books I–IV, but also of Psalms 1 and 2. The wisdom theme of Psalm 1 is taken up in Psalm 108, and the messianic theme of Psalm 2 in Psalm 110.

Psalms 111 and 112 reiterate the wisdom theme introduced in 107:43. Psalm 111 is particularly interesting at this point in the Psalter. It calls to remembrance God's works in the past (111:6) and praises them as faithful and just, done in faithfulness and uprightness (111:7–9). In the light of Book IV, this psalm emphasises the confidence and hope that remain for those who put their trust in the sovereignty of God. However, when viewed in the light of all that has been set forth so far in the Psalter, the psalm takes on a cautionary aspect. It is hard to imagine that a post-exilic audience could appropriate 111:7–9 without remembering the events of the Exile. For a people living with the aftermath of the Exile, this psalm would surely cause them to ponder the covenant disobedience that led to the loss of their land. From this perspective, the call to fear the Lord and follow his precepts (111:10) is more than an exhortation towards a godly life such as we might find in the Book of Proverbs. It implicitly carries with it a reminder of the corporate consequences of failing to live such a life.

Psalms 113–118 form a unit known as the Passover Hallel. This unit celebrates the sovereignty of God over all the nations and the place of God's people among them. It recalls the first Exodus (hence the name 'Passover Hallel') in Psalm 114. The rescue and resettlement of the poor and needy (113:7–9) is celebrated from the perspective of the individual in Psalms 116 and 118 and corresponds to the rescue of God's people from Babylon, the second Exodus.

Psalm 118 ends with a reference to cult participation in the Jerusalem Temple. The next major grouping of Psalms is the so-called Pilgrim Psalter, Psalms 120–134. These psalms, with the superscription 'Song of Ascents', chart the search for a place of security away from hostilities (Psalms 120–121) that culminates in the celebration of life on Mount Zion (Psalm 133) in the house of the Lord (Psalm 134). Given the Zion theology of this psalm grouping, Psalm 119 appears to interrupt the flow of thought from the end of Psalm 118 to the Songs of Ascents. However, Psalm 118 presents God's rescue of the needy as gates through which the righteous may enter (118:19–20). In this respect, Psalm 119, that extols the Torah as the source of wisdom and instruction for a godly life, functions as a commentary on the Torah-adherent life as characteristic of both the righteous who have been rescued and the life to which they have been rescued. In addition to looking back to Psalm 118, it also anticipates Psalms 120–134 in terms of living out the Torah in preparation for pilgrimage to Jerusalem.

Psalms 135 and 136 are two historical psalms of praise and thanksgiving celebrating God's acts of redemption in the first Exodus and the instalment of the Israelites in the land. They are linked to the Pilgrim Psalter by the lexical and thematic connections between Psalms 134 and 135. The Pilgrim Psalter concludes with the exhortation to the servants of the Lord to sing his praise in the sanctuary; Psalms 135 and 136 thus stand as expressions of that praise to be offered in the house of the Lord. Although the psalms' historical retrospectives are limited to Israel's entry into the land, Psalm 135 concludes with a reference to the Lord as the one who dwells in Jerusalem, reinforcing the link with the Pilgrim Psalter. As songs that offer from within Zion praise to God who dwells in Zion, these are representative of the kind of 'God-song' that the exiles of Psalm 137 so vehemently refused to sing on foreign soil.

Before we are in a position to consider the placement of Psalm 137, we must first examine the final grouping of psalms in the Psalter before the Hallelujah Psalms 146–150, the Davidic Psalms 138–145. Psalms 138 and 145 form an *inclusio* around this group of psalms. They focus on praising the name of God because of his greatness and glory. Within these brackets, Psalm 139 is a profession of trust that leads into a series of psalms (140–144) of lament and supplication. Given the overall trajectory from lament to praise in the Psalter it is perhaps surprising that a group of psalms so focused on suffering and distress should be placed so close to the end of the Psalter with its grand finale of praise. However, even after the return of the exiles to the land, the Jewish people still lived with the effects of conquest. They were still subject to foreign powers; first the Persians, then the Greeks. The second exodus had not provided everything that the returnees and their descendants had expected. Life was still harsh and uncertain. They were a people living with deferred hope who were effectively experiencing the unending consequences of the Exile. In this respect, the Psalter addresses 'real life' experience. Rather than presenting an escapist ideal, it testifies to the fact that God is to be praised in the midst of suffering and distress. A further significance to the positioning of this final group of lament psalms will be considered below in the discussion regarding the canonical placement of Psalm 137.

Prominent in this final group of lament psalms is the wisdom perspective of cause and effect, especially in regard to the wicked. The psalmist prays that they will reap the consequences of their own behaviour (140:9) and fall into their own nets (141:10). But not only do these psalms express a desire for the self-destruction of the wicked, they pray too for God's judgement and punishment to fall upon their enemies for what they have done (140:10-12; 143:12). There is a corresponding emphasis on the preservation of the righteous and protection from both wickedness and the wicked (140:1-2, 4-5; 141:3-4, 8-9; 142:6).

So the question we now need to ask is 'Why has Psalm 137 been placed between the historical psalms of praise and thanksgiving (Psalms 135 and 136) and the final Davidic grouping?' In terms of continuity of thought, Psalm 138 would seem to follow naturally from the historical psalms pairing and the Pilgrim Psalter; it expresses praise to God's name in continuity with Psalms 135 and 136, and its reference to bowing down towards the Temple links back to the Songs of Ascents in the Pilgrim Psalter. Just as Psalm 119 appeared at first glance to be an intrusive interpolation between the Passover Hallel and the Pilgrim Psalter, so Psalm 137 seems to interrupt the flow of thought in the latter part of Book V. If the final redactors had been constrained by a fixed historical precedent for keeping Psalm 137 next to its preceding and succeeding psalms, then this would possibly explain its position, but evidence from the Dead Sea Scrolls suggests otherwise.

When the Qumran manuscripts are compared with the Masoretic arrangement of the psalms, there is marked similarity in order between the psalms in Books I–III. However, there are far more instances of variation in order in Books IV and V. This suggests that the order of psalms in Books I–III was fixed much earlier than that of Books IV and V. Likewise, the presence of Psalms 121–132 in order in the Qumran Psalms Scroll 11QPs[a] suggests that a fixed grouping of most of the Pilgrim Psalter existed as a prior arrangement for the final editors of the Masoretic Psalter to draw on, one which was also used in the arrangement represented by the Qumran library. Psalm 137 is attested in the same scroll, where it is preceded by Psalm 139 and followed by Psalm 138. This suggests that there was a common tradition linking Psalms 137 and 138, but nothing more. Indeed, except for Psalms 121–132, the only similarities between the Masoretic and Qumran arrangements of Book V comprise pairings rather than groups, thus suggesting that there was a certain looseness surrounding the ordering of psalms in this book and that the final redactors of the Masoretic Psalter had editorial licence to arrange the psalms to suit their own theological agenda. There is no accidental placement of the 'awkward' psalms, 119 and 137; rather they play a decisive role in the theology of Book V.

The Canonical Placement of Psalm 137
a) Psalm 137 and its Immediate Neighbours

Psalm 137 is positioned immediately after two historical psalms that remember and celebrate Yahweh's covenant gift of the land to the nation. The theme of remembering in Psalms 135 and 136 is thus continued with the repeated use of "remember" in Psalm 137. But the placement of this psalm immediately after Psalms 135 and 136 causes the remembering in Psalm 137 to serve two different purposes. On the one hand, it situates the psalmist's plea to God to remember the suffering of his people and restore them in the context of God's prior redemptive acts. But on the other, it provides a stark reminder to the Jews of the consequences of the failure of the Davidic covenant. In calling upon God to remember when the Edomites stormed Jerusalem and meted out justice, the psalmist is implicitly calling to mind that same time when God withdrew his assistance and forgot his people. The theological crisis brought about by the Exile was centred on the loss of those elements that confirmed Israel's chosen nationhood: the people's presence in God's land and God's presence in the Temple. The positioning of Psalm 137 therefore emphasises the reversal of those very signs of covenant nationhood that were celebrated in the two previous psalms.[25]

---

[25] Allen, *Psalms 101-150*, 241.

Erich Zenger denies Psalm 137 the Deuteronomistic theology of judgement that interpreted the Exile as 'just punishment' for the nation, and he is correct in so far as the psalm is interpreted in isolation.[26] However, the canonical position of the psalm functions in part as a commentary on its interpretation and insists that the nation must take responsibility for the experience of Exile. The prophetic perspective that Babylon will be judged for its treatment of God's people (Jer 51:20–26) is certainly present in the final strophe, but this element does not negate the Deuteronomistic perspective that is created by reading the psalm in light of Books I–III and Psalms 135–136.

Psalms 135 and 136 also represent 'God-songs' that celebrate the presence of God who dwells in Zion. Psalm 137 laments the fact that the exiles could not sing any type of God-song on foreign soil, not least a Song of Zion. When we consider the form of Psalm 137, it appears that this psalm is actually a modified Song of Zion. Since the advent of form criticism, scholars have struggled to assign Psalm 137 to a particular *Gattung* (form). Leslie Allen notes that it "defies straightforward classification in form-critical terms" and Claus Westermann even denies its identification as a true psalm, preferring to describe it nebulously as "something rather like a folk song."[27] Whilst it is unhelpful to attempt to stuff a psalm too tightly into a form-critical strait-jacket (after all, the psalmists themselves were unaware of form-critical classifications), the conformity or otherwise of a psalm to a particular *Gattung* facilitates both a deeper understanding of the psalm and an appreciation for its individuality. In this case, the comparison of Psalm 137 with psalms that are classified as Songs of Zion yields fruitful results.

There are elements within Psalm 137 that correspond with 'genuine' Songs of Zion in the Psalter. Direct address of Zion is one such feature (e.g. 87:3; 122:2, 6–9). The beatitude formula "Blessed/happy is the one who" is another (84:4–5). But this is no standard Song of Zion. The usual celebration of the city's impregnability (e.g. 46:4–7; 48:8; 87:5) is replaced with a reference to its destruction and the perfect verb forms that would usually rehearse the victory of God over Israel's enemies (e.g. 48:4–6; 76:3–9) are now employed to narrate the pain of loss and despair (137:1–

---

[26] Hossfeld and Zenger, *Psalms 3*, 520.

[27] Allen, *Psalms 101–150*, 237; Claus Westermann, *Praise and Lament in the Psalms* (Atlanta: John Knox, 1981), 256.

3).[28] The beatitude formula is no longer applied to those who praise God in his city, but to those who avenge the perpetrators of its destruction. These reversals combine pathos with irony; they emphasise the depth of loss experienced by the exiles but they also cause the psalm to function as a song that manages to mock the very people who set out to taunt them. This Song of Zion cannot offer the usual praise thanksgiving for victory and security, but the imprecations of vv. 7–9 turn the impotence of the exiles in vv. 1–3 into an ironic cry against their tormentors. They asked the exiles for a Song of Zion; the psalmist has responded by composing such a song, but has embedded within it a call for the mockers' downfall.[29]

Thus the reader of the Psalter is confronted by two themes through the placing of Psalm 137 immediately after Psalms 135 and 136. First, the reader is forced to recall the devastation caused by the failure of the Davidic covenant. Second, modifications to the usual Song of Zion present the expectation that God will act decisively to bring about vengeance for his people. This is set in the wider context of God's previous redemptive acts that were remembered in Psalms 135 and 136 and provide hope and confidence that God's long-term promises will prevail. The reader does not have to wait long for confirmation that God is faithful to his promises. The praises and thanksgiving of Psalm 138 constitute a God-song to be sung back on home ground. As such, it is a counterpart to Psalm 137, and the celebration of God's kingship that extends over all the earth (138:4–5) emphasises that the impassioned plea at the end of Psalm 137 was not ill-founded.

b) The Function of Psalm 137 within Book V

There are close links between Psalm 137 and the psalms immediately around it. But when we consider the grand over-arching narrative of the Psalter, a position so close to the end of Book V seems an unlikely place to situate a song whose historical context would make it a better fit in the earlier sections of the Psalter lamenting the failure of the Davidic covenant. Why should it be necessary to emphasise the consequences of the Exile at this point in the Psalter?

A possible answer is to be found in the historical context of the final redaction of the Psalter. By this time, the Jewish people had lived

---

[28] Allen, *Psalms 101–150*, 238.
[29] Savran, "How Can We Sing," 58; Lenowitz, "The Mock-Simha," 157.

with the effects of conquest for many generations. However, their troubles were not limited to the fact that they were still subject to foreign rule. Further tensions arose because of the differing extents to which Jews embraced Hellenism, particularly during the Seleucid period. Conflict was now not only between Jew and Gentile, but between Jew and fellow-Jew. The laments within the Davidic grouping, Psalms 138–145, may very well be intended to speak into this historical context and in this case Psalm 137 would serve an important pivotal role between these psalms and the prior focus on Zion theology in the Pilgrim Psalter.[30]

The final grouping of laments, Psalms 140–144, presents the individual as a victim of evil and evildoers, but Psalm 139 additionally suggests that perhaps the psalmist is tempted to join in with their wickedness. He decries those who hate God and declares his own hatred for them (139–21-22), but at the same time articulates doubts about his own integrity (139:23–24). The presence of these doubts is confirmed by references to protection from the temptations of evil (141:3–4) and a plea for direction in the right way (143:8).

These psalms express the kind of dilemma faced by pious Jews during the Hellenistic period. Torn between their desire to follow the Torah and the attractions of Hellenism, they would surely experience self-doubt as they turned their back on fellow-Jews who embraced Hellenism. All the descriptions of the enemies and opponents then in the final Davidic grouping are characteristics that could be applied by a Jew to his fellow Jew denouncing his neighbour's Hellenism as apostasy. These characteristics extend beyond the lament psalms themselves across the whole final Davidic grouping, thereby adding thematic cohesion to the final redaction. For example, Psalm 138 refers to the proud (138:6); the wicked of Psalm 139 speak against God with malicious intent (139:20), they hate him and rise up against him (139:21); the poison of vipers is on their lips in Psalm 140 (140:3) and they seek to persecute the faithful psalmist (140:4–5; 141:9). But Psalm 145 is clear that in contrast to those who call on him in truth, the wicked will be destroyed (145:20).

---

[30] Harm van Grol, "David and his Chasidim: Place and Function of Psalms 138-145," in *The Composition of the Book of Psalms* (ed. Erich Zenger; Leuven: Uitgeverij, 2010), 332–335; "The Snares Laid for Faithful Lips: Hellenistic Apostasy in Psalm 141," in *The Composition of the Book of Psalms* (ed. Erich Zenger; Leuven: Uitgeverij, 2010), 711–722.

Harm van Grol suggests that the final redactor used Psalm 137 to transition into this final Davidic grouping since the issue of the conflict between 'the own and the foreign' characteristic of the tension between pious and Hellenist Jew is also the key issue in Psalm 137.[31] His argument is persuasive but incomplete. The psalm's refusal to fuse Judahite identity with that of foreigners does anticipate the historical context of the final redactors of the Psalter, but it also provides a retrospective on a previous fusion of Judahite identity with that of foreigners: the idolatry and spiritual adultery committed by both Israel and Judah that led to the downfall of the two kingdoms. When, through the canonical placement of the psalm, readers are forced to recall the removal of the signs of covenant nationhood and the reasons for their removal, Psalm 137 takes on a cautionary purpose. It is not accidentally or awkwardly placed. Rather, it takes up the caution implicit in Psalm 111 and forces readers to confront the mistakes of previous generations and consider whether their current behaviour is directing them down the same path. The impassioned cries for deliverance from the wicked in the final group of laments suggest that the final redactors of the Psalter saw the influences of Hellenism as equally dangerous to national identity as the earlier instances of covenant disobedience.

The great Torah Psalm 119 exhorts the wise to a Torah-adherent life and anticipates Psalms 120–134 in terms of living out the Torah in preparation for pilgrimage to Jerusalem. But the reader of the Psalter must be mindful of the lessons of history. Psalm 137 brings those lessons to the fore and reminds the reader of the consequences of the failure to live a Torah-oriented life. In this respect, Psalm 137 functions as a reminder of the destiny of the wicked, both explicitly in terms of the Edomites and Babylonians and, more importantly, implicitly in terms of the Judahites who disobeyed the covenant. This latter reminder serves as warning to those who approach the Psalter as Psalm 1 exhorted: delight in the law of the Lord and meditate on it day and night; put it into practice, because this is what happens if you do not. The final grouping of lament psalms brings a sense of urgency to the penultimate section of the Psalter. The implicit caution of Psalm 137 must be heeded. The enemies must be silenced, the righteous must be protected from both wickedness and those who perpetrate it, and the integrity of Judaism must be maintained.

---

[31] van Grol, "David and his Chasidim," 332.

Conclusion

The Psalter in its final form is concerned with an exhortation to the wise to read the collection of psalms as Torah. Its wisdom frame is complemented by a messianic thrust that looks forward to the reign of God's anointed one under his divine sovereign rule. Wisdom literature in general is concerned with ethical behaviour that coheres with the orderly arrangement of creation. However, the wisdom thrust to the Psalter is concerned with following Torah, that great body of divine instruction that contains, but is not limited to, the Mosaic law. This causes the ethics of wisdom literature such as are found in Proverbs to fuse with the demands of justice and righteousness (covenant obedience) as presented in the prophets. Although the Psalter does not present an explicit and developed Deuteronomistic theology of judgement, the shadow of the Exile hangs over the whole book.

Psalm 137 in isolation addresses the issue of God's justice for his people who have suffered terribly. In its literary context, however, the psalm reminds the reader that the divine justice that will bring recompense for the victims is the very same justice that demanded their punishment in the first instance. That very same justice could prevail again if Torah-disobedience is rife within the Jewish community and thus the psalm stands as a warning. It appears that the final redactors of the Psalter saw increasing Hellenism as one such threat to the integrity of the Jewish faith and sought to counter this by producing a book of divine instruction to teach the godly. The presence of a group of lament psalms before the final crescendo of praise in Psalms 146–50, and the canonical position of Psalm 137 support the reading of the Psalter as a book of instruction, encouragement and warning. It seems that the Psalter seeks to preserve the struggling post-exilic Jewish communities from Hellenistic apostasy, the penultimate psalm grouping (Psalms 138-145) concluding with the wisdom adage: "the Lord watches over all who love him, but all the wicked he will destroy." The kingship of God will prevail over both the wise and the wicked (let the reader understand).

At the Edge of the Precipice: Psalm 89 as Liturgical Memory

David Cohen

Vose Seminary

In his book *At the Edge of the Precipice* Robert Remini describes a watershed moment in the history of the United States of America as distinguished Senator Henry Clay proposed what came to be known as *The Compromise of 1850*.[1] During this period Remini says "...the Union of American states... came close to being irreparably smashed."[2] Events of such magnitude for many nations throughout history have perhaps been rare but, when they occur, have offered opportunities for both individuals and communities to pause in reflection. Careful and thoughtful reflection can in turn create a space in which some sense can be made of the experience. But why and how might this be so? Essentially it seems to be because such world-shaping opportunities inherently possess the raw material which enables the possibility of imagining a different world. This imagining occurs through embracing the past and present, both of which have contributed to forming the individual and community in the first place.

While ancient Israel, as portrayed in Psalm 89, is an historical world away from Henry Clay and events in the United States of America in his time, the image of precipice unites them.[3] Both groups at particular points in their history, and in their own unique ways, found themselves at the edge of a precipice. Here they were faced with the prospect of plunging into oblivion or, alternatively, being compelled to embrace their past, make sense of their present and re-imagine their future. In simple terms, the life and times of Henry Clay and the life and times of the psalmist in Psalm 89

---

[1] Robert Remini, *At the Edge of the Precipice*, (New York: Basic Books, 2010).

[2] Remini, *At the Edge*, xi.

[3] Robert Remini, *Henry Clay: Statesman for the Union*, (New York: W.W. Norton, 1991), 761–762. Although, in comparing the two histories, it must be acknowledged that the ultimate outcomes were quite distinct, with the United States eventually plunging into civil war in 1861. In Henry Clay's biography, also by Remini, it is noted that Senator Henry S. Foote said "Had there been one such man in the Congress of the United States as Henry Clay in 1860–'61 there would, I feel sure, have been no civil war."

represented a precipice, paradoxically embodying voices of despair and of hope. The image of precipice is helpful in reminding us that it is often only these kinds of momentous, and often traumatic, events in our personal or communal histories which offer a space for significant meaning-making to take place. It also reminds us that a passive response to these opportunities is inadequate. They need to be grasped if their full meaning-making potential is to be realized.

In Psalm 89, kingship personifies ancient Israel's precipice, or, more precisely, the crisis of kingship culminating in their exilic experience.[4] In fact Broyles classifies the psalm as a 'royal prayer' underlining the focus on kingship.[5] Historically kingship in its emergence, consolidation and subsequent self-destruction had led ancient Israel through both the best and the worst of times. However, in a more supra-historical sense, the notion of kingship, and how it is characterized within Psalm 89, draws attention to the existential and theological questions raised by such an institution in a polycentric manner.[6] Psalm 89 addresses these questions by acknowledging existential angst in particular ways and yet, rather paradoxically, offers a sense of hope for the people's future. Both YHWH's, and the people's, uneasy relationship with kings and kingship is voiced in this psalm. Through its inclusion in the Psalter, the psalm not only gives vent to feelings associated with kingship in a form of literature but also, by definition, embeds it as part of the people's liturgical practice and memory.[7] This suggests that their lived exilic experience, as a nation, is transcended by the broader ramifications and understanding of the role of kingship for them as covenant partners with YHWH in the brave new world of post-exilic experience.

In exploring this psalm I propose that, as an act of liturgical memory, Psalm 89 articulates a convergence of four interrelated and equally critical aspects of human reflection: mythic, parabolic, mimetic and parenetic qualities. When appropriately acknowledged

---

[4] David Carr, *The Formation of the Hebrew Bible*, (New York: Oxford University Press, 2011), 342.

[5] Craig Broyles, *Psalms*, (Baker Books: Grand Rapids, Michigan, 2012), 355.

[6] By the term polycentric I am suggesting that each phase of Israel's history — pre-, peri- and post-kingship (human) — is represented in different ways throughout Psalm 89, creating several perspectives on the institution.

[7] It is beyond our scope to explore the specific, historical use of this particular psalm in Israel's liturgical tradition. However, it is entirely reasonable to assume that this psalm, along with the others were used at least periodically if not frequently by both communities of faith and individuals as an expression of worship.

and brought together by using a psalm such as this one in liturgy, these four nested qualities constituted a dynamic space for community reflection on their identity, as a people in covenant with YHWH.[8] It also enabled reflection on how the relationship between themselves and YHWH might be shaped afresh in the face of potentially identity-destroying circumstances.[9] As these mythic, parabolic, mimetic and parenetic qualities engage in dialogue with each other in Psalm 89, a conducive space for meaning-making results at the edge of the precipice. The dialogical process, which is a key to emergent meaning-making, provides ballast for the community to survive the storm. This, in turn, contributes to their resilience in the face of seemingly insurmountable odds. Embracing and yet concurrently transcending the community's circumstances, the four qualities elicit a boldly hopeful stance as they face an uncertain future where life will continue but where life will never be the same. In large part this exploration will focus on defining the four qualities identified above, offering examples of each from Psalm 89. In concluding I will offer some reflections on what these individual qualities and the pattern of their dialogical interaction in Psalm 89 might offer us as individuals and communities of faith in the twenty-first century.

Background Issues

Before considering the four qualities introduced above, it will be helpful to outline some of the critical issues related to Psalm 89 as a backdrop for our current focus. Of particular significance for this exploration is the historical setting of the text, its liturgical usage and the psalm's literary structure.[10] Each provides a lens through which the content and function of the psalm becomes more clearly focused. Much has been postulated around these three issues and

---

[8] 'Space' as used here can be viewed in three ways. First, it can refer to literary space (in this case, as represented in the text of Psalm 89). Second, it can signify a physical space where the psalm is utilized as an expression of the liturgy. Finally, it can be viewed as an intrapsychic space for an individual and/or community. Each 'space' described here can engender a mindfulness in response to presenting circumstances.

[9] The 'dynamic space' envisaged here becomes even more critical when considering Psalm 89 as representative of exilic reflection. At this point in the people's history they had been removed from their 'place'. What's more, their 'place' (the land) had become either a distant memory (for those who survived the deportations) or, a part of the narrative history of a prior generation (for those who were born and/or died in exile).

[10] Of course there are myriad issues which could be addressed here including placement of Psalm 89 at the close of Book III of the Psalter, questions about the rhetorical nature of the psalm, etc. Some of these will be captured in the discussion following.

the following provides only a brief survey of the views pertinent to the discussion here.

Some might argue that the *Sitz im Leben* of any psalm is a moot point and that the issue should thus be dismissed as something which remains unclear and is, therefore, irrelevant. But against such a view it is helpful to remember that, in fact, there *was* an initial historical context for each psalm.[11] This also recognizes that all psalms *do* arise from particular historical circumstances and are descriptive of thoughts, feelings and experiences associated with these contexts, even if the precipitating events cannot be clearly identified.[12] In light of this it seems reasonable to suggest at least viewing "psalms against a larger narrative, that of the history of Israel..."[13] Such a view reminds us that the psalms themselves, and the liturgy in which they reside, arise from 'below'. That is, they are both grounded in and emerge from the complexity and ambiguity of lived history even if the underlying events cannot be accurately adduced.

With the above pre-understanding it is helpful to view Psalm 89 as theology in action *within* history and *through* history.[14] In other words the psalm preserves the lived realities of a people at a particular time, which otherwise risked being relegated to the dusty pages of history. The inclusion of psalms such as this one in the Psalter creates a living liturgical space for following generations to reflect on their own unique thoughts, feelings and experiences.[15] Gerald Wilson alludes to connecting thoughts, feelings and experiences in Psalm 89 when he notes that

> At the conclusion of the third book... the impression left is one of a covenant remembered, but a covenant *failed*. The Davidic covenant introduced in Ps 2 has come to nothing and the combination of the

---

[11] Of course, along with the initial context of a psalm, it is important to acknowledge subsequent redacted forms of a psalm and associated new historical contexts.

[12] For example, Psalm 44 alludes to the events of the Exodus while Psalm 137 is clearly an example of reflection on the Exile.

[13] Harry P. Nasuti, "The Interpretive Significance of Sequence and Selection in the Book of Psalms," in *The Book of Psalms* (eds. Peter W Flint, Patrick D Miller, Aaron Brunell, and Ryan Roberts; (Leiden, NL: Brill, 2005), 317. Here Nasuti is particularly addressing the conjectural issue of Davidic authorship (which is not relevant in a study of Psalm 89) but his point still stands in regard to the historical *Sitz im Leben* of psalms generally.

[14] Here I am taking both a diachronic and a synchronic view of the text.

[15] Erhard Gerstenberger, *Psalms. Part 2, and Lamentations* (Grand Rapids, Michigan: Eerdmans, 2001), 154.

three books concludes with the anguished cry of the Davidic descendants.[16]

As highlighted by Wilson this nexus is not an unfocused, generalized historical overview but, rather, one grounded in ancient Israel's lived experience couched in a theology of covenant. This theology of covenant is not presented as an abstract, ahistorical concept but, rather, a *de facto* principle which has underpinned the identity and mission of this ancient group of people for centuries. Psalm 89, through poetic narrative,[17] recounts history as what could be called *Geschichte* rather than *Historie*.[18] It does this in its own way and for its own purposes echoing the concerns of a particular people in their own particular historical context with one eye on the past and one on the present. Beyond this, Wilson's observations also alert us to the literary/theological function of the psalm in the overall structure of the Psalter.[19] In doing so he reminds us of the far-reaching potential of this psalm for subsequent generations using it as part of their liturgical practice and reflecting on its content.

Liturgical usage is a second important consideration. But can the liturgical usage of Psalm 89 be determined with any confidence? Despite much discussion among scholars around the liturgical usage of most psalms it is important to consider some broad possibilities for Psalm 89. Typically any discussion of liturgical setting can quickly elicit polarized views. As a result the matter can be oversimplified by identifying and adhering to one particular setting *vis à vis* another. Alternatively, the acknowledgement of a multiplicity of settings can result in a lack of any meaningful insight at all. James Ward, in his remarkably perceptive discussion of Psalm 89 and its liturgical usage, helpfully bridges the gap between

---

[16] Gerald Wilson, *The Editing of the Hebrew Psalter* (Chico, California: Scholars Press, 1985), 213.

[17] David J. Cohen, *Why O Lord?* (Carlisle, United Kingdom: Paternoster Press: 2013), 25. The phrase 'poetic narrative' is coined as a way of describing a phenomenon often present in various psalms where clearly a story is being recounted but using typical Hebrew poetic language rather than prose.

[18] Here I am using the term *Geschichte* as describing history as event as opposed to *Historie* which is more related to history as record. In doing this I am following the distinction, albeit rather blurred at times, found in the philosophical works of Heidegger *et al*. For a more detailed discussion on the distinction between *Geschichte* and *Historie* see Alejandro Vallega, "'Beyng-Historical Thinking' in Heidegger's Contribution to Philosophy" in *Companion to Heidegger's Contributions to Philosophy* (ed. Alejandro Vallega *et al*; (Bloomington, USA: Indiana University Press, 2001), 48–65.

[19] Despite the fascinating discussion around these issues it is beyond our scope here to delve too deeply.

these two extremes suggesting that the psalm can have been used as "an exilic lament over the fall of the Judean monarchy..." However, he then continues to note that the psalm "was employed in the regular repeated, national ritual in the pre-exilic period."[20] Ward's observation recognizes the existence of historical *settings* and, in doing so, also acknowledges the over-simplification of limiting the psalm's usage to one setting or another. What he fails to include in his analysis is the obvious incorporation of the psalm into the final form of the Psalter which subsequently became the Hymnbook of the Second Temple. This inclusion established its continuing usage in a post-exilic world. An awareness of this reminds us that usage of psalms emerged from and yet transcended a specific historical instance. In this way they could be viewed as significant at different points in history for different reasons - the idea of polycentrism identified earlier.[21]

The literary issues that Psalm 89 presents are significant, particularly the dramatic shift from the hymnic/oracle sections to what most identify as a royal lament from verse 38 onwards.[22] In examining the broad literary structure of Psalm 89, Gerstenberger notices this dramatic shift. He then briefly ponders its liturgical function and implications saying "we *have to imagine* how the fundamental break in perspective could be accommodated in one and the same psalm and worship service".[23] His observation is both noteworthy and thought-provoking. With the psalm in its current form we *do* have to imagine how these sentiments can in fact co-exist in both literary and liturgical contexts. This in turn causes us to consider what existential effects such a co-existence between hymn/oracle and lament might precipitate for those experiencing the literature as liturgy.

Of course the juxtaposition of hymn/oracle and lament is just one of the myriad literary issues confronting the reader in Psalm 89. There is no doubt that the issue of the unity of the psalm is

---

[20] James Ward, "Literary Form and Liturgical Background of Psalm 89," *Vetus Testamentum* 11/3 (1961), 327. Ward also discussed the concept of psalms like this being used as a regular 'ritual humiliation' although there is no evidence of such activity in the Hebrew Bible itself.

[21] cf. n.6.

[22] This kind of disparity is not without precedent in the Psalter. For example, Psalm 22 begins with a dramatic individual lament only to move abruptly into an ecstatic hymn of praise in the second half.

[23] Erhard Gerstenberger, *Psalms. Part 2, and Lamentations* (Grand Rapids, Michigan: Eerdmans, 2001), 153 (emphasis mine).

contentious.[24] However, Kraus, while arguing that some of the psalm was northern in origin, affirms that "the whole has been welded together in a way that passes understanding..."[25] Whatever the psalm's redactional history, it is important to deal with the text that now exists and ask "Is Psalm 89 simply 'welded together'?" In answer to this, and by considering linguistic connections interspersed throughout the whole psalm, Ward concludes:

> Here we have no accidental juxtaposition of disparate poems but an intelligible unity. The psalm as it stands presents a dramatic movement of ideas, poetically integrated, that proceeds to the logical climax in the poignant plea of the last six lines.[26]

Rather than a 'welding together' which suggests a limited horizon formed by joining disconnected ideas into an ambiguous piece of poetry, Ward views Psalm 89 as a coherent whole, albeit one containing internal paradoxes. The historical and theological scope of Psalm 89, as a piece of literature, is expansive.

When observations about historical setting, liturgical usage and literary structure are considered collectively they suggest that there is something mysterious and yet monumental about Psalm 89. With its placement at the close of Book III of the Psalter and its inclusion in Israel's liturgy despite its seemingly disparate literary units, this psalm reveals an exquisitely crafted piece with a purpose. It is a psalm that recognizes despair, with hopes having been dashed in the crucible of history. But it also embraces glimpses of a nascent imagination of the future for YHWH's covenant people, all emanating from this same reflective liturgical space. This liminal space is where meaning-making can occur. So with these considerations in mind we will now examine the four qualities of Psalm 89, introduced earlier, in some detail to see how they shape this liminal space.

---

[24] M.D. Goulder, *The Psalms of the Sons of Korah* (Sheffield: JSOT Press, 1982), 212. See here for further discussion of associated issues.

[25] Hans-Joachim Kraus, *Psalms 60–150* (Minneapolis: Augsburg, 1989), 202.

[26] James Ward, "Literary Form and Liturgical Background of Psalm 89," *Vetus Testamentum* 11/3 (1961) 323. In this article Ward presents compelling evidence for a linguistic unity to the disparate sections of the psalm. Clifford affirms the earlier work done by Ward saying "vocabulary links throughout the whole poem, and poetic structure all argue that the psalm was a single poem..." (Richard J. Clifford, "Psalm 89: A Lament over the Davidic Ruler's Continued Failure," *Harvard Theological Review* 73/1–2 (1980) 35–36.

The Mythic

Psalm 89 possesses a mythic quality. This term can be employed to describe narratives where life is viewed as being good and where ambiguities and tensions are successfully reconciled and even resolved; the proverbial 'happy ending'.[27] Evidence of this kind of poetic narrative is prevalent in the first section of Psalm 89 from verses 1–37. Familiar themes such as divine faithfulness, love and covenant are all present. Goulder recognizes the mythic qualities here in relation to the broader canonical context of the psalm and its possible significance. He notes:

> The psalm opens on a high note of confidence and gratitude. The hideous doubts of Yahweh's wonders and faithfulness and covenant-mercy being lost in death are gone with the darkness of yesterday.[28]

The gloominess of the 'darkness of yesterday', alluding to the preceding psalm, provides an antiphonal backdrop to Psalm 89 and is important to bear in mind. Given this backdrop, the beginning of Psalm 89 could perhaps be viewed as a dramatic counter-response to the disruption of Psalm 88. The juxtaposition of Psalms 88 and 89 appears to be representative of the cognitive and emotional dissonance for covenant people standing at the edge of a precipice. It is here that their identity has been challenged and their resolve is being tested by exile.

However, before pursuing these ideas of challenge and testing it is important to consider the finer features of the mythic quality evident in Psalm 89. Verses 1–14 possess two images which converge to reinforce a mythic view of reality: covenant and creation, together forming an amalgam which encourages hope. It is clear, even at a superficial level, that both the language and imagery used here recalls the Davidic covenant, and even possibly beyond this with allusions to the Mosaic covenant. McCann has noted the repeated use of the covenantal terms *ḥesed* and *'ĕmûnâ*,[29] both of which could be described as mythic in what they envisage as the expected divine response to a people in covenant with YHWH.[30] As

---

[27] I have addressed the concept of mythic narrative in relation to psalms extensively in David J. Cohen, *Why O Lord?* (Carlisle, United Kingdom: Paternoster Press: 2013).

[28] M.D. Goulder, *The Psalms of the Sons of Korah* (Sheffield: JSOT Press, 1982), 220.

[29] Neither of these terms are easy to translate but can be understood as 'steadfast love' and 'faithfulness' respectively (cf. NRSV).

[30] J. Clinton McCann, "The Book of Psalms," in *The New Interpreter's Bible Vol IV* (ed. Leander E. Keck et al; Nashville: Abingdon Press, 1996), 1034.

well as this, and reinforcing hope in steadfast love and faithfulness, verse 3 makes explicit mention of *bĕrît* (covenant) and clearly connects the term to the revered Davidic covenant as its antecedent. The use of *bᵉrît* is noteworthy as it forms a catchall term for the mythic view expressed in the opening to Psalm 89. Use of this term also connects the poetic narrative here to the broader Hebrew Bible narrative which establishes the people's identity based on an inextricable relationship with YHWH through a covenant.

The creation imagery and language, found in verses 5–14, forms a dyad with covenant. The linguistic connection between covenant and creation is the covenantal term *'ĕmûnâ* (faithfulness). In other words, the faithfulness of YHWH is what undergirds a confidence in divine protection and deliverance for Israel. Coupled with this is the repeated imagery of divine power voiced here as YHWH's consummate power over all creation, both animate and inanimate.[31] In other words, if YHWH is faithful to creation, then YHWH will be faithful to Israel. The dyad of covenant and creation present here is mythic in that it stresses two favourable theological and existential hopes for Israel which together augur well for their continuing preservation. Whether this psalm is viewed as foreshadowing an imminent exilic experience, reflecting on it as a past event, or perhaps both, creation and covenant, together, form a powerful foundation for disambiguating the people's situation.

As if to reinforce this mythic confidence in YHWH's capacity to protect and deliver, the first section of Psalm 89 then proceeds to employ military imagery in verses 15–18. This is followed by a swift transition back to the Davidic covenant in verses 19–37. The culmination of the first section of the psalm reinforces the idea of a God who is in control of the situation. Taken as a whole then, the purview of the psalmist is one which appreciates the potency of YHWH's covenant as reinforced in YHWH's creative action. The kind of potency viewed here is salvific for the people against the backdrop of exile.[32]

---

[31] This kind of language and imagery is of course found elsewhere in the Hebrew Bible. For example, Job 38, Proverbs 8, Psalm 97, *et al.*

[32] I have used the term 'salvific' here understood in terms of the Exodus narrative as a saving *from* oppression *to* a position of liberation. This contrasting of oppression/liberation is particularly relevant in light of the ideal of human kingship championed by YHWH (well summarized in Psa. 72, for example) and the reality of the monarchy, particularly as portrayed in the books of Samuel and Kings.

In regard to kingship, the return to the Davidic covenant at the close of the first section and how the *form* of kingship is described prompts Clifford to note that

> the dominion achieved by Yahweh through his creation victory (vv. 6–19) is shared point by point with the chosen David and his descendants in vv. 20–38... Thus the regent of Yahweh, at least *in potentia*, is the most powerful king on earth.[33]

This also connects with his earlier observations that

> The inclusion of the *ōlām/ /lĕdōr wādōr* (forever/for generation to generation) of v. 2 in v. 5 and the chiasm of *bnh//kwn* (build/establish) in vv. 3 and 5 formally underline the hymnic affirmation that God's choice of David is eternal, like the order established in creation.[34]

Clifford's remarks are clearly supported by the text itself and when covenant and creation are viewed together they constitute a mythic perspective on Israel's history which dominates the first part of Psalm 89.

The Parabolic

Despite the emphatic nature of the mythic perspective in the opening half of Psalm 89, expressing an assured confidence in YHWH as creator and covenant keeper, an underlying dis-ease is present resulting in an antiphony to the dyad of creation and covenant. This underlying antiphony is anticipated by Psalm 88, already highlighted, before the parabolic quality rises to the surface, particularly in the second part of Psalm 89 (vv. 38ff.). So it emerges slowly in the first part of the psalm and then, with shattering abrasiveness, confronts the assertions of the established mythic aura. However, before examining the evidence for the parabolic in more depth it will be helpful to define the term in this context. Anderson contrasts mythic and parabolic narratives observing that "Myth may give stability to our story, but parables are agents of change and sometimes disruption."[35] Parabolic narrative facilitates an articulation of the struggles all human beings have *in* life and

---

[33] Richard Clifford, "Psalm 89: a Lament over the Davidic Ruler's Continued Failure," *Harvard Theological Review* 73/1–2 (1980), 44–45. These sentiments are echoes of Psa. 2:6–9 and Psa. 110.

[34] Clifford, "Psalm 89," 41.

[35] Herbert Anderson, *Mighty Stories, Dangerous Rituals Weaving Together the Human and the Divine* (San Francisco: Jossey-Bass, 1998), 14.

with life at one point or another. Courageously, parabolic narrative is prepared to engage with the uncertainties and ambiguities. This does not necessarily suggest finding resolution but, nevertheless, asking questions which may or may not be answered yet demand to be asked. In Psalm 89 it is not only the presence of these mythic and parabolic qualities that is significant but more importantly their coexistence which forms the basis for a dialogic between the two.

The parabolic potential of Psalm 89 is clear when images of God *over* creation and God *over* covenant are viewed in sharp relief to the historical reality of Israel's exile.[36] The exilic experience itself could be characterized as a parabolic experience, disrupting the people and potentially functioning as an agent of change. So where, and in what way, is the parabolic quality of Psalm 89 evident? Perhaps surprisingly it initially appears in the first half of the psalm despite the overwhelmingly mythic emphasis of verses 1–37 already outlined. The section has a sting in its tail, so to speak.

Although ensconced in a description of the Davidic king, verses 30–32 extend covenantal responsibility beyond the monarch to explicitly include the king's progeny. The languaging of this call is expressed in Deuteronomic terminology and echoes the conditional framework of the Mosaic covenant. It also quite possibly reminds the people of the prayer for an ideal king found in Psalm 72, a king who would act in right and just ways towards the people. With these words and images a sobering picture and a stark contrast between the ideal (what YHWH wanted) and the real (what the kings were mostly like) begins to emerge.

Foreboding dark clouds have formed on the horizon for YHWH'S people creating an unresolved dilemma for this people. In fact Wallace surmises that, whatever the reasons for its demise,

> Psalm 89 reminds the reader, the Davidic monarchy is gone, and what honor can the patron reserve when YHWH seems to be a liar. How can the everlasting house of David no longer exist? Everlasting things should be everlasting.[37]

---

[36] This holds significance whether the reflections here are in anticipation of, or in light of, the experience. I am also suggesting, by using the term 'over' in connection with concepts of covenant and creation, the presence of a paradox between belief in the inherent power of their God and yet perceived divine inaction in the face of the people's exile.

[37] Robert Wallace, *The Narrative Effect of Book IV of the Hebrew Psalter* (New York: Peter Lang, 2007), 17. Also note that he is assuming here the end of the monarchy has already occurred contra others who view the psalm as pre-exilic.

Of course Psalm 89 does not end at this point. However, despite going on to re-affirm the longevity of the Davidic covenant in verses 33–37, the second half of the psalm abruptly and abrasively thrusts us fully into a parabolic disruption. Despite questions around the historical setting of the psalm, Gerstenberger makes an astute observation describing the progression of the psalm as "Leaping from hymnic to plaintive and petitionary elements… in worship, experienc[ing] a kind of cataclysm."[38] It seems that this may well be the point of the psalm being structured like it is. Initially setting the parabolic *among* the mythic provides a primer for the full force of the storm to come, beginning in verse 38.[39] The closing section of the psalm, from verse 38 onwards, sounds typically lament-like in its accusative stance towards YHWH intertwined with questions while, interestingly, also containing echoes of the covenant language used in verses 1–37. The Davidic figure is explicitly recalled with a despairing grasp for some sign of YHWH's *ḥesed* (steadfast love) and *'ĕmûnâ* (faithfulness), coupled as they were earlier in verse 2.

While much discussion may be generated in attempting to identify the literary function of the lament form here, particularly in juxtaposition with the first half of the psalm, its presence has implications beyond literary concerns. The lament, as a contrast to the hymn, helps to construct a liminal space as a forum for expressing the parabolic nature of the community's lived experience. This expression self-evidently occurs at particular junctures in history but then, as with lament psalms, becomes embedded in the liturgy as a continual reminder of the visceral nature of life. Beyond this, both the mythic and the parabolic coexist dialogically within the psalm to create a mimetic quality which also transcends the history of a particular people at a particular time.

---

[38] Erhard Gerstenberger, *Psalms. Part 2 and Lamentations* (Grand Rapids, Michigan: Eerdmans, 2001), 176.

[39] I use the term 'primer' here in the sense of it being a preparation. Although the disruption has begun, as Gerstenberger points out, the person or community utilizing the psalm are not confronted enough to be completely repelled. Rather, they are being gently alerted to the issues at stake for the people. (This kind of 'priming' is not completely dissimilar to the story Nathan tells King David in 2 Sam. 12 following the incident with Bathsheba.)

The Mimetic

Marshall McLuhan said, "We look at the present through a rear-view mirror. We march backwards into the future."[40] McLuhan's approach to our past could be considered to be anamnestic, that is, recalling or remembering the past in order to make sense of the present and, as a result, move into the future. In this sense Psalm 89 could be viewed as an anamnestic piece of literature. It certainly recalls the past and does seem to be an attempt to make sense of the people's presenting circumstances. However a psalm such as Psalm 89, while embracing the importance of remembering, also transcends being remembrance alone as it becomes a part of liturgy. Once this embedding took place the psalm gained a mimetic quality which, by definition, sees it intentionally repeated generation after generation. In this way its use becomes more than a remembrance. It also becomes, in a sense, a re-enactment which mimics their history, 'as if looking in the rear-view mirror.'[41] The dialogue between mythic and parabolic qualities forms a foundation for this mimesis.

Perhaps a clue to this mimetic quality is found initially in the title of Psalm 89. Despite uncertainty surrounding the date and purpose of including titles for certain psalms, Gerstenberger makes an interesting observation in this case noticing that

> Both Ethan and Heman (Ps. 88:1) are listed as famous wise men of the Ezrahite clan. If the final redactors who added this superscription meant to emphasize the monarchic dimensions of the 'corner-stone', they most successfully hid their intention.[42]

While Gerstenberger makes an interesting point about the 'monarchic dimensions' of Psalm 89 he fails to see something else of significance in the attribution: its identification as a *maskîl*. While not an easy term to define, in this context its use perhaps offers some clues to the mimetic quality of the psalm. A *maskîl* could be characterized as an "instructive or skilful song", a "memory passage" or even a "wisdom song performed to music".[43] All these

---

[40] Marshall McLuhan, *The Medium Is the Message* (New York: Random House, 1967), 75.

[41] An example of this can be seen in the *Pesach Seder* celebrated as a remembrance of the Exodus story. Traditionally the story is told by the father in the family using the first person *present* tense. In this way the story is mimetic; both remembered and re-enacted.

[42] Erhard Gerstenberger, *Psalms. Part 2, and Lamentations* (Grand Rapids, Michigan: Eerdmans, 2001), 147.

[43] Gerstenberger, *Psalms*, 147. The term *maskîl* derives from *śākal*, with its cognate definitions of 'insight' and 'understanding'.

suggested ways of understanding the term reinforce the idea of the psalm providing both recall (anamnesis) and re-enactment (mimesis).

The mimetic quality of Psalm 89 forms a repeated affirmation underlining the importance of holding together both mythic and parabolic views. This 'holding together', in turn, enables intentional mimetic reflection on life experience. Nasuti again reminds us of the broad historical substance of this mimesis and its function stating that this psalm sits within an

> historical sequence that includes the origins of the Davidic covenant, its passing on to Solomon (Psalm 72), and its demise at the time of the exile (Psalm 89:39–52). By taking note of the sequence, the reader is led to reflect on the larger narrative of Israel's history and the role of the Davidic covenant within that history.[44]

The 'historical sequence' self-evidently incorporates both the mythic and the parabolic. The true value of one is not found in the dismissal of the other. Rather, it is when the two qualities can coexist (through a process of mimesis) that fertile ground for meaning-making begins to be tilled. The uniqueness of this psalm is where it sits in both the historical sequence of Israel and the literary sequence of the Psalter. Both positions alert us to the edge of the precipice where the people were pondering their identity and continuity as YHWH's covenant people.

A further dimension to the mimetic action here could be described as a re-traditioning of their history by later generations as the psalm was redacted and as they continued to use Psalm 89 in liturgy. This ongoing use of the psalm eventually became a reflection on past events rather than an anticipation of imminent events or processing of current events. Through this shift the psalm embraced both remembering and re-enacting the past. As the community considered their tradition afresh they attempted to make sense of their own experience and those of past generations. All this takes place as the mythic and the parabolic are brought into dialogue with each other through a mimetic act of liturgy.

---

[44] Harry P. Nasuti, "The Interpretive Significance of Sequence and Selection in the Book of Psalms," in *The Book of Psalms* (eds. Peter W Flint, Patrick D Miller, Aaron Brunell, and Ryan Roberts; Leiden, NL: Brill, 2005), 317.

The Parenetic

Psalm 89 possesses one final and important quality which complements the others. It offers the possibility of a future which holds something greater for a community that looks back in order to look forward. The parenetic quality of Psalm 89 is perhaps not explicit but it is, nonetheless, present as the psalm is engaged with through liturgy. It presents implicit exhortation for the future as much as it presents counsel from the past. If mythic, parabolic and mimetic qualities begin to open a space for liturgical meaning-making then the parenetic quality suggests something which can be carried away from the space into the future. How has the opportunity eventuated? Gerald Wilson, in describing the movement in Book III as a whole, perhaps offers an answer to the question when he notes

> These bookends [Pss. 73 and 89] set a tone of agonized reflection and questioning because of the collapse of the Davidic monarchy and the resulting experience of exile. How could God let this happen? And when will he respond in faithful fulfilment of his covenant responsibilities to re-establish the dynasty of David?[45]

The parenetic quality of Psalm 89 emerges from the 'agonized reflection' and from questions such as those posed by Wilson. However, this reflection does not lead to resignation. Rather, it prompts the possibility of a hopeful imagination for a people doubting the very core of their identity and the integrity of their God. Tellingly, this nascent hope is articulated in the form of a question in verse 49 which ponders again the two key concepts of *ḥesed* (steadfast love) and *'ĕmûnâ* (faithfulness) encountered earlier in, and threaded through, the psalm. The question is critical as it opens up a new vista in the covenantal relationship, a way forward which can doubt YHWH yet also express trust in YHWH for the future. Psalm 89 does not present a picture of the protesting voice being silenced but, rather, one of it being given space for expression. In doing this the parenetic quality of this psalm pushes beyond protest to hope.

The climax to Psalm 89, and Book III, is remarkable in both its simplicity and its profundity. The call for YHWH to remember is

---

[45] Gerald Wilson, "The Structure of the Psalter," in *Interpreting the Psalms: Issues and Approaches* (Downer's Grove, Illinois: InterVarsity Press, 2005), 238–9. The 'bookends' referred to here are Psalm 89 and Psalm 73, which opens Book III of the Psalter. In contrast to Psalm 89, Psalm 73 contains none of the parabolic ambiguity. Rather, it presents a picture of confidence in God as one who is good to Israel and the ultimate protector of the people.

clearly covenantal in its overtones and represents a community asking their God to do the same for them as they have sought to do for themselves in recalling and re-enacting their history.[46] The psalm represents an attempt on the community's part to do what they can to reflect, seek counsel and find encouragement from their history but also to move beyond their lament for lost kingship. Now the clarion call is to YHWH to bring the community's hopes to fruition.

How does Psalm 89 achieve this? Rather than abandoning Davidic kingship as a failed ideal it presses the community to imagine it as something more than that which they had previously envisaged or experienced. Mays sheds light on what an expanded notion of kingship might look like, noting

> The point of this carefully drawn parallel between kingship and God and that of David claims that the latter is integral to the former. The Messiah's rule actualizes in the world what is reality in the heavens and cosmos.[47]

If Mays is correct then the picture painted here is something which transcends not only the exilic experience but also the people themselves. This speaks to YHWH's cosmic purposes and, in regard to kingship, takes the people themselves full circle back to the institution of the office.[48] It forms a dual reminder that even though YHWH's kingship was rejected by the people of Samuel's time there remains a close covenantal relationship between YHWH and the anointed king. The closeness between YHWH and the king is pictured in familial terms here in Psalm 89.[49] These two reminders raise an important question which forms the foundation of any hopeful imagination for the future. The dissonance between the demise of human kingship, self-evident in Israel's history, and the promised permanency of the Davidic covenant alongside the fundamental concept of YHWH as king stretches the horizons of possibility for a lamenting people. It prompts a question of what

---

[46] It is also a reminder that the call to remember is based on YHWH's action in the past (e.g. Exod. 3:7ff).

[47] James Mays, *The Lord Reigns* (Louisville: Westminster John Knox Press, 1994), 105.

[48] Cf. 1 Sam. 8.

[49] Cf. vv. 26–27; Psa. 2:7. Broyles notes that the descriptor 'firstborn' is used here of the Davidic king, implying one who transcends the typical limits of human kingship in both power and longevity. Cf. Craig Broyles, *Psalms* (Baker Books: Grand Rapids, Michigan), 357.

kingship might look like for the people now and for future generations.

In perhaps an unexpected twist, Psalm 89 closes with a brief, yet triumphant, doxology. Of course a doxology in itself is not unusual in the Psalter, with similar endings present at the close of Books I, III and IV plus similar echoes at the end of Psalm 150.[50] However, in this case, at the close of Book III, it uniquely draws together the ambivalence and ambiguity of Psalm 89 with a re-affirmation of hope in YHWH. Although the doxology's presence is described by Broyles as not being a 'constituent part' of the psalm, it nonetheless contributes to the rhetorical force of the final literary form.[51] Perhaps the doxology holds an implicit question which asks, 'Where to now?' Psalm 89 thrusts both the Psalter and those who prayed and sang it into a brave new world. Here, irrespective of the existence of a human king, it seems more than coincidental that the following book of the Psalter (Book IV) begins with a purported psalm of Moses. This psalm strongly affirms trust in YHWH and is followed by "psalms after Psalm 90 [which] express proper sentiments of trust in, and praise of, God as the one true king."[52]

Reflections

In a profound way Psalm 89 brings the four qualities described above together in a dialogical process. However, this process was not encountered by chance. It was precipitated by the demise of kingship as Israel had known it and resulted in the Exile. This brought them to a precipice which challenged both their identity and survival. Perhaps, in the previously used words of Robert Remini, Israel came "close to being irreparably smashed" as a people.[53] However, they were not smashed and their covenant relationship with YHWH did not cease to exist. Psalm 89 is, in part, a testimony to this fact. Rather than ignoring the reality of their 'precipice' and potential demise, the questions they had about themselves, God and the relationship between the two were given voice through a psalm which was subsequently embedded in liturgy.

---

[50] Cf. Psa. 41:13; 72:19 and 106:48.

[51] Craig Broyles, *Psalms* (Baker Books: Grand Rapids, Michigan, 2012), 357.

[52] Harry P. Nasuti "The Interpretive Significance of Sequence and Selection in the Book of Psalms," in *The Book of Psalms* (eds. Peter W Flint, Patrick D Miller, Aaron Brunell, and Ryan Roberts; Leiden, NL: Brill, 2005), 318.

[53] Robert Remini, *At the Edge of the Precipice*, (New York: Basic Books, 2010), xi.

Being a poetic song used in liturgy, containing mythic, parabolic, mimetic and parenetic qualities, Psalm 89 should be viewed as far more than a literary masterpiece, lest its inherent power is ignored or lost. The psalm, as a liturgical act, offered an invitation and a pathway for the community to enter into the dialogue. This dialogue, in turn, created a liminal space providing the impetus for making sense out of a world-changing situation in an intentional and enduring way.

The fact that the psalm was embedded in liturgy and included in the final form of the Psalter suggests, of course, that the invitation is open-ended in that it is extended to those beyond the initial audiences. This psalm, as with all psalms, invites us as it speaks beyond its immediate historical context holding a rhetorical force which cannot be understated. Implicit in the text is an encouragement for all to enter a dialogical process in light of their own unique situation of struggle to make sense out of their circumstances. In this way the psalm continues to speak beyond its time in both its content and the model of engagement. It offers people of faith today a model of prayer which opens up the world, providing a vehicle to speak with "shattering evocative speech that breaks through fixed conclusions and presses us always toward new, dangerous and imaginative possibilities"[54] at the edge of the precipice.

---

[54] Brueggemann, *Finally Comes the Poet* (Minneapolis: Fortress Press, 1989), 6.

Psalm 148, Pinnacle of the Psalms

Andrew Brown

Melbourne School of Theology

At auction in the United States on Tuesday, 26th November, 2013, one of eleven surviving copies of the first book ever printed in the American colonies was sold for US$14.165 million. According to Sotheby's, this was "a new world record for any printed book at auction," surpassing the previous record of US$11.5 million.[1] The book concerned is commonly called the Bay Psalm Book, produced by the young Puritan colony of Cambridge, Massachusetts. Its first edition appeared in 1640 in a print run of 1,700 copies. In keeping with other Protestant psalters from the period, this fresh translation from the Hebrew sought to produce a consistent metre for each psalm that would permit its singing in unison.[2]

It is striking that the highest priority for these Puritan settlers' nascent publishing efforts was an independent translation of Psalms from the Hebrew, rather than any other biblical book or classical writing, Christian or secular. Yet such a priority has precedents in Christian tradition. The Psalms played a central role in the Christian monastic tradition, such that the ideal exemplified in the Benedictine Rule was to recite the entire Psalter weekly.[3] The basic component of such systems of spiritual disciplines from late patristic times was the 'Daily Office', a routine of prayer and psalmody running from Vigils in the wee hours of the morning to Compline prior to retiring at night. The office for daybreak in the Benedictine Rule was Lauds, a cycle of psalms that began with the penitential Psalm 51 and ended with Psalms 148–150. The name Lauds itself stems from the rendering of the Hebrew lemma *hālal*, the basis of

---

[1] "Rare Psalm Book Sells for Over $15 Million," http://www.sbs.com.au/news/article/2013/11/27/rare-psalm-book-sells-over-15-million. The title refers to the equivalent in Australian dollars.

[2] S. E. Gillingham, *Psalms through the Centuries* (Oxford: Blackwell, 2007), 158–159; W. L. Holladay, *The Psalms through Three Thousand Years* (Minneapolis: Fortress, 1993), 202–203. See the following reprint of the original: *A Literal Reprint of the Bay Psalm Book, being the Earliest New England Version of the Psalms and the First Book Printed in America* (Cambridge, MA: Charles B. Richardson, 1862 [1640]). http://books.google.com.au/books?id=YDRGAAAAYAAJ

[3] Holladay, *Psalms*, 176–177; S. Terrien, *The Psalms* (Eerdmans Critical Commentary; Grand Rapids: Eerdmans, 2003).

the repeated 'hallelujahs', by the Latin root *laudō*.[4] Lauds still finished with Psalm 148 in the Roman Breviary of 1568, established by the Council of Trent.[5] The same psalm or trio of psalms (148–150) features prominently in other liturgical traditions, Christian and Jewish, from the daily *Amidah* prayer detailed in the Jewish Mishnah to the practice of Lauds in the Ethiopic church.[6]

So the primary agenda for the birth of the new day, after repentance, was praise, and the purest praise to be found in Scripture appeared in Psalms 148–150, and in Psalm 148 in particular. This ample re-use in spiritual service is reflective of the impressive literary and theological qualities of Psalm 148 itself.

The Contexts of Psalm 148

Historical Setting

Many psalms sit very light to any specific historical setting and this in fact may have allowed them to more readily adapt to the spiritual needs of every age.[7] This is definitely the case in regard to Psalm 148, as far as any deliberate reference goes. The single possible exception here is the fact that the 'horn' that Yahweh raises up in verse 14 has sometimes been understood as a reference to a specific deliverer or a specific event of deliverance. But even where so understood, investigations along historical lines have not established any firm historical setting for the psalm on this basis.[8]

It is nevertheless true to say that there is a scholarly consensus concerning the psalm's time of origin. "Overwhelmingly, psalms scholarship is agreed on a postexilic date for Ps 148" and for Psalms 146–150 generally.[9] This is argued at times on the basis of

---

[4] Gillingham, *Psalms through the Centuries*, 52–53; Holladay, *Psalms*, 176.

[5] Holladay, *Psalms*, 222–223. The second-last item in Lauds in the same breviary, immediately before Psalm 148, is The Song of the Three Young Men (or *Benedicite,* not to be confused with the *Benedictus*), which comes from the apocryphal addition to Daniel 3 and may show influences from Psalms 136 and 148.

[6] Gillingham, *Psalms through the Centuries*, 43–45, 50.

[7] Gerald H. Wilson, "The Shape of the Book of Psalms," *Interpretation* 46/2 (1992), 138; J. Goldingay, *Psalms volume 1. Psalms 1–41* (Baker Commentary on the Old Testament Wisdom and Psalms; Grand Rapids: Baker Academic, 2006), 30–31.

[8] Andrew J. Schmutzer and Randall X. Gauthier, "The identity of 'horn' in Psalm 148:14a: an exegetical investigation in the MT and LXX versions," *Bulletin for Biblical Research* 19/2 (2009), 162–163, 182–183; H.-J. Kraus, *Psalms 60–150* (trans. H. C. Oswald; Minneapolis, 1989 [*Psalmen, 2 T., Psalmen 60–150* (5th ed., Neukirchener, 1978).]), 564.

[9] Schmutzer and Gauthier, "Identity," 162. See the references offered there.

language,[10] but I believe this consensus arises more from two dovetailing sets of evidence. The first is the general sense of (sporadic) historical movement within the Book of Psalms, for instance the feeling that one has moved from the Davidic dynasty around Psalm 72 to its collapse in Psalm 89 and on towards restoration from exile around Psalm 107. This is highly visible at 'seams' such as Ps 106:47–107:3.

While such a sense of movement through Judah's history from pre-exilic to post-exilic times might be primarily an editorial achievement, this impression from internal evidence is reinforced by the second set of evidence that comes from external sources. In particular, the important Dead Sea Psalms scroll, 11QPs^a, is mostly composed of psalms found in Psalms 101–150 in our canon (plus Psalm 93), but also includes psalms from outside the Psalter and arranges those common to the Psalter in a radically different order to the familiar canonical one.[11] Other Qumran Psalms manuscript fragments, however, particularly those paralleling earlier parts of our Psalter, tend to support the biblical order.[12] This Qumran evidence, and 11QPs^a in particular, have given rise to "a new view of the stabilization process of the Psalter, in which stabilization occurred gradually from beginning to end with Pss 1–100 assuming relative fixity at a time when Pss 101–150 were still susceptible to rearrangement and supplementation."[13]

Taken in combination, these lines of rather circumstantial evidence account for the quite dominant tendency to view Psalm 148 as appearing relatively late in the development of the book of Psalms, specifically in the post-exilic setting. A post-exilic setting might in fact mesh well with the sense of the Hebrew text of Ps 148:14 that Yahweh has (recently) acted to exalt the strength and dignity of his people, with two provisos: (1) that the post-exilic existence of the returned Jewish community does not always appear particularly exalted in biblical testimony about the post-exilic period, namely Haggai, Zechariah, Ezra and Nehemiah, and (2) we still have little

---

[10] Delbert R. Hillers, "Study of Psalm 148," *Catholic Biblical Quarterly* 40/3 (1978), 328.

[11] An example listing with some explanation is found in Gerald Wilson, *The Editing of the Hebrew Psalter* (SBL Dissertation Series 76; Chico, CA: Scholars Press, 1985), 124–127. Note the one very distinct overlap between the sequence of psalms in this scroll and in the canonical Psalms: Psalms 121–132, the bulk of the 'Songs of Ascent', appear in the same order, suggesting that these songs (or most of them) may have already existed as a stable sub-collection in the given order.

[12] Wilson, *Editing*, 96–121.

[13] Wilson, *Editing*, 73, and see 70–73.

direct evidence for the historical setting of Psalm 148 and should hold any posited setting very lightly.

Genre, Social Setting and Literary Antecedents

More common than attention to any specific historical setting has been the practice, based in form critical traditions, of identifying the genre of Psalm 148 and positing its cultural background. Psalm 148 is commonly labelled a 'hymn', a label whose appropriateness seems self-evident, and more specifically an 'imperative hymn', wherein praising subjects are impelled to praise the LORD.[14]

Mid-twentieth century biblical scholar Gerhard von Rad made an influential suggestion about the background to the literary form of Psalm 148. He drew parallels with certain Egyptian *onomastica*, lists of names of things that exist in the (Egyptian) world whose existence can be attributed (so the writers think) to Egyptian gods. The content of the *Onomasticon of Amenope* that relates to Psalm 148 is mostly oriented towards cosmic and physical phenomena, and the relevant content of the *Ramesseum Onomasticon* more toward classes of living creatures. However, both lists are long and, compared to Psalm 148, rather incoherent, showing little logical connection between categories, and sharing with the psalm only a general sympathy for list-making.[15] Some scholars feel that hymns composed in honour of gods (especially the sun) in ancient Egypt, Mesopotamia and Canaan offer better parallels, and the resemblances here are real.[16] Others feel that study of hymnic traditions within the Old Testament (OT) itself offers more benefits to the researcher.[17]

---

[14] Lothar Ruppert, "Aufforderung an die Schöpfung zum Lob Gottes : Zur Literar-, Form-, und Traditionskritik von Ps 148," in *Freude an der Weisung des Herrn* (Stuttgart: Verlag Katholisches Bibelwerk, 1986), 275; E. S. Gerstenberger, *Psalms, Part 1, with an Introduction to Cultic Poetry* (FOTL; Grand Rapids, 1988), 17; E. S. Gerstenberger, *Psalms, Part 2, and Lamentations* (FOTL; Grand Rapids: Eerdmans, 2001), 451; Kraus, *Psalms 60–150*, 561. Gerstenberger is reluctant to divide the hymn categories too finely.

[15] On the *onomastica*, see G. von Rad, "Hiob 38 und die altägyptische Weisheit," in *Gesammelte Studien zum Alten Testament* (ed. G. Von Rad; München: Chr. Kaiser Verlag, 1958), 262–266; Hillers, "Study of Psalm 148," 329–330; Ruppert, "Aufforderung," 288; Kraus, *Psalms 60–150*, 561–562; L. C. Allen, *Psalms 101–150* (rev. ed., Word Biblical Commentary; Nashville: Nelson, 2002), 392; Patrick D. Miller, Jr., *Interpreting the Psalms* (Philadelphia: Fortress, 1986), 73 n. 17.

[16] Hillers, "Study of Psalm 148," 332–334; Ruppert, "Aufforderung," 286–292. The advocacy of Canaanite precedents seems particularly attributable to F. Crüsemann: Ruppert, "Aufforderung," 289–292.

[17] Hillers, "Study of Psalm 148," 331. See the discussion to follow.

It is popular for form-critical treatments to follow such genre analysis of Psalm 148 by commenting on its 'cultic setting'.[18] The social context for the use of such a hymn, Gunkel says, is the worship of the holy place, and he imagines a psalm like this one sung by a choir.[19] More detailed suggestions involve the calls to praise being issued by worship leaders and the 'rationale' parts constituting a response by worshippers[20], but the lack of firm evidence undergirds the compulsory vagueness of Allen's comment: "A cultic setting is generally ascribed to the hymn, without further specification of usage being possible."[21] To say that Psalm 148 was utilized in worship is both important and a case of stating the inevitable. Yet this psalm, unlike, say, Psalm 118, does not hint at the manner of its own use in worship. The quest to analyse social backgrounds so favoured by form criticism finds little to work with in this instance.

More helpful is an observation often made by form-critics about the internal make-up of the psalm, in that two common constituents of this genre appear in unusual proportion here. The call or summons to praise is the first of these vital components, while the other is the rationale for praise based in the LORD's character, grandeur or actions.[22] The psalms consists of a double cycle of call to praise (1b–5a)/rationale (5b–6)/call to praise (7–13a)/rationale (13b–14), wherein the twin calls to praise are expanded into lists of either spheres or (mostly) the occupants within those spheres that must offer praise.[23]

Inner-Biblical Associations

This detailed recruitment of all parts of creation, animate and inanimate, to praise the LORD is something that marks out Psalm

---

[18] Dominic Coad, "Creation's Praise of God: An Ecological Theology of Non-Human and Human Being" (University of Exeter, Unpublished Ph.D. diss., 2010), 87–88.

[19] H. Gunkel, *Einleitung in die Psalmen* (4th ed.; Göttingen: Vandenhoeck und Ruprecht, 1985 [1933]), 59, 66.

[20] Gerstenberger, *Psalms, Part 2*, 451–452.

[21] Allen, *Psalms 101–150*, 393.

[22] The first pair of terms is Gerstenberger's: Gerstenberger, *Psalms, Part 1*, 17–18; Gerstenberger, *Psalms, Part 2*, 449–451. See also C. Westermann, *Praise and Lament in the Psalms* (Edinburgh: T & T Clark, 1981), 130–132. The second term is my own. Allen uses 'grounds for praise', Allen, *Psalms 101–150*, 390.

[23] E.g., among many examples, Hillers, "Study of Psalm 148," 327–328. In the definitive early form-critical treatment, Gunkel regarded this as an expansion of what was originally an introductory element: Gunkel, *Einleitung*, 36–37, 42.

148 as distinctive in the OT [24], though there are antecedents both within Psalms and elsewhere in the OT where natural arenas such as heavens, earth and seas, and occasionally their occupants, are called upon to praise the LORD. [25] Book 4 of the Psalms seems to carry an emphasis on universal praise; besides the references just cited, Ps 103:20–22 anticipates 148:1–4 by bidding the 'heavenly hosts' to praise, and while Psalm 104 does not have the same hortatory function, it still celebrates Yahweh's maintenance of the created order in great detail.[26]

Thus far we have encountered no clear literary dependence of Psalm 148 on another text, but there is one other biblical text sometimes suggested as a direct antecedent or model for this psalm: the account of the seven days of creation in Gen 1:1–2:4.[27] Some commentators come out strongly in favour of influence of the latter on the former, or at least the strong resemblances between the two[28], while others are more hesitant.[29] There is a suite of terminology common to the two passages, including 'heavens and earth', especially where artfully reversed at the conclusion of each passage (Gen 2:4b; Ps 148:13)[30]; the use of the passive (niphal) form of *bārā'* meaning 'to be created' (Gen 2:4a; Ps 148:5), and multiple terms from vv. 7–10 of the psalm.[31]

Yet there are differences as well, such as the explicit naming of sun and moon in Ps 148:3 in contrast to the careful avoidance of their names in Gen 1:14–18, or the atmospheric phenomena appearing in Ps 148:8 which find no real parallel in Genesis 1. More broadly, the order of the two series is not the same, contra the brief comments of Rogerson and McKay. It is not possible to clearly align our text's

---

[24] Ruppert, "Aufforderung," 282.

[25] E.g. Ps 96:1, 11–12; 97:1; 98:1, 7–9; 100:1; Isa 44:23; 49:13.

[26] See Ruppert, "Aufforderung," 283, 293–294; Hillers, "Study of Psalm 148," 331.

[27] See subsequent note on the place of Gen 2:4.

[28] Ruppert, "Aufforderung," 293; F. L. Hossfeld and E. Zenger, *Psalms 3: A Commentary on Psalms 101–150* (Hermeneia; Minneapolis: Fortress, 2011), 639 (note that Zenger is the author of the commentary on Psalm 148); James L. Mays, *Psalms* (Louisville: John Knox, 1994), 445; A. Weiser, *The Psalms* (OTL; London: SCM Press, 1962), 838.

[29] Hillers, "Study of Psalm 148," 328. Despite Hillers' citation of von Rad as advocating direct dependence, i.e. taking the opposite stance to his own, with the exception of citing a direct link at Ps 148:4, Gunkel seems to err on the side of caution also: Gunkel, *Einleitung*, 92.

[30] I would suggest that Gen 2:4 is not just a conclusion to Gen 1:1–2:3, since it contains the *tôlĕdôt* formula that I am convinced functions as a heading in Genesis. Gen 2:4 has a 'seam' function that performs a 'janus' role in Genesis 1–3, referring both backwards and forwards in its context.

[31] Ruppert, "Aufforderung," 293. See the verse-by-verse commentary.

units in order with the contents of the creation week.³² We could certainly speak of the two texts' consistency of world-view, for example the apparently non-mythological portrayal of the ocean depths (*tĕhōmôt*) and large sea animals (*tannînîm*) in v. 7,³³ creation by command (v. 5), and the listing of humanity last among created things. Beyond that, it is possible that the seven-stanza structure represents a deliberate nod on the psalmist's part toward the Genesis creation account. Combined with the frequency of common terminology, this lends considerable weight to the argument for a conscious relationship between the texts.³⁴

The Placement of Psalm 148 in the Book of Psalms

The dominant new trend in Psalms scholarship in the last fifty years or so has been the perception of an intentional purpose behind the existing canonical shape of the Book of Psalms. This has constituted in part a reaction against the general form-critical tendency to regard the present arrangement of the Book of Psalms as merely a symptom of historical process, so that there are sub-groupings that bear witness to occasional collating efforts but little in the way of meaningful final shape or thematic flow.³⁵ The quest to understand the scattered genres found in Psalms operated as an alternative way to unveil a kind of order within the book based on various literary classes of psalms and their social uses. This approach has indeed borne fruit; it is helpful, after all, to recognise that Psalm 148 is a communal hymn that impels all 'beings' to participate in praise, and to compare this with analogous hymns within Psalms, e.g. Psalm 95:1–7b.³⁶

But the newer trend, probably sparked in part by the advocacy of canonical understanding by Brevard Childs in his 1979 *Introduction to the Old Testament as Scripture*,³⁷ has been to seek meaning and, furthermore, editorial intention in the canonical shape of the whole

---

[32] J. W. Rogerson and J. W. McKay, *Psalms 101–150* (The Cambridge Bible Commentary on the New English Bible; Cambridge: Cambridge University Press, 1977), 184–185.

[33] The degree of mythology remaining in the presentation of these and other entities in the psalm is disputed. See the commentary on vv. 7–8, below.

[34] Ruppert, "Aufforderung," 180.

[35] Gunkel, *Einleitung*, 435, 453–454; Wilson, *Editing*, 1–5.

[36] Westermann, *Praise and Lament in the Psalms*, 131.

[37] For Childs' rather tentative movements from a form-critical background towards consideration of the canonical shape and editorial intention of Psalms, see Brevard Childs, *Introduction to the Old Testament as Scripture* (Philadelphia: Fortress Press, 1979), 511–517, 520–523.

book, though not always to the exclusion of historical factors. Childs' student Gerald Wilson offered in his 1985 monograph *The Editing of the Hebrew Psalter* the seminal modern work advocating meaningful structure and sequence in the Book of Psalms.[38] Many publications taking a sympathetic stance have appeared since, indicating that the landscape of Psalms scholarship has changed for good since that time.[39]

The approach has with good reason paid careful attention to the role of Psalm 1 as an introduction to the Psalter; Psalm 2 as either part of a joint introduction with Psalm 1 or else (as I think) an introduction to Books 1 and 2 of the Psalter; psalms at the 'seams' where the five Books meet, especially 72–73 and 89–90; intentional shaping within each Book; the psalm titles as clues to editorial perception and intention, and so forth.[40] Avoiding for present purposes the question of the degree of legitimacy of this perspective in general terms, it is relevant to ask about the implications of such a holistic stance for the final chapters of the Book of Psalms, the chapters surrounding Psalm 148.

In Wilson's own model, Psalms 146–150 constitute a kind of hallelujah chorus that concludes, not Book 5, but the entire Psalter. But his focus is on what he regards as the twin frames of the major part of the book, Psalms 2 and 144 and then Psalms 1 and 145. Wilson rightly draws attention to the way the kingly implications of the final set of psalms with Davidic titles, 138–145, are met very soon in the concluding hallel psalms with the exhortation, "Do not put your trust in princes/In mortal men, who cannot save," (146:3), and, "The LORD reigns forever," so that Yahweh's kingship is

---

[38] For Wilson's conclusions at that stage of his research, see Wilson, *Editing*, 209–228. A brief, updated analysis with helpful diagrams is Gerald H. Wilson, "Shaping the Psalter: A Consideration of Editorial Linkage in the Book of Psalms," in *The Shape and Shaping of the Hebrew Psalter* (ed. J. Clinton McCann; JSOTSup 159; Sheffield: Sheffield Academic, 1993). For biographical background on Wilson, see http://www.thesacredpage.com/2006/03/gerald-wilsons-contribution.html.

[39] Examples are numerous, but typical of sympathetic treatments is J. C. McCann (ed.), *The Shape and Shaping of the Hebrew Psalter*, (JSOTSup 159; Sheffield: Sheffield Academic, 1993). An example of scepticism towards perceptions of intentional unity is Norman Whybray, *Reading the Psalms as a Book* (JSOTSup 222; Sheffield: Sheffield Academic, 1996).

[40] The literature is considerable, but a snapshot may be found in David M. Howard, Jr., "The Psalms and Current Study," in *Interpreting the Psalms: Issues and Approaches* (ed. D. Firth and P. S. Johnston; Downers Grove: IVP Academic, 2005), 24–29. See in the same volume, Gerald H. Wilson, "The Structure of the Psalter," in *Interpreting the Psalms: Issues and Approaches* (ed. D. Firth and P. S. Johnston; Downers Grove: IVP Academic, 2005), 229–240.

emphasized over that of any hoped-for Davidic king.⁴¹ He also sees the praise of Psalms 146–150 as an answer to the agenda set by the final verse of Psalm 145 as the psalmist challenges both himself and "every creature" to praise Yahweh.⁴² But his schema seems in practice to leave these psalms rather neglected, their climactic significance acknowledged but left aside from the main investigation.⁴³ One unanswered question is whether the positioning of Psalm 148 in its context is significant for its meaning.

There are literary features that help to unify Psalms 146–150. The most obvious is the *hallû-yāh* frame around each of these psalms, a feature only found otherwise in Psalms 113 and 135.⁴⁴ The general impression as one reads through the Psalter, finding single uses of *hallû-yāh* in Psalms 104–106, at the end of Book 4, then further uses in Psalms 111–117 and 135–136, and then, following the final Davidic group, in 146–150, is of a gathering chorus of praise. The intense use of *hallû-yāh* in Psalms 148 and 150 creates a sense of climax for this gathering chorus. As Wilson observed, it is possible to see the final line of Psalm 145 as announcing a praise agenda for the hallel psalms: "Let every creature praise his holy name for ever and ever,"⁴⁵ while its first line and second-last line both declare the 'praise' of Yahweh using the corresponding noun, *těhillâ*.

Then there are specific resonances between neighbouring psalms within these five. We should firstly note that Psalms 145 and 146 are linked by alignments of language concerning the lifting-up of the downcast (145:14; 146:8), provision of food (145:15–16; 146:7), protection of the vulnerable (*šômēr*, 145:20a; 146:9a) and judgment of the wicked (145:20b; 146:9b), all functions expected of a righteous king, and embedded in twin psalms emphasizing the kingship of Yahweh.⁴⁶ So we should not posit any radical break

---

⁴¹ Wilson, *Editing*, 226–227; David M. Howard, "Editorial Activity in the Hebrew Psalter: A State-of-the-Field Survey," in *The Shape and Shaping of the Hebrew Psalter* (ed. J. Clinton McCann; JSOTSup 159; Sheffield: Sheffield Academic, 1993), 63. Scripture quotations, where not my own translations, are taken from NIV®, copyright © 1973, 1978, 1984, 2011 by Biblica, Inc.™ Used by permission. All rights reserved worldwide.

⁴² Wilson, *Editing*, 193.

⁴³ Note the way Psalms 146–150 do not appear in Wilson's diagram of Book 5, and hardly in the associated discussion, in Wilson, "Shaping the Psalter," 80–82.

⁴⁴ Psalms 104–106, 115–117 only have *hallû-yāh* at the end, and Psalms 111–112 only at the beginning.

⁴⁵ Gordon Wenham, *The Psalter Reclaimed: Praying and Praising with the Psalms* (Wheaton: Crossway, 2013), 71.

⁴⁶ Nancy L. deClaissé-Walford, *Reading from the Beginning: The Shaping of the Hebrew Psalter* (Macon, GA: Mercer University Press, 1997), 100.

between Psalms 146–150 and what precedes. Then Psalm 147 picks up the Zion reference in 146:10 and speaks in 147:2 of the restoration of Jerusalem and the regathering of the exiles, making the post-exilic historical setting of this psalm series virtually indisputable. In keeping with Psalms 145–146, we read that "The LORD sustains the humble, but casts the wicked to the ground" (147:6).[47] While carrying a clear creation theme over from Psalm 146 in connection with the stars in v. 4, and turning to cold phenomena in vv. 15–18 in preparation for 148:8[48], Psalm 147 maintains its particular focus on Israel at regular intervals throughout (vv. 12–14, 19–20).

At the other end of Psalm 148, whose tone is mostly universal, the sudden turn back to focus on Israel in 148:14, with the use of the notable expression *ḥăsîdîm*, 'saints', prepares the way for the strong particularity of Psalm 149[49], which immediately refers to the *ḥăsîdîm* again in v. 1 and retains this focus on Israel's righteous to the identical final word, *ḥăsîdîm*, before the exiting *hallû-yāh* frame. Pss 148:14 and 149:1 also share the key term *tĕhillâ* already mentioned.[50] Then Ps 149:3 exhorts praise with dancing (*māḥôl*), timbrel (*tōp*) and harp (*kinnôr*), while Ps 150:3b–4a features the same three terms in reverse order. Psalm 150 also shares other things with Psalm 148 besides abundant use of the verb *hālal*, particularly a focus on the heavens at the beginning of each psalm and the sense of universality expressed by the final verse of Psalm 150, "Let everything that has breath praise the LORD."[51]

To what degree some of these links within Psalms 146–150 are deliberate is hard to establish, and similarly, to what degree they are the work of editor/s of the book as opposed to original psalm authors.[52] Certainly the sheer consistency of the opening and closing *hallû-yāh* framing otherwise rather distinct psalms seems

---

[47] Compare 145:20; 146:9.

[48] S. E. Gillingham, "Entering and Leaving the Psalter," in *Let Us Go Up to Zion* (ed. Iain W. Provan and Mark J. Boda; Leiden: Brill, 2012), 385–386.

[49] See deClaissé-Walford, *Reading from the Beginning*, 101–102.

[50] Hossfeld and Zenger, *Psalms 3*, 630, 635, 639; Gillingham, "Entering and Leaving," 386.

[51] Various writers expound the links between Psalms 149–150 and Psalms 1–2; I would agree with Susan Gillingham that Psalms 2 and 149 share in common the theme of the submission of the nations to the kingship of Yahweh, while Psalm 150 functions not as a frame with Psalm 1 so much as a climax to the swelling praises of the book as a whole: Gillingham, "Entering and Leaving," 387–393.

[52] Zenger, for instance, sees the ending of Psalm 148:14 as a deliberate editorial addition to aid the transition to Psalm 149: Hossfeld and Zenger, *Psalms 3*, 635, 638.

editorial, and the absence of some of these in the Septuagint (LXX) and other versions confirms the impression that this outermost structure came late in the piece. To my eye the sequence of these five psalms does not seem to be the only meaningful one that could have been chosen, though Psalm 150 is, as Brueggemann points out, eminently suitable for its position. He aptly calls it "the most extreme and unqualified statement of unfettered praise in the Old Testament."[53] A more appropriate ending for the Psalter is hard to imagine. But as I will argue in my conclusion, Psalm 148 at the centre of these final hallelujah psalms has a certain pride of place and represents the pinnacle of the book.

The Structure of Psalm 148

One 'sacred canon' of ancient Near Eastern (ANE) backgrounds is the idea that the ANE cosmology was tripartite, and this sometimes imposes too heavy an interpretive burden on OT Scripture, including Psalm 148. In a classic example, Dahood classifies vv. 1–6 as concerned with the heavens, v. 7 as concerned with the 'nether world', and vv. 8–13b as concerned with the terrestrial world, before a final historical reflection in vv. 13c–14.[54] In fact, Othmar Keel has shown from ANE analogues that a bipartite, 'heaven-and-earth' formula is "at least as significant as the longer tripartite formula", displaying a world-picture that is arguably at its base bipartite.[55] Psalm 148 clearly plays a significant part in Keel's treatment; he believes that the psalm's structure matches an ancient conception of the cosmos in bipartite terms.[56]

This leads us to the structure of Psalm 148. In such a highly ordered, carefully constructed psalm, there is no mistaking the key parallel structures. "Praise the LORD from the heavens" (1a) and "Praise the LORD from the earth" (7a) are clearly parallel openings to their respective sections, just as the twin "Let them praise the

---

[53] W. Brueggemann, "Bounded by Obedience and Praise: The Psalms as Canon," *Journal for the Study of the Old Testament* 50 (1991), 67.

[54] M. Dahood, *Psalms* (3 vols., vol. 3, Anchor Bible; New York: Doubleday, 1970), 352. Dahood himself seems puzzled by the dissymmetry of his own scheme on pp. 353–354. See also Coad, "Creation's Praise of God," 83.

[55] Othmar Keel, *The Symbolism of the Ancient World: Ancient Near Eastern Iconography and the Book of Psalms* (Eisenbrauns: Winona Lake, 1997 [1972]), 30. Arguably tripartite formulae in the OT would be Exod 20:11; Ps 33:6–8; 96:11.

[56] Keel, *Symbolism*, 26, 30, 40; J. Goldingay, *Psalms volume 3. Psalms 90–150* (Baker Commentary on the Old Testament Wisdom and Psalms; Grand Rapids: Baker Academic, 2008), 728.

name of the LORD, for [rationale]" constructions (5a, 13a) clearly correspond. Between these pivotal points, vv. 1–4 consist (after the opening *hallû-yāh*) of a series of seven imperative 'hallels' compelling praise from heavenly entities, before the exhortation (what is known in Hebrew grammar as a 'jussive' form of *hālal*) with rationale in vv. 5–6. Then vv. 7–12 consist, after the initial imperative hallel, of a tumbling rush of twenty-three earthly entities (in the grammatical role of 'vocatives') who are likewise bidden to praise the LORD. Then follows another exhortation to praise beginning in v. 13a, beginning with the same jussive form of *hālal*. That the total number of units, seven + twenty-three, adds up to thirty seems deliberate. The finely-geared structure of the entire psalm suggests that an element like this was not left to chance, but expresses the completeness of the praising assembly by means of a numerological device.[57]

The clear correspondences just identified lead many commentators to posit a psalm of two main sections, vv. 1–6 and 7–14.[58] To incorporate the entire content of the psalm, this proposal sees the first section as culminating in twin bicola (vv. 5–6) and the second section more fully in twin tricola (vv. 13–14), an arrangement that satisfies me.[59] One variant on this arrangement is to offset all or part of v. 14 from the rest. Hence Hillers affirms the bipartite structure of the psalm, but treats v. 14 as "a brief appendix" or "closing petition."[60] A redaction-critical version posits that part or

---

[57] Ruppert, "Aufforderung," 279–280; Hossfeld and Zenger, *Psalms 3*, 632; Gerstenberger, *Psalms, Part 2*, 447, 449–450; Pierre Auffret, *La sagesse a bâti sa maison* (Orbis biblicus et orientalis 49; Fribourg/Göttingen: Éditions universitaires/Vandenhoeck & Ruprecht, 1982), 390–391, 393, 399. It seems possible to carry numerology too far; without properly grasping all the principles of Duane Christensen's 'logoprosodic analysis' method, something is wrong when its outcome is a seven-strophe structure that neglects the clear correspondences between vv. 1–6 and vv. 7–12 and finds as the 'meaningful centre' of the psalm, through syllable-counting, the term 'and mist' [or 'smoke'] (*wĕqîṭôr*) from v. 8: Duane L. Christensen, "Psalm 148:1–14: Translation, Logoprosodic Analysis, and Observations," http://www.bibal.net/04/proso/psalms-ii/pdf/dlc_ps148–001-f.pdf.

[58] F. Delitzsch, *Psalms* (trans. F. Bolton, Commentary on the Old Testament in Ten Volumes 5; Grand Rapids: Eerdmans, 1871), 404, 406–407; Allen, *Psalms 101–150*, 390–392; Auffret, *La sagesse*, 385–387; Kraus, *Psalms 60–150*, 561.

[59] Allen, *Psalms 101–150*, 390–392; Auffret, *La sagesse*, 385–387; Évode Beaucamp and J.-P. de Relles, "Le chorale de la création en marche: Psaume 148," *Bible et vie chrétienne* 72 (1966), 31–32.

[60] Hillers, "Study of Psalm 148," 327.

all of v. 14 is likely to have been a later subscription or a redactor's attempt to integrate Psalms 148 and 149.[61]

It is also helpful to outline the psalm more finely in terms of its poetic structure. Each of the first twelve verses consists of a poetic line of two balanced halves, called a 'bicolon', while as mentioned above vv. 13–14 both arguably consist in our Hebrew texts of three parts in balance, or tricola. Typically each colon in these combinations has three 'beats' or stressed syllables, so that even to read the Hebrew text gives an impression of great regularity.[62]

It is possible furthermore to arrange these bicola and the final two tricola in pairs, which results in a psalm composed of six quatrains (four-line stanzas) and an extended final stanza. This is reasonably well supported by the content of the psalm, where, for instance, the sixth stanza (vv. 11–12) would consist of classes of humans, and the third and seventh stanzas (vv. 5–6, 13–14) of rationales for praise. None of the paired verses sit poorly together. Such a combination into (mostly) quatrains yields seven units of which the seventh is climactic, and in terms of the bipartite structure, breaks down into three and four stanzas respectively.[63] When combined with the creation theme that dominates the psalm, it is a short step to find here a deliberate structural allusion to the seven days of the creation week.[64]

Commentary

Stanza 1: vv. 1–2

> Praise the LORD.
>
> Praise the LORD from the heavens;
> Praise him in the highest places.
> Praise him, all his emissaries;
> Praise him, all his forces.

---

[61] Gerstenberger, *Psalms, Part 2*, 447, 450–451; Ruppert, "Aufforderung," 277–278; Hossfeld and Zenger, *Psalms 3*, 630, 635, 638–639. No-one that I have found follows R. A. F. MacKenzie's proposal that v. 14b–c belongs as a title to Psalm 149. R. A. F. MacKenzie, "Ps 148:14bc: Conclusion or Title?" *Biblica* 51/2 (1970), 221–224; Hillers, "Study of Psalm 148," 328. Kidner thinks instead that Ps 148:14 *inspired* Psalm 149: Derek Kidner, *Psalms 73–150* (Tyndale Old Testament Commentaries; Leicester: InterVarsity, 1975), 489.

[62] A rabbinic reading is available at http://www.mechon-mamre.org/mp3/t26e8.mp3.

[63] Terrien, *The Psalms*, 917–919; Beaucamp and de Relles, "Le chorale de la création," 31–32.

[64] Ruppert, "Aufforderung," 279–280; Hossfeld and Zenger, *Psalms 3*, 632.

We have discussed the fact that the initial *hallû-yāh* functions at a kind of trans-psalm level, binding together Psalms 146–150 and culminating the spasmodic series of hallel psalms that appears late in the Book of Psalms. It is an entirely consistent opening for Psalm 148, which uses the pertinent verbal root *hālal* twelve times including these framing hallelujahs at its two ends, a frequency only exceeded in the OT by Psalm 150 (13x).

Verse 1 proper also begins with the imperative *hallû*, and in this first instance makes the object of praise explicit, 'the LORD' (or Yahweh), as the framing term *hallû-yāh* does, but now using the fuller holy name. The second imperative "praise him" simply uses the pronominal suffix to refer to the LORD, beginning a pattern that will persist through verse 4. This verse does not immediately invoke praising agents, but calls for praise from or in the heavenly sphere (here taking *haššāmayim*, 'the heavens', and *mĕrômîm*, 'the highest places', as synonyms).[65]

Verse 2 then moves to invoke the praise of beings that reside in the heavens. The word translated 'emissaries' here is *mal'ākîm*, often rendered 'angels' or 'messengers', the former term by now compromised by centuries of accreted popular conception. Again we meet immediately with a synonym, *sĕbā'āyw*, traditionally rendered 'hosts'.[66] I have opted for 'forces', permitting a mildly military connotation, conscious that 'hosts' has fallen out of present-day English usage. The image is probably the numerous ranks of soldiers and servants that an ancient monarch could assemble at need; and the LORD is the ultimate monarch. Holladay affirms that in the post-exilic setting of this psalm, it is indeed angels, i.e. spiritual beings on a lower tier than deity, that would have been in the writer's mind.[67] Just as a human monarch

---

[65] There is no perfect English equivalent for *šāmayim*: 'heaven/s' most often denotes an unseen, transcendent realm, the divine realm, in modern English, while 'sky' is a purely physical term. While I believe that some distinction between physical heavens and spiritual heavens is already emerging in OT times, *šāmayim* can cover both, making the translator's decision difficult.

[66] The plural is actually the 'qere' reading in the Leningrad Codex that lies behind the standard Hebrew text, *Biblia Hebraica Stuttgartensia* (BHS), at this point. The text itself reads as singular, 'his force' (= the 'kethiv').

[67] Holladay, *Psalms*, 61. This makes the concept somewhat less fraught than the difficult 'sons of God' in Gen 6:2–4; Job 1:6; 2:1; Ps 29:1.

would have a large court of attendants at his command, so it is in the court of the heavenly King.[68]

This call to the heavenly assemblies to participate in praise has a precedent in Ps 103:20–21.[69] From a literary point of view it is worth pointing out already that the two cola of verse 1 rhyme, as do the two cola of verse 2, although rhyme is less significant in Hebrew verse than English verse.[70]

Stanza 2: vv. 3–4

> Praise him, sun and moon;
> Praise him, all shining stars.
> Praise him, heavens of the heavens,
> And waters above the heavens.

The focus in verse 3 remains on praising entities in the heavenly realm, but has moved from what we would regard as animate, though spiritual, beings, to inanimate beings: sun, moon and stars. It is important to remember, though, that in the ancient world the line between animate and inanimate beings in the heavens was not so clearly drawn. Augustine's meditations on Psalm 148 in his handbook for the Christian life, the *Enchiridion*, reveals his uncertainty about whether the sun, moon and 'other stars' ought to be included among the various ranks of angels, or whether, as "some believe," they are "merely luminous bodies, without either sensation or intelligence."[71] Though the parallelism with 'emissaries' (*mal'ākîm*) in verse 2 encouraged us to see the 'forces' (*ṣĕbā'āyw*, 'hosts') in the same verse as animate beings, the very uncertain distinction between animate and inanimate in heavenly entities means that sun, moon and stars could well fall within the categories of verse 2.[72] We notice again that, unlike Gen 1:14–19,

---

[68] H.-J. Kraus, *Theology of the Psalms* (trans. K. Crim; Minneapolis, 1986 [Theologie der Psalmen, 1979]), 49, Walther Eichrodt, *Theology of the Old Testament* (2 vols.; London: SCM Press, 1967), 2:194 202.

[69] Ruppert, "Aufforderung," 283; Allan E. Harman, *Commentary on the Psalms* (Fearn, Ross-shire: Mentor, 1998), 450.

[70] Rhyme is both less necessary in Hebrew, and more likely accidental due to the limited number of noun ending possibilities. In essence, play in the sound of word-endings is common in Hebrew poetry but not limited to line endings at all. W. G. E. Watson, *Classical Hebrew Poetry: A Guide to Its Techniques* (JSOTSup 26; Sheffield, 1986), 229–234.

[71] Quoted in Quentin F. Wesselschmidt, *Psalms 51–150* (Ancient Christian Commentary on Scripture, Thomas C. Oden; Downers Grove: InterVarsity, 2007), 423.

[72] Certainly *ṣĕbā'āyw*, 'hosts' or 'forces' includes reference to the heavenly bodies that we regard as physical in Gen 2:1. On the overlap in the conception of stars and angels in the OT, see Delitzsch, *Psalms*, 406; Eichrodt, *Theology*, 2:196.

there is no apparent nervousness about dignifying sun and moon with names here; but they clearly do obeisance to the LORD.

It is hard to sufficiently express the sonic qualities of verse 4. Counting doubled letters, the Hebrew features six 'sh' sounds and nine 'm' sounds, a pronounced use of the poetic device called 'consonance', or similarity of consonant sounds.[73] Consonance is really more important in Hebrew poetry than (the closely related) rhyme, while this verse features both, since both cola end with 'the heavens' (*haššāmayim*). The 'sh' and 'm' sounds here recall 'sun' (*šemeš*) in verse 3 and anticipate the more important 'name' (*šēm*) of Yahweh in verse 5, yielding an extended sound play reminiscent of the sea surging on a stony shore.[74] Furthermore, there is an inversion of sounds at the halfway point between the two cola also, yielding a chiasmus of sound or palindrome effect that covers all but the outermost terms.[75] Such devices are an integral part of crafting and communicating meaning in biblical poetry, and at a more subtle level, also in prose.

The concepts in this verse are challenging for the modern reader. The nearest we can approach the concept of heavens above nearer heavens is the distinction between 'sky' and 'outer space', and this is not unhelpful. However, it remains a strictly physical pairing, whereas the concepts here are inclusive of a spiritual realm also. And what the waters above the skies could be is quite perplexing. One common solution is to regard them as the clouds[76], but this is emphatically *not* the psalmist's idea, as convenient as it would be for us. Genesis 1 presents the sun and moon as embedded *in* the 'firmament' (*rāqîa'*) in some sense, while it is there to separate the higher waters from the more familiar lower waters—with the result that the 'upper waters' are portrayed as beyond the orbit of sun and moon! And these upper waters cannot have been some primordial

---

[73] This would be a good time to access the audio of this verse at http://www.mechon-mamre.org/mp3/t26e8.mp3 to experience this. Listen for these 'sh' and 'm' sounds early in the reading.

[74] Watson, *Classical Hebrew Poetry*, 242–245; Auffret, *La sagesse*, 390.

[75] Auffret, *La sagesse*, 388–389. This palindromic or 'envelope structure' in the sound in this verse may have required the abandoning of the otherwise quite regular rhythm (almost 'metre') in this psalm. Most cola in the psalm have three beats, as already mentioned, but this verse is 3-4, and I know of no manuscript evidence that offers a 3-3 alternative. Watson comments that, though it is unsettling for the Westerner, Hebrew verse tends to periodically break up an otherwise consistent rhythmic poetic pattern in this way: Watson, *Classical Hebrew Poetry*, 98.

[76] E.g. Kidner, *Psalms 73–150*, 487–488.

vapour canopy that collapsed, because they are here called upon to praise Yahweh, implying that they still exist, like the *rāqîa'* itself (Ps 150:1), for the psalmist.

Let me clarify the world-picture involved here if I can. Much has been written about this, but drawing on comments made about ancient worldviews by Peter Harrison,[77] I would suggest that the psalmist's worldview (and that of both Old and New Testaments) assumes a correspondence between 'earth' and 'heaven', or human and divine realms, with the heavenly realm situated above the earthly. Just as the heavenly King has a court of attendants analogous to human emperors, and a heavenly throne (Ps 103:19; 123:1; Heb 8:1; 12:2), and heaven has (or is) a sanctuary (Ps 150:1a; Heb 8:2), so the heavenly realm has, I am suggesting, its waters corresponding to our oceans, and which may be understood to enclose our terrestrial skies (hence their blue colour).[78] Then this heavenly realm would have its own skies, the 'heavens of the heavens' (v. 4a). I take as confirmation of this proposal that in verse 8, atmospheric phenomena do not belong to the heavenly realm, addressed in 148:1–4, but to the earthly sphere.[79]

With this reference to the highest heights of the heavenly realm, inarticulate agents of praise as in v. 3, both the psalmist's survey of seven praising agents in vv. 2–4 and his seven imperative calls to praise in 1–4 are complete,[80] implying the call of everything that exists in the heavens to praise the LORD.[81]

Stanza 3: vv. 5–6

Let them praise the LORD's name;
For he commanded and they were created.

---

[77] Peter Harrison, *The Bible, Protestantism, and the Rise of Natural Science* (Cambridge, UK: Cambridge University Press, 1998), 13–17, etc.

[78] Keel, *Symbolism*, 36. The Egyptian picture on the same page clearly shows that the heavens (presented in Egyptian conception as a woman), complete with embedded stars, can be sailed upon by the boat that carries the sun, clearly demonstrating its watery nature.

[79] It may be objected that I am reading a Platonist model into the ancient Hebrew cosmology at this point, but the two are not absolutely different. The Hebrew concept seems to me less developed or philosophically construed, and more obviously 'vertical' in its physical understanding of the cosmic hierarchy, but has in common with Platonism the idea of correspondences between heavenly and earthly spheres.

[80] The initial, framing *hallû yāh* can legitimately be discounted for this counting purpose as editorial, meaning that the artistry of the original song did not include it in the number of these imperatives.

[81] Watson describes the form of these two lists of entities in 148:1–6 and 7–12 as 'meristic lists', intended to be all-embracing: Watson, *Classical Hebrew Poetry*, 322.

> He set them up to last forever and ever,
> He made a decree and it never becomes obsolete.

These two verses form the climax of the first major section of Psalm 148. Having named first the sphere of praise (v. 1) and the agents of praise (vv. 2–4), the psalmist offers the rationale for the praise that the heavens' occupants must give. 'Let them praise' represents a different, jussive form of *hālal* in contrast to the preceding seven (or eight) imperatives. The rationale here is creation-based, and particularly the way their creation represented unquestioning and unchanging compliance to his royal will. We are reminded of the irrevocable "laws of the Medes and the Persians" in Dan 6:8, 12, 15, and indeed the likely historical setting of this psalm matches the explicit setting of the events in that chapter of Daniel. We may assume that our psalmist knows all about absolute monarchy. If Yahweh wants a world, at this point a heavenly world, he gets it, and that permanently. Commentators like to highlight the word for 'created' here, *bārā'*, which is the same word used in Gen 1:1 and related contexts. Although it does not always refer to physical creation, it always has God as its subject in OT Scripture in the active (qal) stem, just as Yahweh is clearly the understood agent of this passive, niphal form (*nibrā'û*).[82] The resemblance of this form to the one found in Gen 2:4 has already been noted.

The term I have translated as 'becomes obsolete', *ya'ăbôr*, can be construed in two main ways. If it is understood in a transitive sense, it can mean to cross or transgress a boundary.[83] Interestingly, this meaning applies in certain creation or providence-related contexts in company with the noun here translated 'decree' (*ḥoq*), namely Job 14:5, Prov 8:29 and Jer 5:22. Each of these uses is relevant but slightly different, but all support this transitive sense of crossing a limit or boundary. The alternative is the intransitive sense, 'to pass away' (hence 'become obsolete), which is used (negatively) of the 'laws of the Medes and Persians' in Esth 1:19 and of the Feast of Purim in Esth 9:27–28, though not with *ḥoq* per

---

[82] On this verb's use in reference to creation, see G. von Rad, *Old Testament Theology* (trans. D. M. G. Stalker; 2 vols.; Edinburgh/London: Oliver & Boyd, 1962, 1965 [Theologie des Alten Testaments, 1957, 1960.]), 1:142; Eichrodt, *Theology*, 2:103; Kraus, *Theology of the Psalms*, 36, 63.

[83] William L. Holladay (ed.), *A Concise Hebrew and Aramaic Lexicon of the Old Testament*, (Grand Rapids: Eerdmans, 1988), 263; Francis Brown, S. R. Driver, and Charles A. Briggs (eds.), *The Brown-Driver-Briggs Hebrew and English Lexicon*, (Peabody, MA: Hendrickson, 1996), 717. This discussion pertains to the qal stem of this verb.

se.⁸⁴ The former, transitive sense therefore has stronger precedent in Scripture, but is a little more difficult grammatically in Ps 148:6 since an explicit subject for the verb is lacking in 6b. I have therefore taken the simpler option of understanding *ḥoq*, 'decree', as the subject and the verb as intransitive.⁸⁵ In effect, God has decreed that the heavenly realm and its occupants should exist, and so they will for as long as his will decrees.⁸⁶

Stanza 4: vv. 7–8

> Praise the LORD from the earth:
> Huge aquatic animals and all vast depths,
> Fire and hail, snow and smoke,
> Violent wind performing his command;

Corresponding to the address to the heavens' occupants in verse 1, verse 7a initiates the second major section in this psalm, turning the address to terrestrial things.⁸⁷ More quickly than in verse 1, the listing of entities of earth begins, and they will come at a rapid-fire pace in vv. 7b–12, without the intervening verbal imperative, *hallû*, seen in vv. 1–4a. So *hā'āreṣ* (the earth) identifies the new domain, and 7b immediately names the first two occupants, *tannînîm* and *tĕhōmôt*. These terms pertain to the oceans, but rather than being treated as the third part of a tripartite cosmos, the oceans are included under the broader category 'earth' here, as already discussed. Both terms have mythological overtones in ANE literary analogues and in certain OT texts,⁸⁸ but here and in most OT occurrences, especially in the case of *tĕhōm*, appear devoid of any mythological overtones, and act as descriptors of natural

---

⁸⁴ Brown, Driver, and Briggs (eds.), *Lexicon*, 718.

⁸⁵ If the Hebrew term *ya'ăbôr* were recast as either a plural or instead as passive, the transitive meaning would become viable, but there is no textual support for the change. LXX's *pareleusetai* is supportive of the intransitive meaning. See Hillers, "Study of Psalm 148," 326. Holladay thinks both meanings are intended(!): Holladay, *Psalms*, 60, 325.

⁸⁶ The idea that the laws of the Medes and Persians in Daniel 6 and Esther 1 cannot be rescinded even by the emperor himself, once decreed, is a separate problem.

⁸⁷ I have mentioned Dahood's translation of *hā'āreṣ* here, normally 'the earth', as 'the nether world', following an earlier suggestion by Cross & Freedman based on ANE analogues: Dahood, *Psalms*, 351, 353. But the clearly bipartite structure of the psalm and the plainly terrestrial nature of the contents of vv. 8–12 show that this idea has waylaid Dahood's handling of this psalm.

⁸⁸ For *tannînîm*, see Ps 74:13; Isa 27:1; 51:9, and perhaps Job 7:12. Elsewhere it can mean a variety of snake (Exod 7:9–12; Deut 32:33) or crocodile (Jer 51:34; Ezek 29:3; 32:2). *Tĕhōmôt* or the singular *tĕhōm* has been since about 1900 often associated by scholars with Tiamat from Mesopotamian myth. It does occur in theophanic passages (Ps 77:16; Isa 51:10; Hab 3:10), although many such uses refer in their contexts to the exodus event.

phenomena.[89] So while commentaries influenced by the 'history-of-religions' tradition tend to perceive a mythological element in this psalm[90], many recent commentators acknowledge that, as with Genesis 1, such associations as once existed are now 'dead links', and the terms thoroughly 'demythologized'.[91]

Verse 8 adopts a 4–4 rhythm, unique in the psalm, in order to pile up terms related to atmospheric phenomena. Some of the terms present challenges; while 'hail' and 'snow' seem clear from their OT use and match each other well, recalling 147:16–17, 'fire' and 'smoke' are more debatable. My choice of these terms works on the assumption that the two are meant to match one another in an inverted or envelope structure. However, *qîṭôr* is rarely attested in the OT, and LXX's *krystallos* may reflect a different Hebrew term, *qeraḥ*, meaning 'frost' or 'ice'. However, I would opt with Alter to read *qîṭôr* and take the meaning that is normal for it in its other contexts (esp. Gen 19:28), 'smoke';[92] *'ēš* would then retain its more common meaning, 'fire' (although 'lightning' is certainly a permissible meaning), the two together possibly suggesting volcanic phenomena.[93] The remainder of verse 8 is clearer, while we ought not to miss the clear message that natural phenomena take place in obedience to the command (*dābār*) of the heavenly King.[94]

Stanza 5: vv. 9–10

> Mountains and all hills,
> Fruit trees and all cedars,
> Animals wild and domestic,
> Those that crawl and birds on the wing

Having already named seven earthly entities in quick succession, phenomena of ocean and sky, the second major section (or strophe) of Psalm 148 moves now to a properly terrestrial domain. Rhythmically these verses return to a 3–3 bicolon structure, and Auffret rightly identifies a rhythmic match between lines one and

---

[89] The same is true where each term occurs in Genesis 1 (1:2 for *tĕhôm*, 1:21 for *tannînîm*).

[90] Gunkel, *Einleitung*, 92; Weiser, *The Psalms*, 838; Terrien, *The Psalms*, 921. Kraus begins this way and backtracks: Kraus, *Psalms 60–150*, 563.

[91] Coad, "Creation's Praise of God," 85–86; Hossfeld and Zenger, *Psalms 3*, 637; Goldingay, *Psalms volume 3. Psalms 90–150*, 732.

[92] R. Alter, *The Book of Psalms: A Translation with Commentary* (New York: Norton, 2009), 510; Hillers, "Study of Psalm 148," 326.

[93] Here, for a change, I agree with Dahood, *Psalms*, 354.

[94] Compare Ps 147:15, 18.

three of this stanza, while the rhythms of lines two and four seem deliberately reversed.[95]

We are in the department of Days Three and Five–Six of the creation week, and some of these terms reflect equivalents in Genesis 1. Identical terms are 'fruit trees' (*'ēṣ pĕrî*), 'wild animals' (*ḥayyâ*), 'domestic animals' (*bĕhēmâ*), and 'crawling animals' (*remeś*) (Gen 1:11, 24–25; Ps 148:9b–10). "Birds on the wing" (*ṣippôr kānāp*) is similar to *'ôp kānāp* in Gen 1:21. Zenger thinks these and other correspondences are intentional on the author's part, and we must admit that this accumulation of terms is strongly suggestive.[96]

'Mountains' and 'hills' are not specifically mentioned in Genesis 1 but are certainly well attested in OT meditations on creation, often symbolizing a kind of permanence that whispers the eternity of God (Gen 49:26; Deut 33:15; Job 26:14; Pss 36:6; 125:2). And like the classes of animals, 'fruit trees' represents domesticated trees, while 'cedars' (*'ărāzîm*) is quite possibly broader than a single tree species and may stand for the tall, undomesticated forest tree.[97] All of the creatures mentioned here are still inarticulate, but the movement, as generally in Genesis 1, is from inanimate to animate but inarticulate; articulate praise will soon follow.

Stanza 6: vv. 11–12

> Kings of the earth and all peoples,
> Princes and all governors of the earth,
> Both young men and young women,
> Elders and youngsters together:

The terms in this stanza are also carefully arranged. The inverted arrangement in the bicolon of verse 11 is clear in English translation, with the outer terms being roughly synonymous and complemented by *'ereṣ*, 'earth', which is of course a theme word for this second section of the psalm. 'Princes' (*śārîm*), by contrast, is not equivalent in meaning to the very general 'peoples' (*lĕ'ummîm*), but a certain resemblance in sound warrants the use of alliteration in the translation above. The focus emerging from verse 11 is one on humans in elite positions, and there is an international feel that

---

[95] Auffret, *La sagesse*, 392.

[96] Hossfeld and Zenger, *Psalms 3*, 632, 636–638; Alter, *Book of Psalms*, 509.

[97] Ludwig Koehler and Walter Baumgartner (eds.), *The Hebrew and Aramaic Lexicon of the Old Testament* (2 vols.; Leiden: Brill, 2001), 1:86.

makes sense in terms of a Persian-era setting. While we have noted that the sequence of entities in the psalm does not directly match that found in Genesis 1, the move to humans here in stanza six is still reminiscent of that creation account.

What we notice, then, about verse 12 in terms of content is the shift from the powerful to ordinary classes of people. That everyone is included is expressed in twin 'merisms', expressions intended to cover the entirety of a class by naming its extremes—male and female rather self-evidently, and then those towards the younger and older ends of the human spectrum, all expressed in rhythmic symmetry in the Hebrew. With twenty-three earthly entities' praise (vv. 7–12) to match that of seven heavenly entities (vv. 2–4), the roster of thirty is complete, having moved incrementally and poetically from the outermost extremes of the cosmos to the centre of human society, the ordinary person in all his and her variety. If there is any sense of progress in importance within this list, it culminates not in the king but in the commoner and the child.

Stanza 7: vv. 13–14

> Let them praise the LORD's name,
> For his name alone is lifted to the highest;
> His majesty over earth and heavens.
>
> And he raised up a horn for his people,
> [A point of] praise for all his loyal ones,
> For the Israelites, who enjoy his close presence.

This is the most debated part of the psalm in terms of structure and possible editing. I have chosen to read this as a pair of tricola, with Auffret, Allen, Alter and others[98], yielding a deliberately longer 'rationale' for praise in comparison to verses 5–6, in view of its greater importance. Understood this way, the first tricolon (v. 13) is designed to undergird the praise of earth and its inhabitants in particular, although "earth and heavens" moves to embrace both classes of praising agents in reverse order in a deliberate framing device. There is no entity that has been named, not even the 'highest heavens' of verse 4b or the 'highest places' of verse 1b, that can match the exaltation (*niśgāb*, here "lifted to the highest") of the

---

[98] Auffret, *La sagesse*, 386; Alter, *Book of Psalms*, 511; Allen, *Psalms 101–150*, 389; Beaucamp and de Relles, "Le chorale de la création," 32; Terrien, *The Psalms*. BHS arranges this section as three bicola, with considerable support, e.g. J. P. Fokkelman, *The Psalms in Form: The Hebrew Psalter in its Poetic Shape* (Leiden: Deo, 2003), 153, 172. Issues relating to possible editing are discussed in the introduction.

LORD's name, which is played off against 'heavens' (*šāmayim*) doubly here, to the advantage of 'name' (*šēm*), as it was in verses 4–5. Indeed, Kraus emphasizes the name of the LORD as the central motif of this psalm.[99] Sun, moon, stars and heavenly powers, ocean depths (*těhōmôt*) and sea monsters (*tannînîm*) might be worshipped as deities in other cultures; here they are bound to offer worship to their Creator. The rationale for praise here is no longer their createdness and obedient permanence, as it was in 5b–6, but is now Yahweh's exaltedness in relation to them.

But then in the final verse the rationale changes. Praise has been anchored in creation, then recently exaltation, and now its rationale is redemption.[100] Gunkel identified this move as characteristic of the hymns in Psalms, and it accords well with the twin poles of Christian theology, creation and redemption.[101] The past tense translation, "he raised up," is guided by the vowel points of *wayyārem* in the Masoretic (Hebrew) text, which imply a completed action, perhaps with the end of exile in mind. If repointed as an imperfect form, *wěyārēm*,[102] we have in view a future redemptive action, in terms very like those found in 1 Sam 2:10, at the climax of Hannah's song. That verse is highly susceptible to messianic interpretation, and the LXX, perhaps under influence from that context, also reads the form as imperfect here, and therefore probably inferring messianic connotations. It is hard to choose between the two here, given that the text was purely consonantal for so long, but messianic expectation gathered pace in the period between the Testaments, and LXX's construal may exemplify that trend.

Another interpretive question here concerns 'praise' (*těhillâ*), the cognate noun of the 'hallel' verbs so abundantly used early in this psalm. Is it praise directed *to* Israel, or praise *from* Israel to God? The LORD might be inherently more worthy of praise, but if we retain a place for the intention of the writer in establishing the meaning of our text, there is a structural aspect of this verse that

---

[99] Kraus, *Psalms 60–150*, 563–564; Kraus, *Theology of the Psalms*, 20–22, 32–33. Gunkel identifies this way of referring to Yahweh as a feature of the hymns: Gunkel, *Einleitung*, 41, 49. The exaltation of the LORD's name is celebrated (again using the root *śgb*) in Isa 12:4, and of LORD generally, in Isa 2:11, 17; 33:5.

[100] In neighbouring psalms personal redemption or rescue from harm, or more so God's delivering nature, forms a rationale for praise (Pss 146:7–9; 147:6; 149:4), but here the corporate redemption and care of Israel is in view.

[101] Gunkel, *Einleitung*, 51.

[102] The vowel points formally entered the Hebrew text tradition long after the consonants.

deserves attention. Amongst the varieties of parallelism seen in Hebrew poetry is what is called 'stepped parallelism', wherein the first element of several in a colon is elided (left out) but assumed in the second colon, permitting further development of subsequent unit(s), and this elision/expansion process may proceed further in the case of a third colon.[103] Verse 14 is a clear example:[104]

Verb	Object	Beneficiary[105]	Appositional Phrase
And he raised up	*a horn*	*for his people*	
	[A point of] praise	*for all his loyal ones*	
		For the Israelites	*who enjoy his close presence*

It is clear that the retention of the sense of the initial elements of the earlier cola without explicit restatement makes room for further development of later elements while the same overall length and rhythm is maintained for each colon.

The raising of the 'horn' for Israel most likely originally connoted the restoration of her dignity and reputation in the world, meaning that the 'praise' would be that directed to Israel from other nations. But because it might be that Yahweh has given Israel *cause* to praise Him, I have chosen augmenting words ('a point of') that leave the understanding somewhat open-ended.[106] The 'horn' may not refer to a specific person or asset, since this OT expression often stands figuratively for power and renown, e.g. Ps 89:17, 24.[107] Yet there is specificity about the appropriation of this OT concept in Luke 1:69:

---

[103] Alastair G. Hunter, *An Introduction to the Psalms* (T&T Clark Approaches to Biblical Studies; London: T & T Clark, 2008), 15. It is described a little differently than I have in Watson, *Classical Hebrew Poetry*, 150–151.

[104] Auffret, *La sagesse*, 394.

[105] This is a semantic term; see http://www-01.sil.org/linguistics/GlossaryOfLinguistic Terms/WhatIsABeneficiaryAsASemanticR.htm Formally these are prepositional phrases, but in syntactical terms they might be described as 'benefactive datives' introduced by the '*lamed* of interest' (or more broadly, as 'adverbial modifiers'): B. K. Waltke and K. M. O'Connor, *Biblical Hebrew Syntax* (Winona Lake: Eisenbrauns, 1990), 75, 207–208.

[106] The possibilities are explored fairly thoroughly in Hossfeld and Zenger, *Psalms 3*, 630. One writer concludes that it is Yahweh's praise for his people that is seen here: Duane Warden, "All Things Praise Him (Psalm 148)," *Restoration Quarterly* 35/2 (1993), 107.

[107] Delitzsch, *Psalms*, 409; Allen, *Psalms 101–150*, 390, 394; Terrien, *The Psalms*, 921. See especially Schmutzer and Gauthier, "Identity," 161–164, 180–183. I have cited the English verse reference location.

"He has raised a horn of salvation for us in the house of his servant David." References such as this one and Ps 18:3 were evidently soon thought of in specific, messianic terms, if not originally so intended.

There is also specificity about the way this psalm finishes. Prior to the final, fitting 'hallelujah', the focus of what was mostly a psalm of such universal scope has closed in on the one people of Yahweh's intimacy—from the generality of creation to the particularity of election. This brings us to consider in closing the meaning of the psalm overall.

The Significance of Psalm 148

For such a creation-focused hymn, it is odd how little attention Psalm 148 garners in many treatments of creation themes in the Psalms.[108] It is true that the emphasis here is on creation as a *fait accompli*, as an existing order, rather than on the work of creation, apart from verses 5b–6. It certainly is a valuable insight into a post-exilic Jewish cosmology, as explored in our introduction. But it is more than that. It is a valuable contribution to a biblical theology of creation, one with many resonances with, if not deliberate allusions to, the supreme biblical creation text, Gen 1:1–2:3.

What of the nature of its creation theology? How does it cast the triangular relationship between God, nature and humanity? The present climate in biblical studies is highly suspicious of a 'speciesism' that would accord preferential status to human beings within God's created order. Concerning creation in Genesis 1, Ellen van Wolde questions the idea that humans appear last in the creation week because they are most important, instead positing a network of relationships between created things that share equal status.[109] More militantly, Norman Habel reads the same account as emphasizing "the intrinsic value of Earth as the centre of the cosmos and the source of life." The appearance of humans

---

[108] There is isolated mention of Psalm 148 in James L. Mays, "'Maker of Heaven and Earth': Creation in the Psalms," in *God Who Creates* (Grand Rapids: Eerdmans, 2000), 86. It seems to rate no mention at all in Richard J. Clifford, "Creation in the Psalms," in *Creation in the Biblical Traditions* (Washington, DC: Catholic Biblical Association of America, 1992), 57–69. William Brown's recent work on the creation theme in the OT mentions the psalm in a single endnote: William P. Brown, *The Seven Pillars of Creation: The Bible, Science, and the Ecology of Wonder* (New York: Oxford University Press, 2010), 282.

[109] Ellen van Wolde, "Facing the Earth: Primaeval History in a New Perspective," in *The World of Genesis* (ed. Philip R. Davies and David J. A. Clines; JSOTSup 257; Sheffield: Sheffield Academic Press, 1998), 25–27.

produces an inevitable, "radical conflict" between Earth and humans.[110] Nature would be fine if only we were not here! Talk about a 'Gnostic return in modernity'![111] It is the creation of humans that becomes the Fall. The triangle is broken. Not all 'ecotheology' is so cynical; some would simply search Scripture more carefully for a theology of nature, or refute the Lynn White thesis that Judaeo-Christian biblical belief is primarily responsible for modern over-exploitation of nature by refuting the idea that biblical creation teaching is skewed in an anthropocentric direction.[112]

The strong nature focus of Psalm 148 attracts those concerned to discover an eco-friendly theology. It presents humans as one class of created beings among many that praises God.[113] "Here all creatures, including ourselves, are simply fellow-creatures expressing the theocentricity of the created world, each in our own created way, differently but in complementarity."[114] Fretheim, opposing anthropocentricism in theology, perceives here "a symbiosis of praise; every element in all of God's creation is called to praise together, and the response of one affects the response of the other."[115] Bauckham, furthermore, is keen to emphasize that Psalm 148 denies that creation is mute but for the priestly mediating role of humans in articulating praise on its behalf. "Creation praises God very well without us."[116] Beaucamp and de Relles instead see a greater role for humans as leaders of the creation symphony of praise "by delegation".[117] So creation is not mute without humans, but humans are graciously granted the right to lead the chorus. This is, I believe, the subtle implication of the placement of humans last

---

[110] Norman C. Habel, "Geophany: The Earth Story in Genesis 1," in *The Earth Story in Genesis* (ed. Norman C. Habel and Shirley Wurst; Sheffield: Sheffield Academic, 2000), 45–46.

[111] Here I am borrowing the title of Cyril O'Regan, *Gnostic Return in Modernity* (Albany, NY: State University of New York Press, 2001).

[112] Richard Bauckham, "Joining Creation's Praise of God," *Ecotheology* 7/1 (2002), 46–47; Lynn White, Jr., "The Historical Roots of Our Ecological Crisis," *Science* 155 (1967), 3–4.

[113] Margot Kässmann, "Covenant, Praise and Justice in Creation: Five Bible Studies," in *Ecotheology* (Maryknoll, NY/Geneva: Orbis/WCC Pubns, 1994), 36.

[114] Bauckham, "Joining Creation's Praise of God," 48.

[115] Terence E. Fretheim, "Nature's Praise of God in the Psalms," *Ex Auditu* 3 (1987), 28. See pp. 16–17 for the complaint about anthropocentrism.

[116] Bauckham, "Joining Creation's Praise of God," 49–51, quote on latter page.

[117] Beaucamp and de Relles, "Le chorale de la création," 34.

in the list of created beings in Psalm 148, and the analogy holds for the similarly climactic structure of Gen 1:1–2:3.

An associated question here is whether creation's praise in this psalm is a metaphorical idea, or whether creation does in some sense have an actual 'voice'. A more traditional evangelical position is that the call to praise is rhetorical. "This hymn that features rhetorical calls to the elements of creation to praise their God is an expression of the praiseworthiness of Yahweh."[118] Fretheim resists this as a premature domestication of the text, but also warns of the existence of a contrasting position tending to animism or panpsychism—that the earth, Gaia-like, is alive, or that 'mind' permeates nature.[119] The team behind the Earth Bible project, in their opening essay to the volume on the Psalms and Prophets, take from Psalm 148 and like texts that creation can really address God in praise. Interpreted against the preceding context, there seems to be some kind of opening for panpsychism implied.[120]

The middle position recently advocated by several evangelicals is that creation's praise in Psalm 148 is real, not just a rhetorical way of calling humans to praise God more enthusiastically, yet is not meant to be a return to animism:

> The passages about creation's praise are, of course, metaphorical: they attribute to non-human creatures the human practice of praising God in human language. But the reality to which they point is that all creatures bring glory to God simply by being themselves and fulfilling their God-given roles in God's creation.[121]

Perhaps I can clarify just a little further. Psalm 19:1–4a puts it even more strongly, not just invoking creation to praise God but saying that it already does. It is not in the sense of verbal communication, as 19:3 makes clear[122]; it is in the sense of glorifying God, which is to say that inanimate creation praises God *to us* more than to God.

---

[118] Allen, *Psalms 101–150*, 395. See also Goldingay, *Psalms volume 3. Psalms 90–150*, 735.

[119] Fretheim, "Nature's Praise," 22–23 and 20, respectively. Very similar is Coad, "Creation's Praise of God," 87–89.

[120] The Earth Bible Team, "The Voice of Earth: More than Metaphor?" in *The Earth Story in the Psalms and the Prophets* (ed. Norman C. Habel; Sheffield: Sheffield Academic, 2001), 25–27.

[121] Bauckham, "Joining Creation's Praise of God," 47. See also Fretheim, "Nature's Praise," 26–28; Coad, "Creation's Praise of God," 89.

[122] Here the 2011 NIV has improved the translation found in the 1984 edition.

By their splendour and majesty, created things allude to the far greater splendour and majesty of the LORD.[123]

Can we justify according Psalm 148 a privileged place within the final five hymns that close and climax the Psalter, as my title would imply? Psalms 146–150 manifest a fascinating theological tension between the universal and the particular, between Yahweh's sovereign rule over all creation and his selective redemption of the 'faithful ones' (*ḥăsîdîm*) of Zion. Psalm 146 seems to balance the themes. Psalm 147, while still mindful of creation, tips the balance towards the particular election of Israel. Following the mostly universal Psalm 148, Psalm 149 is very particular indeed, to be followed again, finally, by the universality of Psalm 150.[124] To borrow the words of Matt 22:14, the effect is an oscillation: "Many are called—but few are chosen—but many are called—but few are chosen...but (finally) many *are* called." Like many scriptural paradoxes, we cannot cut this theological Gordian knot; we actually need to retain the tension to retain the truths involved. But I am encouraged that the Book of Psalms finishes on the note, "many are called."[125] Psalm 150 expresses this theme last, at the denouement of the book, but Psalm 148 expresses it fullest and best.[126] Theologically profound and artistically superb, Psalm 148 stands out even among its peers, the final hallel psalms, as "a fine climax of praise."[127]

For additional resources relating to this psalm, including visual content, please go to: https://firstthreequarters.wordpress.com/2014/01/21/special-features-of-psalm-148-english-text-version/

---

[123] Ps 148:13; Job 26:14.

[124] This is especially true if the 'sanctuary' (*qōdeš*) in view in 150:1 is the heavenly one, rather than a temple structure (if one existed when the psalm was penned) in Jerusalem.

[125] Wenham, *Psalter Reclaimed*, 185–186.

[126] It nonetheless retains an admonitory note: all things are bidden to praise... what if any should refuse?

[127] M. Goulder, *The Psalms of the Return (Book V, Psalms 107–150)* (JSOTSup 258; Sheffield: Sheffield Academic, 1998), 293. Terrien says, "Psalm 148 goes beyond other hymns in that it unites distance and intimacy." Terrien, *The Psalms*, 922. Alter calls it "one of the most majestic of these six concluding psalms of praise." Alter, *Book of Psalms*, 509. See again Wenham, *Psalter Reclaimed*, 186.

INVITATION FOR PAPERS

MST's journal *PARADOSIS* brings together theological minds in the on-going advancement in Christian thought and practice. We believe that theological and biblical disciplines should never exist on their own; they require a broader field of vision. Therefore *PARADOSIS* will showcase articles in biblical studies and theology which manifest this.

Particular interest will be shown in those submissions which are of an inter-disciplinary nature, especially those that connect biblical, historical or theological insights with current church trends or challenges to Christian thought in a wide variety of current contexts.

The majority of papers in each edition will coalesce around certain themes and the Executive Editor will receive suggestions regarding potential future themes or guest authors for individual issues. Each issue will have its own Issue Editor on her/his own field of expertise (proposed themes for the coming years are listed below). In this way the journal will examine reasonable expressions of the proposed theme from the range of theological disciplines, framework and perspective to suit a scholarly, student or pastoral readership.

Articles accepted for publication are 'peer reviewed', being read and assessed by at least one pertinent scholar in the appropriate field.

We extend our invitation to all, both in Australia and internationally.

Dr Justin Tan
Executive Editor

2016: *Christology*
2017: *Christian/Biblical Ethics*
2018: *Christian Spirituality*

NOTES FOR CONTRIBUTORS

Submission requirements

Manuscript

> Papers should not exceed 8000 words, although the Editor retains the discretion to publish papers that vary from this length.

> It is preferable that submissions be prepared in Microsoft Word format. When using citation management software tools, please remove all field codes before submission.

All papers are to be written in English, and must conform to MST style requirements. This can be found on the MST website (http://www.mst.edu.au/wp-content/uploads/2015/07/MST-Essay-Guide-15.pdf). Refer also to the style used in the current issue.

> Any Greek and Hebrew words written in original script should use SBL Greek/Hebrew (or SBL BibLit) Unicode font. An English translation should be provided in brackets where the meaning is not readily apparent from the context. No transliteration is necessary unless judged necessary.

> Authors are advised to use gender inclusive and non-discriminatory language.

> Any visuals should be integrated into the document, or sent separately as separate jpg or gif files with an explanation as to their position in the paper.

Submission

> Papers to be considered for inclusion are to be submitted directly to the Executive Editor (jtan@mst.edu.au), via electronic mail.

> A declaration that the submitted articles are your own work and that you have acknowledged the work/s of others used in the articles in the references, etc. must be included with any submission.

> A covering letter that includes the author's full name, titles, affiliations, with complete mailing addresses, including email, telephone and facsimile numbers, should be attached to the paper.

Review of Submissions

All submissions will be sent to referees for anonymous recommendation.

The Editor holds the right to make editorial corrections to accepted submissions.

Copyright

PARADOSIS is published by MST Press, the publishing arm of the Melbourne School of Theology. The copyright for any published papers will remain with the author. MST publishes these papers on the following conditions:

- They do not appear elsewhere (including web pages) for 12 months from the date of publication in *PARADOSIS*.
- Whenever they are printed elsewhere (including web pages), the following notice will be included: "This article first appeared in the __ issue of the *PARADOSIS* series".
- MST retains the right to use the paper in any MST publications, reprints, or in electronic form (ie. Online, CD-Rom, etc.).
- MST retains the right to use a portion or description of the paper with the author's name in our promotional material.
- Authors are themselves responsible for obtaining permission to reproduce copyright material from other sources.
- The author will be presented with one copy of the publication.

Disclaimer

The opinions and conclusions published in the *PARADOSIS* series are those of the authors and do not necessarily represent the views of the Editors or the Melbourne School of Theology.

www.ingramcontent.com/pod-product-compliance
Lightning Source LLC
Chambersburg PA
CBHW070617300426
44113CB00010B/1563